CHAPLIN

CHAPLIN
A Life

Stephen Weissman, M.D.

Arcade Publishing • New York

Arcade Publishing books may be purchased in bulk at special discounts for sales promotion, corporate gifts, fund-raising, or educational purposes. Special editions can also be created to specifications. For details, contact the Special Sales Department, Arcade Publishing, 307 West 36th Street, 11th Floor, New York, NY 10018 or arcade@skyhorsepublishing.com.

Arcade Publishing® is a registered trademark of Skyhorse Publishing, Inc.®, a Delaware corporation.

Excerpts from *My Autobiography* by Charples Chaplin, published by The Bodley Head. Reprinted by permission of the Random House Group Ltd.

Visit our website at www.arcadepub.com.

Visit the book's web site at www.chaplinalife.com.

10 9 8 7 6 5 4 3 2 1

Library of Congress Cataloging-in-Publication Data is available on file.

ISBN: 978-1-61145-040-8

Printed in the United States of America

To Carole and Annie

Contents

Introduction

A FEW YEARS AGO I RECEIVED A PHONE CALL from an acquaintance I had made at a film festival, resulting in the following conversation:

"You might want to check this out. Some cocky young author has written an article about your father insinuating that your grandmother was a doxy."

"A what?"

"A chippy, a tart, a . . . houri!"

"*What?*"

"Oh! And that she had syphilis."

"WHAT?"

"Yeah, well, I put it in the post for you. Check it out."

I had dinner with my stepson that night. I told him, "Apparently some jerk has published an article calling my grandmother a syphilitic whore!"

My stepson was nonplussed and practical: "Well, get in touch with whoever wrote it, thank him for the information, then tell him that by the way, your grandmother worked in the same establishment as his grandmother, his mother, his sisters, aunts, and all his female cousins!!!"

The article arrived in the mail a few days later. Its cocky young author turned out to be a notable psychoanalyst, Stephen Weissman, M.D. The article was riveting and perceptive and diligently researched. (It has since been published in Richard Schickel's *The Essential Chaplin*.) It also rang true. I was duly shocked. I was intrigued.

I phoned a friend who is the "Central Intelligence authority" on who is doing what on Chaplin—the Langley of Chapliniana. I asked him if he had heard of Steve Weissman.

"Weissman? The shrink? Sure have! He's had your father on the couch for years!" A posthumous psychoanalysis of my father? Oh dear! "He's doing a book. Something special. Big-time, if you ask me."

To make a long story short, I contacted Dr. Weissman, who confirmed that he was writing a book and promised to send it to me when it was finished. He kept his promise and here is the book.

It is unlike anything that has ever been written about my father. Weissman weaves a psychologically astute narrative of Chaplin's life and art, brilliantly exploring the relationships between experience and creativity.

A mixture of gritty social history, romance, and medical science, the book begins with Weissman dissecting Chaplin's parents' tempestuous courtship and disastrous marriage, coming to surprising conclusions. He then takes us into the world of the Victorian music hall. He is an expert, giving wonderful anecdotes about George Leybourne, Alfred Peck Stevens (the Great Vance), Joe Saunders, the male impersonators Vesta Tilly, Nellie Power, Ella Shields. He brings to life the streets of South London, the grim Hanwell orphanage, and finally, with a fresh insight, the Hollywood of the teens and the twenties.

Did Chaplin spin personal tragedy into universal comedy, creating the Little Tramp as a parody and a memorialization of his alcoholic father? Are Chaplin's film heroines sublimated, half-remembered, half-repressed memories of his tragic and adored mother? Weissman probes into the psychological explanation of the closest human bonds. It is uncanny how intuitively correct a trained outside investigator's conclusions can turn out to be.

This book, always provocative and at times heart-wrenching, is an enlightening read, an important addition to an understanding of my father's genius and art, and a unique meditation on the mystery of creativity.

—Geraldine Chaplin

Chaplin

A Family Romance

THE ENTRY IN THE REGISTER of the Hanwell School for Orphans and Destitute Children reads:

> Chaplin, Charles, aged 7, Protestant.
> Admitted on the 18th June, 1896.[1]

He made the twelve-mile trip to the orphanage in a horse-drawn bakery van. Rattling and bumping along lanes lined with chestnut trees, past orchards and wheat fields, the wagon rolled through the fragrant green English countryside. For the seven-year-old, it was a breath of fresh air compared to the grim, gray pavements and thick, smoky fog of the stifling tenement slums of South London from which he had come. Even years later as a grown man, Chaplin could recall the adventure of that van ride.

Until, that is, he was greeted by the first harsh intimations of the starkly regimented life that awaited him. Before donning their scratchy school uniforms, new children were routinely stripped, inspected, and deloused in order to prevent outbreaks of verminous epidemics. Young Charlie soon became one of a sorry group of thirty-five plucked youngsters who suffered the stigma of shaven, iodined heads and miserable quarantine that year.

Far worse than the combined ringworm and delousing regimen was the loss of his mother. With wisdom and compassion, the Lambeth Board of Guardians shipped Charlie off to Hanwell accompanied by Sydney, his older half brother and protector. But after four short months the Hanwell authorities decided that Sydney should be transferred to another institution where he could learn a trade, now that he had turned twelve and was preparing to make his own way in the world.

It was then for the first but not the last time that young Charlie Chaplin found himself desolate and utterly alone. Fourteen months feels like an eternity for a child that age, and Chaplin always remembered this period as one of the most unhappy in his life.

After returning to Hanwell thirty-odd years later at the height of his success, he told a friend:

I wouldn't have missed it for all I possess. It's what I've been wanting. God, you feel like the dead returning to the earth. To smell the smell of the dining hall, and to remember that was where *you* sat. . . . Only it wasn't you. It was you in another life — your soul-mate — something you were and something you aren't now. Like a snake that sheds its skin every now and then. It's one of the skins you've shed, but it's still got your odour about it. O-oh, it was wonderful. When I got there I knew it was what I'd been wanting for years. Everything had been leading up to it, and I was ripe for it. . . . Being among those buildings and connecting with everything — with the misery and something that wasn't misery.[2]

Fortunately for moviegoers, some of the skins Chaplin shed in the intervening years were made of celluloid. If you include all those old one- and two-reelers starting with Sennett and the Keystone days, along with seven or eight full-length film classics, they amount to more than eighty films — a remarkable number of moltings, even for Charlie, who lived to the age of eighty-eight and proudly fathered ten children of his own.

Sifting through Chaplin's celluloid moltings, it's not hard to pick up the scent of his childhood. Of course there's still room to wonder about the precise details. Was the Hanwell School bakery truck a closed van like the one that hauled off the recently orphaned gamine (Paulette Goddard) in *Modern Times*? Or was it an open, flat-bedded affair like the one in which the foundling (Jackie Coogan) got shipped off to the orphanage in *The Kid*? And if Chaplin's orphanage-haunted memories of delousing were not the source of his endless preoccupation with that wonderful flea-circus gag that eventually found its way into Calvero the clown's comeback performance in *Limelight*, where did it come from?

Calvero's oscillations between a flea-bitten tramp apologetically scratching himself and an expert trainer of acrobatic insects proudly placing his personal corps de ballet on display is executed with comic brilliance. But to say Chaplin mastered his old orphanage terror of being discovered flea-ridden by transforming it into a piece of exhibitionistic funny business does little to advance our understanding of how the creative process operated. Such a crude interpretation relies entirely upon Freud's primer on the psychology of jokes to explain the subtle mechanisms of comedy. It assumes that the comic mind operates as a seething id-cauldron automatically transforming childhood fears into schoolboy gags which are periodically belched and farted up from the steamy depths of the unconscious.

Of course, like everyone else, including his audience, Charlie did think along the lines of this eructatative-flatulent model of slapstick humor. When he was hot, Chaplin came up with a gag a minute. Sometimes his boiling brain overflowed at such a rate that the studio stenographers couldn't keep up with him. But at those times he was only mining his unconscious for the raw material of humor. The subtler process of comic refinement operated at an entirely different pace, with artistic methods and a timetable of its own.

For instance, it took more than thirty years from the original conception and filming of that flea gag before it found its way, uncut, into a finished film. Studio notes reveal that Chaplin first shot that idea while making *The Kid* — a most fitting occasion from a free-associative point of view, since it was his first film that dealt with his orphanage experiences as a child. But funny as it was, the gag didn't work in that film and ended up on the cutting-room floor.

Later, on at least three separate filmmaking occasions (*The Circus*, *The Great Dictator*, and an incomplete work, *The Professor*), Chaplin toyed with but resisted the temptation to use the flea routine. Judging from scant remaining footage of *The Professor*, revealing Charlie in a flophouse scene as Professor Bosco, the impresario of his own corporeal flea circus, the gag was going to serve as the comic centerpiece for that film. Interestingly, Chaplin family tradition had it that, at the time of Charlie's birth in London, Charlie Sr. was out of town playing Professor Bosco's Empire Palace of Varieties in Hull. But even though he had connected his cherished flea gag with memories of his dead father, Chaplin still did not feel ready to use it. As a colleague once put it, "Chaplin had a mind like an attic. Everything was stored away in case it ever came in handy."[3]

The flea gag didn't find its place in one of his movies until he made *Limelight*, the film in which he belatedly came to terms with his parents' marriage and his conflicted feelings toward his alcoholic father, whom he had always blamed for their family falling apart. It was a time in Chaplin's life when, at the age of sixty-three, he had finally begun to settle into a stable family situation of his own. Having at last set aside his lifelong ambivalence about marriage and fatherhood, he felt the need to put some painful memories of his own father to rest.

Also woven into those fictionalized recollections of the man whose name he bore and whose trade he plied was Chaplin's mounting fear that, like his father before him, he too was about to be spurned and forgotten by his once-doting public. And so when Chaplin made *Limelight*, his final opus, he created the character of Calvero the clown — a composite of himself and his father, a faded music hall star and flea-bitten has-been. While filming both a magnificent final comeback for himself and a forgiving tribute to his father's memory, Chaplin brought the flea business back to where it began. For as seven-year-old Charlie well knew, he would never have had to deal with fleas and orphanages in the first place if it had not been for his father's refusal to rescue his mother from the Lambeth poorhouse.

Hannah Hill Chaplin's precipitous decline from headliner to breadliner was a devastating defeat for the formerly "lighthearted and gay" music hall comedienne,[4] better known to her fans and admirers as "that charming little chanter, Lillie Harley"[5] — or Lily Harley, the usual spelling. After losing her singing voice, her theatrical bookings, her sons, and her pluck, she ultimately plunged from poorhouse to madhouse, where she was labeled both a lunatic and a pauper, much to her young son's dismay.

While half blaming his alcoholically impaired father for not coming to his mother's aid, the small boy couldn't shake a nagging feeling "that she had deliberately escaped from her mind and had deserted us."[6] Except for two brief remissions, the former songbird spent the rest of her life as a madwoman who, having regained her singing voice, sometimes required the soundproofing of a padded seclusion cell because of her theatrical tendency to belt out militant Christian marching songs on inauspicious occasions.

Preferring to drown his disappointments over his waning theatrical career, Charlie's father drank himself to death by the time Charlie was twelve. Left to make his way alone at an early age, the son of these two once semisuccessful vaudevillians on occasion had to sleep on the streets, busk for pennies to the tune of hurdy-gurdies, and scavenge for his supper. But ever mindful of his former station in life even in the face of dire poverty, he desperately struggled to keep up a facade of shabby gentility in order not to lose that most precious of all Englishmen's possessions, his sense of social class. Once, on unexpectedly encountering a former playmate, young Charlie casually dismissed his tattered and patched appearance by ad-libbing that he was just on his way home from a carpentry lesson. But inwardly the youngster cringed at the sorry spectacle of his own poverty and daydreamed of creating a successful vaudeville act playing a millionaire tramp.

Like Dickens, who was haunted by his boyhood encounter with the bootblacking factory and his parents' stint in debtor's prison, Charlie Chaplin never forgot his family's calamitous plunge into poverty and those feral moments of his childhood spent on the streets of South London. He recalled them over and over again in his immortal persona the Little Tramp. Not only did Charlie's character relive and sometimes triumph over his boyhood tribulations, but at times his tramp also appeared determined to correct the respective plights of Chaplin's parents, albeit with slapstick.

In spite of his puny, ineffectual appearance, Charlie's wobbly, waddling tramp-hero brings a ferocious determination to the saving of wistful young women beset by poverty, unemployment, loneliness, institutionalization, incurable physical illness, prostitution, stolen babies, and other dire predicaments. And when under the influence, as he was on at least a dozen separate filmmaking occasions, Chaplin's Little Tramp weaves his woozy way through booby-trapped obstacle courses filled with lethal pitfalls and comic pratfalls designed to destroy all but the most nimble of alcoholics. Through choreographic miracles of their creator's invention, Chaplin's drunks are always watched over and kept from harm's way by their guardian angel.

In his most memorable final fade-outs, the Little Tramp shuffles offscreen into the sunset, desolate and alone. What is most striking about Chaplin's nostalgic renderings both of his family and of the lonely predicaments of his boyhood in these scenes is the bittersweetness of his comic vision and the re- markably forgiving way in which he commemorated his feckless parents.

Family Secrets

I once had in mind a picture which was a burlesque of sentimentality. The opening scene was a long, long stair. The camera was following an old lady carrying a bucket of water.
Struggling up each step, you know, painful with rheumatism,
getting to one landing, and up another. And when she gets on
the fourth or the fifth landing, a man suddenly opens a door and
hits her a terrific punch right in the face. He turns white, says,
"Oh, I beg your pardon, lady. I thought you were my mother."
And she says, "You have a mother?" He weeps and says, "Yes, I
have a mother."

— Chaplin[1]

CHARLIE CHAPLIN'S STAGESTRUCK COCKNEY PARENTS met in
1881 while touring in a provincial theatrical production of
Shamus O'Brien, an Irish melodrama. For the teenage would-be
music hall stars, landing roles in the play marked the start of
promising show business careers. Meeting so auspiciously lent a
magical quality to their backstage romance, which in turn helped
fuel their attraction to one another. As their son Charlie put it at
age seventy-five, they were very soon "sweethearts."[2]

Their mutually idealizing experience — encountering a professional and social counterpart at such a critical turning point — was like gazing into a looking glass and discovering a soul mate. Their roller-coaster romance, tempestuous courtship, and disastrous marriage began with this adolescent infatuation. It was a case of first love mistaken for true love.

That these two ambitious Londoners came from such similar working-class backgrounds contributed to the illusion of ideal compatibility. He was a butcher's son, she a shoemaker's daughter. But despite their shared dream of self-betterment, they were fundamentally different people. When she jilted him in 1883 and ran off to South Africa to marry a wealthy member of the British aristocracy whom she had just met, Chaplin's mother revealed just how far her social ambitions exceeded his father's. His father (referred to henceforth as Charlie Chaplin Sr.) set his sights on becoming a music hall star. But Hannah Hill had bigger fish to fry.

If we read between the lines, theatrical success was a stepping-stone to much grander, if not grandiose, life plans. The stage name she picked — Lily Harley — suggests the extent of her determination to rise above her station in life.

Vivacious, flirtatious, and impulsive, the sixteen-year-old Hannah had just run away from home. Nothing if not a risk taker, she determined to escape the usual fate of a teenage working-class girl in South London. Rather than resign herself to the vocational and social dead ends to which unmarried young women of her class were routinely consigned in the rigidly class-conscious world that was late-nineteenth-century London, she hoped to baffle destiny by becoming Lily Harley. That gamble was a terrible risk. But if her luck held up, she hoped to become a romantic adventuress just like the famous actress whose name she echoed in her own. Lily Harley yearned to become the next Lillie Langtry.

Better known to her adoring public as the Jersey Lily, Langtry was a renowned actress who had been a mistress of the Prince of Wales, the future Edward VII, whom she playfully addressed as "Bertie." As Lily Harley well knew, Langtry's life was living proof that commoners and kings could mingle freely. Or, as Hannah Hill probably reasoned to herself before deciding to run away from home and seek a career in the theater, talented young actresses of Langtry's ilk could end up marrying wealthy aristocrats if they met the right people and got the right breaks.

Along with Lillie Langtry, two other women served as inspirational fixations for Lily Harley's teenage dream of emancipation via an expert blend of sexual seductiveness and feminine wiles. One was Josephine de Beauharnais, who, a hundred years earlier, had conquered the most powerful man on the Continent and parlayed her conquest into becoming empress of France.

The other figure in Lily's pantheon of female seductresses was a young woman who grew up in the slums of seventeenth-century London, Nell Gwyn. The Cockney-born actress and former child prostitute had ended up as royal mistress to Charles II, whose reign had marked the end of Oliver Cromwell's austere Puritan revolution. Defiantly proud of her loyal service to her beloved monarch, Nell delighted in describing herself as "His Majesty's Protestant whore." And she was equally proud of bearing the royal bastard, the Duke of St. Albans.

Chaplin later recalled a vivid childhood memory of a full-length, life-size portrait of Nell Gwyn that had a place of honor in his mother's front room when he was a child of two or three. He also recalled his own fascination a few years later as a spellbound seven-year-old, when his mother was more economically pressed, watching her improvisations of scenes from Gwyn's life that she performed in their one-room slum garret for his edification and her own amusement: "She would enact Nell Gwyn, vividly describing her leaning over the palace stairs holding her baby, threatening Charles II: 'Give this child a name, or I'll dash it to the ground!' And King Charles hastily concurring: 'All right! The duke of St. Albans.'"[3]

Minus the life-size portrait, similar improvisational sketches were also accorded to Lily's other favorite, Josephine de Beauharnais. Lily's performances of scenes featuring Napoleon and Josephine for seven-year-old Charlie were so unforgettable that many years later he periodically toyed with film treatments and screenplays for possible movies about Napoleon's life.

And in a remarkable real-life scenario that a thirty-five-year-old Chaplin arranged in 1924 with a sixteen-year-old aspiring actress, he insisted she play Josephine to his Napoleon while he initiated her into sex in his boudoir. Not unlike the original Beauharnais-Bonaparte relationship, the question of who conquered whom is entirely debatable. Subsequently forced to marry that starstruck, status-seeking teenager after the seduction resulted in an unplanned pregnancy that she refused to terminate, Chaplin placed her on prominent public display at a fabulous costume ball at William Randolph Hearst's palatial home, where they dressed in historically authentic Napoleon and Josephine costumes (designed and sewn by the wardrobe department of his film studio). Rather than admit to the Hollywood community the mortifying truth, that the great Chaplin had met his Waterloo in the bedroom of his Hollywood mansion, the star saw this flamboyant display of his new Josephine as a public relations ploy that would quell the widely circulating rumors of his secret shotgun wedding by depicting their marriage as both voluntary and happy.

The entire Napoleon-Josephine display in 1924 can also be seen as an unconscious reenactment of his star-crossed parents' courtship and marriage in the early 1880s. The crucial psychological importance of Charlie Chaplin Sr. as the original Napoleon figure for Chaplin's midlife drama cannot be overestimated. Without him, or Charlie's image of him, it would have be an entirely different story.

Chaplin's mother undoubtedly envisioned herself as Josephine in her performances for her son back in 1896. But Lily's enactments of famous historical scenes from Bonaparte's life, coupled with her romanticized description of Charlie Sr. as resembling Napoleon, captivated the father-hungry child and satisfied his curiosity about his social origins. When young Charlie begged her on repeated occasions to tell once more the tale of how she and his absent father first met and became sweethearts while touring in *Shamus O'Brien*, Lily employed her well-developed powers of theatrical embroidery. She breathlessly informed Charlie that his handsome and brooding father had been a dead ringer for France's first emperor.

One glance at a photograph of Charlie Chaplin Sr. on the sheet music cover of "The Girl Was Young and Pretty" — a masher ballad he successfully popularized at the height of his fame in the 1890s — clearly reveals that he was no Napoleon look-alike. And that observation in turn confirms that, when they first met in *Shamus O'Brien*, they had seen each other through the distorting lens of looking-glass love. She needed to see him as a Napoleonic consort whose looks matched her own grandiose ambitions.

Exactly how, when, and why the scales of romantic idealization first fell from Lily Harley's eyes is unclear. Given that Charlie Chaplin Sr. died in 1901 from severe and chronic alcoholism, it is entirely possible that he had already started drinking heavily when he and Lily first met in 1881.

But considering the scope of her ambitions, it is equally possible that when she jilted Charlie's father only three years later, it was because she was under the impression that she had just landed a bigger fish. That man was a member of the English aristocracy by the name of Sydney Hawkes. Or at least that was what he claimed to be.

Ardently pursuing eighteen-year-old Lily, Sydney Hawkes talked her into running away with him to South Africa, where they planned to get married and live on his wealthy family's plantation estate. Instead, Lily ended up with an out-of-wedlock pregnancy and, quite likely, a case of syphilis, which she probably contracted as the result of a brief encounter with prostitution in the South African gold rush of 1884.

We know through hospital records in England that Lily was diagnosed in 1898, at age thirty-three, with psychotic symptoms caused by third-stage neurosyphilis of the brain. And she also suffered from migrainelike head pains in 1895, when she was twenty-nine. Taking into account the well-established progressive course of meningovascular syphilis and reasoning backward, it is probable that Lily Harley first contracted primary syphilis in South Africa.

We also know from South African historical records that the enticement of gullible young Cockney girls to that country with false promises of marriage, after which some of them were raped and forced into lives as white slaves in the boomtown dance halls on the Witwatersrand by fast-talking pimps from London's East End, was a common occurrence in the much more famous gold rush of 1886. Whether a similar, if less violent, seduction scenario was also the case for Lily Harley two years earlier — when a less sustained and less lucrative gold rush had just taken place — is not known.

As to Sydney Hawkes, a Cockney con man and East End Jew who sweet-talked the ambitious gold digger from across the Thames in South London to South Africa under false pretenses, his reasons for doing so are unclear. If Hawkes was only the bookmaker that Chaplin family lore and previous Chaplin scholarship have always agreed he was, luring Lily halfway around the world at great expense and effort just to have his way with her seems unlikely.

But if "bookmaker" was a euphemism for pimp, his slick seduction of a would-be seductress by promising her the world makes perfect sense. Provided, that is, the term "pimp" is being used in a broad enough sense to include a fancy man — a fast-talking hustler who encourages a vulnerable woman's love for him and then exploits those feelings by getting her to turn tricks with customers he provides, in order to support the two of them in the lavish style to which he is accustomed.

While it is difficult to picture Hawkes luring Harley to South Africa out of love, it seems unlikely that Lily would have named their love child Sydney after she returned to England unless she still had residual feelings for the father, even though he had lied to her and used her.

Forty years later, in 1925, Lily's second son Charlie made a film in which his alter ego attempts to console and rescue a downhearted prostitute who is trapped and stranded in the hollow life of a good-time girl in a gold-rush boomtown saloon far from home. Chaplin claimed at the time he made it that this picture was the one for which he most wanted to be remembered by posterity.

Less a matter of conjecture are the events that followed Lily's return from South Africa in 1884. Sadder, wiser, more than a little bit pregnant, and probably infected with syphilis, Lily wasted no time in seeking out and reestablishing contact with her former sweetheart, Chaplin Sr. Although she had no way to know it, the microorganism that causes syphilis (*Treponema pallidum*) may by then have been permanently lodged in her body like a silent, ticking timebomb.

Lily was first diagnosed with syphilis when she became psychotic in 1898. In the 1890s, before the Wassermann test was developed, that disease was widely known as "the great mimic." The medical nickname underscored that syphilis could easily imitate other conditions, physical and mental. Sometimes a missed diagnosis of masquerading syphilis was made only at the time of autopsy. But in thirty-three-year-old Lily's case, the admitting physician's diagnostic impression that his patient was suffering from a case of syphilis masquerading as madness was probably based on his finding classic neurological signs compatible with syphilis on physical examination.

If in 1898 Lily Harley developed a syphilitic brain infection that had begun to drive her crazy, when and how did the *Treponema pallidum* spirochete first enter her central nervous system? That monthlong siege of unremitting headaches that Lily had developed three years earlier, in 1895, offers a possible clue. Diagnosed at the time as migraine headaches, they might actually have resulted from meningovascular syphilis. The term refers to an inflammation in the walls of the blood vessels of the brain lining, or meninges. And the inflammatory response in those blood vessels is caused by the immune system's futile attempt to destroy the invading microorganism and prevent it from entering the brain itself. Those irritated blood vessels can cause a patient to suffer from blinding headaches, indistinguishable from regular migraines.

Indistinguishable, that is, except that typical migraine attacks don't last a month. And in the 1890s (or the 1990s) migraine headaches didn't result in medically indigent and otherwise healthy young women requiring monthlong hospitalizations at public expense, as Lily Harley did in 1895 in the Lambeth Infirmary. Assuming her "migraine attack" was due to a case of meningovascular syphilis and plotting backward, it is then possible to postulate that she first contracted primary syphilis eleven years earlier in South Africa in 1884. Although it could have occurred later, this timetable is compatible with the well-known chronological progression of that disease, which most frequently manifests itself five to ten years after the infection but can appear for the first time as much as thirty years later.

That none of Lily's children developed congenital syphilis does not help pinpoint the timing of her original infection. Contrary to popular belief, syphilis at any stage in a pregnant woman does not invariably cause congenital syphilis in her child. That none of her children ever showed signs of congenital syphilis does not mean that she was free of that disease at the time of her pregnancy with that child. Nor of course is it the case that a woman had to be a prostitute in order to contract syphilis. Women who are active with only one partner their entire lives can and do contract sexually transmitted diseases.

The only medical fact we know for certain is that when Lily Harley first became psychotic in 1898, the admitting physician entered in her medical records an explanatory diagnosis of syphilis. He never specified the stage — primary, secondary, latent, or tertiary.

The first hint we have that Charlie knew about his mother's disease came from the late-life recollections of another glamorous and promiscuous showgirl, Louise Brooks. As an eighteen-year-old starlet in the Ziegfeld Follies in 1925, she had a two-month casual fling with the married movie star in which they both knew the score from the start. Looking back on their amorous interlude many years later, Louise recalled with good-natured amusement Chaplin's odd habit of painting his penis with iodine to protect himself from contracting a venereal disease. As she put it, "Charlie came running at me with his little red sword."[4]

At the time of their affair, Chaplin had come to New York for the premier of *The Gold Rush*. But he remained there for two months, comfortably ensconced in a posh Manhattan hotel suite with Brooks. He stayed with Louise for such a long time in order to avoid what he perceived as the nauseating prospect of returning home to Hollywood and his money-grubbing, minnow-brained teenage wife who had recently given birth to the unwanted child that had made him so miserable.

Shortly after he and Louise parted company, Charlie sent her a hefty check (unsolicited) as the expression of his deep gratitude for her company at what had been such an extraordinarily lonely and painful time in his life despite the fabulous reception his masterpiece had received and the fact that it had made him the toast of New York. When he finally arrived back at their Beverly Hills home, his wife was completely bewildered by her insomniac husband's taking as many as eight or ten showers and baths a day. Like Chaplin's compulsive penis painting, his compulsive showering was probably a germ phobia. If his self-cleansing rituals were a transient case of syphilophobia, it's noteworthy that they developed shortly after he completed *The Gold Rush* and established a casual sexual liaison with a sophisticated and intelligent woman of the world who was willing to love him with no strings attached.

Conclusive evidence that Charlie knew about his mother's syphilis came from Jerry Epstein, who was a close friend of Chaplin and served as his assistant producer on *Limelight*. In addition to telling me of Hannah Chaplin's syphilis, which Charlie revealed to him while working on *Limelight*, Epstein also put me in touch with David Robinson, who generously provided a copy of Hannah's psychiatric records verifying that diagnosis.

Robinson omitted the story of Hannah's syphilis in his own 1985 biography — probably out of consideration for Chaplin's family. (As Geraldine Chaplin notes in her introduction to this book, her first reaction upon learning about my article was to assume that I was a brash biographer who was calling her grandmother "a syphilitic whore" for sensational effect.) In any case, once I published my 1996 article discussing Hannah Chaplin's mental illness and establishing that it had been diagnosed as a case of syphilis, the story of her incurable venereal disease became a matter of public record.[5]

And so in 2001, when a new edition of his own Chaplin biography came out, Robinson mentioned her medical history in passing — without addressing the more controversial conjectural issues concerning her problematic sexuality raised in that article.

In an unpublished autobiographical novel, *Footlights*, which he later used as a treatment for the script of *Limelight*, Chaplin discreetly referred to his showgirl mother's sexuality as her "tragic promiscuity." And in the film *Limelight*, when the hero Calvero saves the beautiful ballet dancer–heroine Terry from a suicide attempt, he erroneously assumes that she is trying to kill herself because she has just contracted an incurable venereal disease. (Moreover, from a psychoanalytic perspective, the hysterical paralysis of Terry's ballet dancer legs in *Limelight* can be understood as a classic symbolic expression of her unconscious conflicts over becoming a streetwalker, a line of work her older sister engaged in to support Terry's training as a ballet dancer — a fact we learn from *Footlights*.) Equally noteworthy is the fact that Hannah Chaplin and Terry were both ballet dancers at the Empire Theatre, whose famous promenade, Charlie nostalgically recalled, was "frequented by the smartest courtesans" of the Edwardian Era.[6]

Returning to David Robinson's strategic decision to steer clear of any in-depth exploration of Hannah Chaplin's indisputable medical history of syphilis, our two biographies approach Chaplin's life from very different viewpoints. As he put it in his 1985 preface:

Readers who like biographers to supply post-Freudian interpretations for every action and incident may be frustrated. I have no personal liking for that genre of biography; I do not feel qualified for psychoanalysis; and finally I think that Chaplin's singular life story would defy the process.[7]

Improvisations

One of my earliest recollections was that each night before Mother went to the theatre Sydney and I were lovingly tucked up in a comfortable bed and left in the care of the house-maid. . . .

Every night, after she came home from the theatre, it was her custom to leave delicacies on the table for Sydney and me to find in the morning — a slice of Neapolitan cake or candies — with the understanding that we were not to make a noise in the morning, as she usually slept late.

Mother was a soubrette on the variety stage, a *mignonne* in her late twenties, with fair complexion, violet-blue eyes and long light-brown hair that she could sit upon. . . . Though she was not an exceptional beauty, we thought her divine-looking. . . . she was dainty and attractive and had compelling charm. She took pride in dressing us up for Sunday excursions, Sydney in an Eton suit with long trousers and me in a blue velvet one with blue gloves to match. Such occasions were orgies of smugness, as we ambled along the Kennington Road.

— Chaplin, age 75[1]

F OR THE REST OF HIS LIFE, CHAPLIN CHERISHED this nostalgic image of the emotional security and financial prosperity his family had enjoyed when he was a cosseted and pampered child of three. Four years later, a new boy at the orphanage, the seven-year-old would inform his fellow inmates that, unlike some less fortunate children, he and Sydney had parents. Nor were they charity cases whose parents had been obliged to make them permanent wards of the state. Their stay at Hanwell was to be temporary. He and Syd would be leaving as soon as their actress mother got her career back on track. Their mother was the famous music hall star Lily Harley, whose salary of twenty-five pounds per week had, until recently, provided them with a life of luxury. It might be only a matter of a few weeks, a month at most, before she would come and bring them home. They would then be back on Easy Street, or, more precisely, on Westminster Bridge Road. (Actually, their "posh digs" there were not very far from the working-class neighborhood where Lily herself had grown up.)

In a three-room flat on the road — with Nell Gwyn adorning the front room — Lily and the boys had delighted in the luxury of their la-di-da lifestyle, complete with a maidservant to look after their daily needs. Sunday was their favorite day. Lily's most ostentatious indulgence was her weekly Sunday morning strolls with Charlie and Syd, parading up and down Kennington Road for all her former friends and acquaintances from the old neighborhood to see, if they chanced to pass by. Smartly turned out in jewels and finery, she loved showing off her boys, who were dressed to kill in children's outfits whose expensive elegance advertised and celebrated her success as a music hall star.

Lily's actual success, however, was as something rather different. What she was, during this period of magical prosperity in Charlie Chaplin's early childhood, was a well-paid backup singer and mistress of an immensely successful music hall star, Leo Dryden. Exhaustive research in the *Era* (the nineteenth-century

British equivalent of *Variety*) finds no mention of Lily Harley playing musical hall venues anywhere in England, Ireland, Scotland, or Wales as a solo artiste performing under her own name during this period.

The absence of a performer's name in that show business newspaper of record was not definitive proof that his or her career was dead, dormant, or budding. Struggling players treading the boards in obscure venues could and did fall through the cracks. Failure to appear in the *Era* was suggestive but not hard evidence, as some of Chaplin's previous biographers have assumed. In truth, it is impossible to trace any nineteenth-century music hall performer's career with complete confidence by relying exclusively on the *Era*. That does not apply to music hall stars earning twenty-five pounds per week, however. Stage appearances by an actor or actress earning that much were duly noted in the *Era*. When Charlie's glamorous actress-mother tucked him in, kissed him goodnight, and dashed off to the theater, it is clear she could not have been appearing as an artiste in her own right. She may have been wearing glittering stage makeup and diaphanous theatrical gowns, but Lily Harley was not the superstar that her impressionable and adoring young son thought she was.

Given the fact that Lily and the boys lived with Leo Dryden *en famille* during this two-and-a-half-year period, it's likely that her financially successful show business career consisted at most of appearing onstage as a backup singer in her lover's act. It is not known if Charlie and Syd were encouraged to think of Leo as a father, an uncle, or simply a close friend of Lily's at the start of their liaison, but by the time Lily joyfully gave birth to their half brother Wheeler Dryden two years later, Charlie and Syd had certainly come to consider him a father figure. But when Leo then stole their six-month-old baby brother and ran away to Canada, they began to think of him as a monster who had devastated their mother and plunged her into a severe depression.

The only rational explanation for Leo's cruelty was that by stealing the baby he was depriving Lily of an ongoing meal ticket. No matter how destitute his ex-mistress became or how much he continued to prosper as a music hall star, Dryden was off the hook permanently for child support payments. Leo's fame and prosperity had undoubtedly contributed to Lily's attraction to him in the first place. She probably thought when she "divorced" Charlie Sr., Cockney-style, that Leo Dryden or someone like him would be a much more successful match.

Whether she left her husband for Dryden or met Dryden after she left her husband is uncertain. What is indisputable is that, once again following her penchant for picking men to exploit who then exploited her, Lily mistook Leo's glitter for substance and hitched her wagon to his star. Seven years earlier, her blind ambition had led her to tread that same self-destructive path with Sydney Hawkes. But having failed then as an eligible, childless young woman who sought prominence by marrying into the aristocracy, this time she set her sights on the more realistic goal of "marrying" a wealthy superstar and having his baby.

Viewed from Charlie Chaplin Sr.'s perspective, the experience of being twice rejected by the same woman was a painful reminder of his naïveté and her crass opportunism. After five years of marriage, he had returned home from a successful tour in the States (where he played the Union Square Theatre in New York City) to discover that he had once again been abandoned.

His namesake son was one and a half years old at the time. For the next seven years, father and son spent little if any time together, although they lived only a few minutes apart. During that period, as Charlie grew more mobile and more observant, there were increasingly frequent sightings of his sorely missed father, which he later recalled with devastating accuracy. Whether father and son saw each other so infrequently was Lily's doing or Charles Sr.'s is unclear. But carefully filed among the many visuals in Chaplin's childhood memory are a series of tracking and panning shots of drunks in motion — meticulously observed studies of the subtle variations in gait, posture, and tilt of body angle, all of which would serve as choreographic templates for his future repertoire of impersonations of alcoholics. Not surprisingly, Charlie's ticket to Hollywood would be earned on the basis of the skill with which he played a comic drunk. In fact, long before he ever made a film, at least one theater critic had already declared Chaplin "the world's greatest impersonator of inebriates and the biggest laughmaker on the vaudeville stage."[2]

But unquestionably during the first few years after their "divorce," Charlie Sr. was completely marginalized by his successor, who was financially supporting both of the children. The one known visit young Charlie paid his estranged father during this time was arranged by his mother. It took place at the nearby Canterbury Music Hall on Westminster Bridge Road, where the wide-eyed boy, then only three or four, sat in a red plush velvet seat in the orchestra pit while his father performed onstage. Considering the strained feelings between Lily and Charlie Sr. at the time, it's unlikely that she took him backstage to visit his father after the show that night. (If she had, Chaplin would surely have mentioned it.) In any event, young Charlie never said what he saw his father perform that night. Still, enough is known of his father's fifteen-year career in music hall to describe the kind of material his impressionable child might have observed. A talented character actor with a fine light baritone voice, handsome good looks, polished manners, an affable smile, and an aura of bonhomie, Charlie Sr. specialized in playing elegant swells, bon vivants, champagne-swilling men-about-town.

Arriving onstage resplendent in a tall silk hat, a frock coat with matching trousers, starched cuffs with an equally stiff bib dickey, and a formal batwing collar with a fastidiously knotted and billowing cravat, he sang (and dramatized with running stage patter) songs about the high life.

With a glass of bubbly in one hand and a walking stick in the other, he offered bone-weary laborers temporary respite from their hard lives through vicarious identification with the life of ease his stage character personified. After his act was over, it would be his great pleasure — in fact it was a job requisite — to meet and greet those same blokes at the bar and encourage them, by convivial example, to spend as much of their hard-earned money on beer, wine, or champagne as they could afford — or ill afford. His own conspicuous consumption of the most expensive wines and spirits on the refreshment list was, of course, on the house, courtesy of a management that carefully calculated the precise value of his artistry by the amount of drinking his act inspired.

If Lily Harley exploited her good looks and charm by playing flirtatious coquettes and adorable *mignonnes* to seduce her audiences, Charlie Sr. was a professional charmer in his own right. Off-stage, they must have been a pleasing couple when they were young. Given their respective onstage personae, it's easy to understand the original basis of their attraction and to imagine the powerful chemistry between them as teenage sweethearts.

But Charlie Sr.'s feelings for Lily Harley had been deeper than that. His acceptance of her on her return from South Africa in 1885 was remarkable. Arriving back in London broke, friendless, and pregnant, she made a beeline for her ex-sweetheart. Moving into a rooming house with her, he supported her emotionally and financially through the third trimester of her pregnancy with another man's baby, married her three months later, and adopted and raised the child Syd as his own.

Based on their history, it's easy to see why, when Leo walked out on her and the boys, Lily again made a beeline for Charlie Sr. By then, however, he was living with another woman whom he had "married," Cockney-style, by sharing a home and having a child with her. Although he had finally become a major headliner and was, for the time being, in a financial position to help Lily, he was not inclined to do so. Suing Charlie Sr. first beseechingly and then in the courts, Lily was unsuccessful on both counts.

Since voluntary child support was not forthcoming, in the court hearing that followed, bitter accusations of adultery were traded back and forth. Rather than decide the question of who wronged whom, the court decided in favor of the children by awarding their mother fifteen shillings a week child support. But Charlie Sr., still deeply hurt by Lily's betrayal of him with Leo Dryden, responded by simply refusing to keep up the payments. Setting out to support her brood, Lily sang for their supper till her voice literally gave out.

Young Charlie Chaplin never forgot the night his mother's voice cracked. Not only did it mark the fatal downturn of their already declining fortunes, but Lily's swan song also was, he claimed in his autobiography, his first night in show business as a performer. It was at the Aldershot Canteen, a dingy, smoke-filled hall jammed with rowdy drunken soldiers who delighted in heckling (and pelting) performers who failed to please them, driving the unlucky ones off stage. By now, not only was Lily forced to accept lesser bookings in noisier halls, which put a further strain on her delicate voice, but her straitened circumstances also forced her to dispense with the childcare services of her housemaid, which is why five-year-old Charlie was backstage that night.

I remember standing in the wings when Mother's voice cracked and went into a whisper. The audience began to laugh and sing falsetto and to make catcalls. It was all vague and I did not quite understand what was going on. But the noise increased until Mother was obliged to walk off the stage. When she came into the wings she was very upset and argued with the stage manager who, having seen me perform before Mother's friends, said something about letting me go on in her place.

And in the turmoil I remember him leading me by the hand and, after a few explanatory words to the audience, leaving me on the stage alone. And before a glare of footlights and faces in smoke, I started to sing, accompanied by the orchestra, which fiddled about until it found my key. It was a well-known song called "Jack Jones" that went as follows:

> Jack Jones well and known to everybody
> Round about the market, don't yer see,
> I've no fault to find with Jack at all,
> Not when 'e's as 'e used to be.
> But since 'e's had the bullion left him
> 'E has altered for the worst.
> For to see the way he treats all his old pals
> Fills me with nothing but disgust.
> Each Sunday morning he reads the *Telegraph*,
> Once he was contented with the *Star*.
> Since Jack Jones has come into a little bit of cash,
> Well, 'e don't know where 'e are.

Halfway through, a shower of money poured onto the stage. Immediately I stopped and announced that I would pick up the money first and sing afterward. This caused much laughter. The stage manager came on with a handkerchief and helped me to gather it up. I thought he was going to keep it. This thought was conveyed to the audience and increased their laughter, especially when he walked off with it with me anxiously following him. Not until he handed it to Mother did I return and continue to sing. I was quite at home. I talked to the audience, danced and did several imitations including one of Mother singing her Irish march song. . . .

And in repeating the chorus, in all innocence I imitated Mother's voice cracking and was surprised at the impact it had on the audience. There was laughter and cheers, then more money-throwing; and when Mother came on the stage to carry me off, her presence evoked tremendous applause. That night was my first appearance on the stage and Mother's last.[3]

Lily's theatrical dreams were rapidly eclipsed. But there was still the hope of an occasional windfall booking. While making the rounds of the agencies on the off chance she might fill some last-minute hole in a playbill, she was obliged to supplement those meager pickings by mending holes in other people's clothes. After a brief stint as a ballet dancer at the Empire Theatre, she became a seamstress, doing fancy needlework for affluent women, a talent she had acquired earlier by sewing her own theatrical costumes.

Her wounded confidence only added to the quiver in her already failing voice whenever she faced an audience. But her old gusto returned when she played private command performances for her two most loyal fans, Charlie and Syd. Cheering herself up by basking in the admiration of her two spellbound sons, who still considered her divine, the twenty-nine-year-old violet-eyed soubrette slipped into her fading sequined gowns, donned her feathers and rhinestones, and serenaded the boys with her music hall routines, including her signature numbers as that coquettishly charming *mignonne*, Lily Harley.

Necessity forced her to pawn, one by one, her jewels, her fashionable clothes, and her prized possessions — including the beloved Nell Gwyn portrait. But she held on to her theatrical gowns, props, and wigs for as long as she could in the hope of staging a comeback. These were the last to go.

Given her need to pay the rent and make ends meet on a needleworker's wages, which would have placed their family income at or near the poverty line and forced them to live in the worst slums in London, it's reasonable to assume that she may have reluctantly supplemented her funds by exposing her children to a steady stream of awkwardly introduced "friends" and "uncles" who visited or spent the night.

After tracing every street address where Chaplin lived during this grim period in his life, one researcher concluded that his boyhood memories of his family's Dickensian poverty were exaggerated because he and Lily never lived in the foul, dank, rat-infested hovels of the notorious London underworld of that time. Anticipating such disbelief about the extent of his child-hood poverty, Chaplin confided to a friend, Konrad Bercovici:

> I shall never be able to tell anybody all the poverty and all the misery and all the humiliation we — my mother, my brother, and I — have endured. I shall never be able to tell, for no one would believe it. I myself at times cannot believe all the things that we have gone through.[4]

As to precisely what those humiliations were, three decades later Charlie told Konrad that he was toying with the idea of writing a real shocker. His personal memoir would be a sensational exposé on how the children of the poor learn the facts of life at a tender age. But instead of frankly revealing his showgirl mother's unconventional sexual mores and hard-pressed survival tactics, when he finally did publish his autobiography at age seventy-five, Chaplin alluded to them with great dignity, saying simply: "To gauge the morals of our family by commonplace standards would be as erroneous as putting a thermometer in boiling water."[5]

In that book Charlie recalls in loving detail how his beautiful young mother bravely coped with the oppressive drudgery of the menial labor she had fought so desperately to circumvent, nostalgically describing the wonderful legacy of her lunch breaks and work breaks in the snug and tidy slum garrets they called home. He wrote of a fastidious housekeeper and fiercely devoted mother, undaunted by poverty, who was determined to inspire both of her sons to better themselves by providing them with a primary education in the fine points of acting and the art of stagecraft.

During her respites from the tedium of fancy needlework, Lily would rummage through the playbills in her trunk and take the boys on trips down memory lane. She would not only enact whole scenes from plays but also render perfect imitations and satirical takeoffs of the distinctive performance styles and quirky personality traits of the famous actors and actresses of the day, from both the legitimate stage and the music halls. Teaching by example, she showed the boys how to "do" people. Her talent for mimicry passed to Charlie, who became famous for it, giving remarkable impromptu performances that people remembered for the rest of their lives.

There on a stool sat Charlie Chaplin before a dozen cheering guests. His eyes were blazing, his hair was awry, with clenched fingers he shook his hands at the ceiling . . . frenzied words were pouring from his mouth. The torrent of eloquence was uninter-rupted. He was speaking in the broadest Cockney and, for a moment, I had a shuddering memory of a séance I had once attended in which the medium had been possessed by a Cockney "control." There was the same white face, the same distended pupils, the same twitching lips. Charlie was possessed by one of the fiercest spirits of an intolerant world — by one of those tattered English demagogues who nightly gesticulate at Hyde Park. Often on Spring evenings, I have listened to these orators, fascinated by the abandon with which they denounce the rich, drawn by the impotent fluttering of their thin, dirty hands. But I shall never listen to them again, for none of the denunciations I ever heard in Hyde Park could equal in their searing bitterness, the speech which Chaplin made that night. It was one of the most dangerous condemnations of the existing order which can ever have been delivered. Yet we cheered and cheered, as though we too were part of the shivering crowd in Hyde Park, and we cheered not only a brilliant performance but a superb exercise in economic argument. . . . You have only to listen to him describe a Cockney newspaper-seller, joking at his rags, referring with a wink to the arm he has lost in the war, trying to cough because the fog is creeping into his lungs — there is no tragedy of life's seamy side which Charlie does not know.[6]

The theater was Lily's lifeblood. And unlike those fully costumed rehearsals of her own act, which were intended as preparation for the personal comeback for which she still hoped, the improv performances in her everyday work clothes were meant to inspire a love of theater in her sons and to serve as rudimentary tutorials in acting, by deconstructing seamless performances into their component parts. This deconstruction — a running commentary of asides — was offered as she broke stride in mid-performance and explained to the boys what she had been doing and why she was doing it. There's no way to judge how good her acting lessons were, but, more important, she was teaching her sons to observe and analyze an actor's technique rather than simply enjoy the performance like an ordinary member of the audience. Despite her lack of stage success, Lily thought like a pro and tried to teach her young sons to do the same.

She was delighted to discover how amply her efforts were repaid. Charlie was a quick study and gifted mimic (very much like five-year-old Jackie Coogan, the child actor in *The Kid*, who would later remind Chaplin of himself at the same age). Anxious to win Lily's approval, Charlie could barely control his desire to show off his virtuosity. Dashing home from neighborhood outings, he would crack Lily up with his routines. His most memorable was his gleeful impersonation of a local character by the name of "Rummy" Binks:

> When I saw Rummy shuffle his way across the pavement to hold a cabman's horse for a penny tip, I was fascinated. The walk was so funny to me that I imitated it. When I showed my mother how Rummy walked, she begged me to stop because it was cruel to imitate a misfortune like that. But she pleaded while she had her apron stuffed into her mouth. Then she went into the pantry and giggled for ten minutes.
>
> Day after day I cultivated that walk. It became an obsession. Whenever I pulled it, I was sure of a laugh. Now, no matter what else I may do that is amusing, I can never get away from the walk.[7]

Rummy's alcoholic shamble later became the Little Tramp's signature gait. But the real question concerning Charlie's childhood effort to achieve a perfect imitation of the drunken shuffles is whether Rummy was a stand-in for Charlie's father. Rummy Binks was the doorman at the Queen's Head pub, Charlie Sr.'s favorite watering hole. But whether it was that hapless carriage attendant or, unconsciously, Charlie's pixillated papa who was the object of his fastidious scrutiny, it is clear that the youngster cast a connoisseur's eye upon his subject.

Any paternal input into young Charlie's satirically biting but hilarious impersonation of an impaired alcoholic was never discussed with his mother. Lily would never have countenanced the glee with which young Charlie raced home to regale her with his comic impressions of the drunken shuffles if she thought the boy was being disrespectful of his father. While she frankly told Charlie that she left his father because he drank too much, she was also careful when reminiscing of her days with Charlie Sr. to speak of him "with humor and sadness," not bitterness.[8]

Frustrated though she may have been over her former husband's refusal to support them now that they were down and out, she did not bear a grudge or encourage young Charlie to do so. While the boy clearly sided with his mother and blamed his father for abandoning them, she was well aware that there were two sides to the story of their marriage. From her perspective, she may have been unfaithful to him because he drank too much; in his mind, his drinking was perhaps a response to her unfaithfulness.

She never told her sons the role her infidelities played in their marital difficulties, but otherwise she did try to be fair to her ex-husband. The bitterest irony of Charlie Sr.'s music hall career was that the more economically and professionally successful he became in his bibulous stage role, the worse his alcoholism became. His was a hazardous profession. His stage character imposed his death sentence.

*   *   *

One final way in which Lily laid the groundwork for Charlie's future success was by convincing both him and his brother that they were special. Very special. Or, as Chaplin put it,

> in spite of the squalor in which we were forced to live, she . . . kept Sydney and me off the streets and made us feel we were not the ordinary product of poverty, but unique and distinguished.[9]

While it's easy to see why Lily never told her sons the real story of her relationship with Sydney Hawkes, it was typical of her theatrical tendency to go overboard and soothe Syd's craving for a father of his own with hushed whispers of his lordship in South Africa and dramatic hints of a secret two-thousand-pound inheritance that Syd would be receiving from his birth father when he came of age. Hearing Lily's stories, Charlie found himself half wishing he was a bastard too, rather than the son of a mere music hall star, even if that man did — his mother insisted — happen to be the spitting image of Napoleon.

Later, when Lily desperately turned to religion, embracing God in the hope He would restore her voice in response to her prayers, nothing would do for wide-eyed Charlie after listening to his mother's dramatizations of Bible scenes but to plan to die and go to Heaven in order to meet sweet Jesus (whose life, like Napoleon's, Chaplin would later consider playing in film).

Unfortunately, neither the charitable assistance of the Christ Church congregation of Westminster, which Lily had begun to attend on a regular basis, nor the spiritual consolations of her own private brand of theatrical fundamentalism could stave off her despair over the bleak poverty that threatened to engulf her small family. Unable to support herself with the genteel fancy-dressmaking needlework she had been doing for the more affluent women in her congregation, Lily was obliged, in order to make ends meet, to rent a sewing machine and do sweatshop piecework for pennies. The shift from skilled needlework to unskilled machine work marked one further step down in her rapidly accelerating social descent.

It was roughly at this point that she developed those blinding migraines, which forced her to lie for hours, and sometimes days, in a darkened room with, by doctor's order, moist tea-leaf bandages over her eyes. While it's easy to see why these headaches were attributed to the eyestrain of sweatshop piecework for twelve and fourteen hours a day, in hindsight we know that the deadly syphilis agent *Treponema pallidum* had begun to invade her central nervous system as well.

Hospitalized at the Lambeth Infirmary, Lily was discharged after a month and resumed her increasingly grim and humorless struggle to support herself and her children. Even as late as four months before the boys' entry into Hanwell, she managed to play a one-night stand at a small club at New Cross. Whether that booking came through the generosity of a kindhearted manager helping a friend for old times' sake or merely a last-minute vacancy in the bill that needed filling is unknown. In either case, by the time the bakery van rolled up to deposit Charlie at the orphanage, Lily's show business days were over. Her descent from the stage at Aldershot to the Lambeth poorhouse had taken only two years. But during that time, and in spite of her many failures, she had nonetheless managed to instill in her son a dream that would help prepare him to survive the hardships that awaited him.

The Invulnerable Child

Even when I was in the orphanage, when I was roaming the streets trying to find enough to eat to keep alive, even then I thought of myself as the greatest actor in the world. I had to feel that exuberance that comes from utter confidence in yourself. Without it you go down to defeat.

— Chaplin[1]

FOR CHARLIE, ENTERING THE HANWELL ORPHANAGE meant the loss of his hair, his clothes, his mother, his belongings, his dignity, his autonomy, and free access to Syd. For Lily, it meant food for her sons and a roof over their heads. Giving up her stage name for her legal name in order to apply for relief as a pauper was the penultimate comeuppance for the formerly proud and glamorous ex-actress. But from Hannah Chaplin's perspective, the workhouse and orphanage were safer bets than the slums of London.

Not everyone saw it that way. The Poor Laws created living conditions that denigrated and humiliated *adult* members of the underclass seeking relief at public expense in order to discourage them from doing so. In his 1903 study of the London poor titled *People of the Abyss*, which he researched by living among them, the American author Jack London described a woman who preferred suicide (by drowning) over the poorhouse because of the psychological humiliation and physical deprivation she anticipated. Regarding her choice, London wrote: "I, for one, from what I know of canals and workhouses, should choose the canal, were I in a similar position." He added that "the one attribute common to all [long-term] workhouse inmates . . . is . . . unhesitating obedience, passing into servility."

Fortunately for Charlie and Syd, they were not exposed to a workhouse experience for very long. A more enlightened welfare policy had already begun to separate *some* indigent children from their pauper parents by transferring them from poorhouses to orphanage schools like Hanwell instead of subjecting them to the indifferent care their parents received as punishment for their failure to be self-sufficient members of society.

Charlie spent three weeks in the poorhouse before they shipped him to Hanwell. From the start, he relied on the same coping strategy he followed throughout his eighteen-month stay at the orphanage. When life became unbearable, he went somewhere else and became someone else. As he later put it:

> My brother Syd and I were sent to the poorhouse. English people have a great horror of the poorhouse: but I don't remember it as a very dreadful place. To tell you the truth, I don't remember much about it. I have just a vague idea of what it was like. The strongest recollection I have of this period of my life is of creeping off by myself at the poorhouse and pretending I was a very rich and grand person. . . . I was of a dreamy, imaginative disposition. I was always pretending I was somebody else and the worst I ever gave myself in these daydreams and games of "pretend" was a seat in Parliament for life and an income of a million pounds. Sometimes I used to pretend that I was a great musician, or the director of a

great orchestra; but the director was always a rich man. Music, even in my poorhouse days, was always a passion with me.[2]

Precisely who young Charlie became was far less important than the psychological self-protective device he employed. As a self-soothing seven-year-old in an orphanage, he resorted instinctively to that similar "let's pretend" game that his plucky seamstress-mother had already modeled for him when she escaped the painful daily reality and oppressive poverty of her own life by dressing up as Lily Harley or "doing" Nell Gwyn or the empress Josephine.

And so when Chaplin at age fifty passed that same legacy on to his own son Charlie Chaplin Jr. by recalling how he had coped with adversity as a pauper in the poorhouse and inmate in the orphanage by pretending that he *already* was "the greatest actor in the world," there is good reason to believe that he was describing an actual childhood experience, not concocting some retrospective cock-and-bull story for his namesake son's edification (or his own self-glorification).

By pretending to be a world-famous somebody instead of an orphanage nobody, seven-year-old Charlie transformed his world from menacing to manageable. While obediently conforming to the dehumanizing routine of an orphanage inmate, he established his identity and retained his dignity by telling himself he was unique. He was not like the other 1,147 inmates at Hanwell. C*H*A*R*L*I*E C*H*A*P*L*I*N (fascinating letters he was learning to spell and write for the first time) already was the most famous actor in the world. A direct descendant of Napoleon Bonaparte and Charles II, he was invulnerable.[3]

Ironically, it was a belated visit from the original source of inspiration for those dreams of grandeur that broke Charlie's heart and actually threatened to shatter his feelings of invulnerability. Admitted on June 18, 1896, Chaplin did not see his mother until August 10, 1897. Hanwell stood twelve miles outside London. Time and again, during those first thirteen months of what he later labeled "my incarceration," whenever he pictured his mother in his mind's eye, the homesick boy always saw glamorous Lily. Time and again he described the beautiful actress to his fellow inmates. And so, when the drastically aged and bedraggled Hannah Chaplin finally showed up on visiting day, Charlie was shocked and mortified. A close friend and confidant, Harry Crocker, recalled:

> It was his realization of the extreme poverty of the family which threw him into an absolute panic of self-consciousness and moral despair. "My poor mother!" he sighed. "Upon certain occasions even she caused me anguished embarrassment. What a traitor to her I felt! But my consciousness of poverty was too overwhelming! She came to the institution one day — she had been a very good-looking woman, a beautiful woman . . . but . . . she never recovered her looks, and she couldn't afford to dress well. . . . she came with an oil can — she'd been shopping — and the association of her with the oil can as my mother, and all the boys seeing her was too much. I cried: 'Why do you come with that mother?' I sobbed, pointing to the oil can. 'Why do you come at all? They'll see you, they'll all see you.' I shed terribly bitter tears." Charlie writhed at the memory.[4]

Understandably, Chaplin completely revised that orphanage memory in *My Autobiography*; just as he entirely omitted any mention of his mother's relationship with Leo Dryden, modified the story of her contretemps with the immigration authorities, and touched up a number of other embarrassing facts and painful memories. *My Autobiography* was written in six drafts over eight years. After finishing the sixth version, Chaplin spent another year editing out the bitterness. (As he put it, there was a lot of bitterness.)

So what was daily life at Hanwell really like for children at risk in 1896? Anthony J. Mundella, M.P., a Liberal politician and social reformer who chaired a parliamentary committee investigating conditions at Hanwell and other "barrack schools," addressed that question in a report he published the year Charlie was admitted. According to his report, there was no deliberate cruelty, little severe physical hardship, and plenty of discomfort.

Hanwell consisted of 136 acres of grounds with buildings on 20 acres. The inmates slept in dormitories with twenty-two to forty-nine beds per room. Each child was allotted the rough equivalent of a six-by-six-foot area of floor space. Clothes were kept in baskets that hung from the foot of iron beds. The bedding afforded adequate warmth, but the dormitories and washrooms were sometimes poorly heated. The lack of fresh air throughout the entire school resulted in a pervasive and distinctive smell of overcrowded bodies and general stuffiness. One whiff of that familiar odor triggered a flashback that staggered Chaplin when he revisited Hanwell in 1931. Returning to his suite at the Carlton, his emotional memories jogged by that long-forgotten aroma as if by a Proustian madeleine, Charlie wept like a child (and for a child) for nearly an hour.

Each inmate had been issued flannel underclothes, a school uniform, and heavy, stiff boots that were worn all day, all year round. Mundella wrote:

> One of the reasons why the children were not sent out of doors more frequently is that they are not sufficiently provided with outdoor clothing. . . . we have ourselves seen the children in the yards too thinly clad and suffering from colds and chilblains. It appears to be considered unnecessary to supply the children with extra clothing unless they go beyond the school precincts, and yet in the yards, which are often draughty and sunless, and in which there is little inducement to play, the children need more warmth than if they were walking briskly.[5]

There were separate living quarters, separate playgrounds, separate water fountains, and separate libraries for the older inmates of each sex, with a common dining room, an outdoor swimming pool, and an infants' school for children under seven, to which Charlie was admitted for the first few months because of his small size. Infants who misbehaved were punished by standing in a corner or in front of the class for "half an hour or so." Older boys received a few strokes of the cane for "repeated disobedience, dirty habits and bad language."[6]

While their overall conclusion was that the Hanwell inmates were somewhat subdued and apathetic, the Mundella Committee did not consider the mild mental dullness they observed a direct result of cruel or unusual punishment, chronic hunger, or low-grade starvation. Compared to their better-fed and better-dressed counterparts in traditional English boarding schools and working-class homes, Hanwell children lived in spartan conditions. Compared to the barefoot and shivering children sleeping in doorways and under the arches of the streets of London, life at Hanwell may well have been almost utopian.

"Even the teachers suffer from mental depression due to the dull monotony and want of mental life in the whole establishment," the Mundella report concluded. "Undoubtedly the general tendency of living in the school is to, as it were, run all our children in a mould." As Chaplin recalled it, "we marched in military order from class to class, and to and from meals."[7]

As a seven-year-old, Charlie received three ounces of meat a day, a pint of milk, and enormous amounts of starch — about twelve ounces of bread and four ounces of potatoes. The diet "leads to overfeeding on the one hand and . . . malnutrition on the other."[8] But thanks to Charles Dickens and his fictional counterpart Oliver Twist, in 1896 it was entirely permissible for Hanwell inmates to ask for "more." Like Chaplin, both Dickens (age twelve at the Marshalsea) and Hogarth (age ten at the Fleet Street Debtor's Prison) were children of impecunious parents;

each later brilliantly satirized his residual childhood feelings about "the system" in his respective art form.

What role did Chaplin's encounter with "the system" later play in shaping his comic vision? It left him — as it had Dickens — with a sense of burning indignation toward established authority. In his novels, Dickens's residual feelings of outrage and wounded pride took the form of satirical ridicule of the social system, what one critic, Walter Bagehot, referred to as his "sentimental radicalism." In his films, Chaplin's feelings of resentment toward the Hanwell system of law and order took the form of what the critic Robert Benchley dubbed "Charlie's ass-kicking humor."[9] Benchley was specifically referring to those old slapstick one- and two-reelers in which moviegoers of all nations vicariously delighted in the universally intelligible silent film spectacle of physically intimidating authority figures and massive bullies receiving well-aimed and well-deserved kicks in the pants from Charlie's pint-sized Little Tramp.

While it was behemoths like Roscoe "Fatty" Arbuckle, big-bellied Mack Swain, and mountainous Eric Campbell whose heavy haunches served as the Little Tramp's favorite targets, it takes scant stretch of the imagination to reinsert a mighty two-hundred-pound giant by the name of Captain Hindrum into his rightful place in the rogues' gallery of Charlie Chaplin's childhood imagination.

Every Friday — Punishment Day — the ex-naval officer dispensed Hanwell justice in an elaborately choreographed ritual purposely designed to instill unquestioning obedience in the abject inmates. "There was a sadistic streak in the old Captain and his fury and brutality in administration of his punitive duties were a horrible thing to witness," Chaplin recalled.

> At ten o'clock we marched in order into the huge, gloomy armory with monotonous gray walls. We were left to stand at silent attention, staring at the implements of torture — a vaulting horse, an

easel with straps upon which hung the cane, the birch and the cat. After a half hour of suspense and anticipation of the horror to come, there entered solemnly the doctor, a master, two assistants and the dread Captain Hindrum, the disciplinarian.[10]

Striding up to a spread-eagled victim whose trousers were down and buttocks exposed with his wrists strapped to the vaulting horse, with the swoosh of "a cane as thick as a man's thumb" Hindrum left "three pink welts as wide as a washerwoman's finger across his bottom," while the entire assemblage of five hundred boys looked on in terrified amazement.[11] By no means a defiant or rebellious child in spite of his growing contempt for authority, Charlie managed to suffer only one unjust flogging, which left a more indelible impression on his mind than on his bottom. "They tried to break my spirit at Hanwell," he recalled, but "they never succeeded."[12]

Before entering Hanwell, Charlie had been a carefree child roaming the streets of South London with virtually no adult supervision. While Hannah Chaplin now sewed ten to twelve hours a day, streetwise Syd kept an eye on his kid brother and taught him the ropes:

> I was about five, and Syd nine. . . . In our street there was a book shop with an outside shelf of bargain books. . . . "Gee," said Syd, "let's get some of those. You go and get some and bring them around the corner." . . . the proprietor failed to notice me and I had the wild exhilaration of success of theft. Syd congratulated me and piled the books up evenly against the wall. . . . after a second armful . . . I essayed a third pilfering expedition but luck deserted me. Through the window I felt the eye of the proprietor upon me, but I was fascinated and could not stop. He came out . . . just as I was making off with the third load. . . . I'll never forget it, Syd was lying beside our collection . . . with a small stick, whistling as he played the stick like a flute. And I arrived with the shopkeeper.[13]

After calling a "rozzer," who scared the hell out of the boys, the kindly shopkeeper and the amused bobby let them off with a stern warning and a free book apiece.

It would not be surprising if that good-natured bobby later turned up in Chaplin's cinematic imagination as the smiling comic policeman who crosses paths with Jackie, the pint-sized hustler in the first window-breaking scene early in *The Kid*. And it is also likely that Charlie and Syd's boyhood game of book snatching was replayed in 1918 as that food-snitching game at a Lambeth-looking food stall in *A Dog's Life*, in which the two Chaplin brothers nostalgically reprised a slightly modified version of their original childhood caper. In that same film, streetwise Charlie (the screen character) also succeeds in nicking a wallet in an extended gag sequence that was an in-joke between himself and Syd, alluding to Syd's experience of "finding" a purse with seven gold sovereigns while peddling papers on a London bus. Syd's lucky "find" was used to finance the one and only seaside holiday their family ever took. Instead of confronting Syd with her suspicions, Lily set her scruples aside by telling herself "God had sent it as a blessing from Heaven."[14]

Not only were the two brothers less than fully law-abiding citizens before entering the orphanage, but Charlie had never been really scared by any adult authority figure before he met Captain Hindrum. A former upstairs neighbor recalled:

In those days I had a room in Walcot Gardens. In the evenings when we were trying to work, the kids in the court below used to make such a hubbub that we could not get on. When I looked out, there was that lad . . . with an audience around him. I used to jump down flights of stairs furious, and then I would listen. The boy was the most marvelous mimic I ever saw.

When he saw me, he would say "Ladies and gentleman, a slight impression of the bloke upstairs who comes down to chase us," and as I listened my face grew red and I knew the kid was a genius. . . . He thought no one who ever lived was like his mother. The lad thought she was the cleverest player in the world, a great lady and his ideal.[15]

The crime Charlie was accused of, and said he never committed, was arson. Some other kids had set scraps of papers on fire in the lavatory when Charlie happened to be there. Unable to refute the circumstantial evidence against him, unwilling to peach, and disinclined to risk more severe punishment by protesting unsuccessfully, the young Charlie pleaded guilty and took the beating.

As for the crime: while fire setting may seem like a harmless prank, twenty-six children had perished in a fire in the orphanage in 1889, just seven years earlier. As for the punishment: flogging was then a universal practice that transcended all social classes, from the hallowed halls of Eton to the meanest charity orphanage. Throughout the nineteenth century, corporal punishment was a standard form of child discipline in English institutions. But while the Mundella Committee considered a few strokes of the cane a mild rebuke for bad behavior, for Charlie it was an experience with authority he never forgot or forgave.

One reason why Chaplin's screen character's ass-kicking antics in those early films were so immensely popular with early-twentieth-century moviegoers is that they resonated unconsciously with his audiences' personal experiences with that universal child-rearing practice. Playing to a generation whose rumpas and dumpas, fannies and tushies, bottoms and bums had all known the sting of authority, Charlie made them laugh until their sides split. Given our current penchant for gentler forms of child discipline, it is not surprising that the Little Tramp's crude comic antics have lost much of their freshness and charm for twenty-first-century audiences. In fact it would not be surprising if many of today's parents would strenuously object to their children viewing many of those early one- and two-reelers that first made Chaplin world famous by 1915, because they contain too much of what is known in modern educational parlance as gratuitous violence.

But if Charlie Chaplin's early comedies now seem primitive and outdated, his comic character has managed to endure thus far as an archetypal figure who has already joined the immortal ranks of characters like Falstaff and Don Quixote. For the deepest message beneath all of the Little Tramp's slapstick antics was and is to give as good as you get: when kicked in the pants by life's indignities, pick yourself up, dust yourself off, hang on to your self-respect, and repay the compliment in full measure. Or as Chaplin put it in 1925: "The whole point of The Little Fellow is that no matter how down on his ass he is, no matter how well the jackals succeed in tearing him apart, he's still a man of dignity."[16]

While it would be absurd to suggest that the mature Chaplin's hard-knocks credo had fully developed by the time the eight-and-a-half-year-old boy left the orphanage to rejoin his mother, there is every reason to believe that the seeds of his survival philosophy and Charlie's coping mechanism — using his creative imagination to deal with adversity — had both been firmly planted and were beginning to take root.

"Life Is a Tragedy . . . in Close-up, but a Comedy in Long Shot"

In the creation of comedy, it is paradoxical that tragedy stimulates the spirit of ridicule, because ridicule . . . is an attitude of defiance: we must laugh in the face of our helplessness against the forces of nature — or go insane.

— Chaplin[1]

UNAWARE OF HIS MOTHER'S SYPHILIS and its implications, the stunned and dismayed child would ultimately blame her breakdown on starvation and exhaustion brought on by the pace of sweatshop piecework on a rented sewing machine. But in truth she had been diagnosed as syphilitic before being transferred to the Cane Hill Lunatic Asylum in Sussex on September 15, 1898. Her admission note read:

> Has been very strange in manner — at one time abusive and noisy, at another using endearing terms. Has been confined in padded room repeatedly on account of sudden violence — threw

a mug at another patient. Shouting, singing and talking incoherently. Complains of her head and depressed and crying this morning — dazed and unable to give any reliable information. Asks if she is dying. States she belongs to Christ Church (Congregation) which is Church of England. She was sent here on a mission by the Lord. She says she wants to get out of this world.[2]

Hannah Chaplin's first psychotic episode lasted two months, after which the homeless, unemployed needleworker was discharged to recuperate. Her illness was brought on by overwork and malnutrition — and neurosyphilis.

Her nine-year-old son never witnessed the breakdown itself, but he did observe firsthand the working and living conditions leading up to it. Charlie and Sydney Chaplin lived with their struggling mother for the first six months after Charlie's discharge from Hanwell and Syd's return from vocational training school.

But at the precise point in time when Hannah Chaplin first became floridly psychotic, her sons had already been living in another charity institution for a full month. After two school nurses took Syd aside to gently break the news, he tried explaining it to Charlie. But Charlie kept insisting she had done it on purpose and "deliberately escaped from her mind."[3]

The consoling image of his mother taking a break from reality was preferable to the terrifying thought of her experiencing a break with reality. Young Charlie tried to convince himself that her madness was an extended work break. She was not really crazy. She was only taking a much needed rest. But the sight of Syd weeping finally made him understand.

Many years later, as a grown man at the height of his artistic powers, Chaplin would try to make sense out of this senseless childhood tragedy by exploring two of the three causes of his mother's breakdown — malnutrition and stress — in two of the most hilarious and memorable comic sequences in his canon and in motion picture history.

Examining the ludicrous but serious premise that someone could be driven crazy by starvation to the point of visual hallucinations and cannibalism or, alternately, so famished as to eat a shoe as if it were a gourmet delicacy, Chaplin left them rolling in the aisles in *The Gold Rush*. And having been driven mad by the frenzied pace of work on a factory assembly line,[4] his homeless screen character in *Modern Times* would be discharged to recuperate from his nervous breakdown after a brief stint in a mental institution.

In modern life, as in *Modern Times*, Chaplin's "sentimental radicalism" would later be reinterpreted as Communist radicalism by members of the House Un-American Activities Committee (HUAC) during the Cold War and Red scare of the late 1940s. While Oxford University would award him an honorary doctorate for his screen character's subversive comic antics, the FBI would reward him with a two-thousand-page security file as a dangerous political instigator. Like his favorite author Charles Dickens, Chaplin also found the earliest roots of his twentieth-century sentimental radicalism in the events of his nineteenth-century London boyhood.

It is not known what Hannah Chaplin did or how she supported herself during the eighteen months Charlie was in Hanwell. Her show business career was over. Her formerly pretty features had become so coarsened by stress, poverty, malnutrition, and illness that she would strike both of her sons as dowdy, careworn, and one or two decades older than her actual age of thirty-three at the time they were finally reunited in 1898.

By then, the former free spirit, adventuress, and would-be royal courtesan had been an upstanding member of the Church of England for three years. Her faith was such that, shortly before the family reunion, she underwent a formal baptism ceremony at Christ Church. She first became a member of that congregation in 1895; records of her original conversion by the Reverend F. B. Meyer describe her as "an actress who lives apart from her husband."[5]

In view of her increasing faith and decreasing health, it seems highly unlikely that during the eighteen months she and the boys were apart she would have been capable of or interested in supplementing her income with financial contributions from lovers or patrons as she probably had done as a pretty and vivacious young woman in her midtwenties.

Looking back on his mother's stormy life passage from actress to needleworker to madwoman, sixty-five years later in *My Autobiography* Chaplin assumed that she first turned to religion in hopes of regaining her singing voice. Yet her monthlong ordeal of blinding pain from syphilis-induced headaches, which started around the same time she converted to Anglicanism, suggests that she was first drawn to Christ Church as a direct result of her unremitting physical suffering, which made her think of Christ's. Not only did Charlie's miracle-hungry mother profess deep and abiding feelings of personal identification with that ordeal, she was also deeply moved by Christ's compassionate forgiveness of sinners and their sins, particularly adultery.

Reviewing that especially miserable period in their lives, Chaplin vividly recalled his childhood fascination with his mother's austere but riveting dramatizations of scenes from the Bible, which were clearly the match of those lusty Nell Gwyn impersonations they were replacing:

> . . . she gave the most luminous and appealing interpretation of Christ I have ever heard or seen. She spoke of His tolerant understanding; of the woman who had sinned and was to be stoned by the mob, and of His words to them: "He that is without sin among you, let him first cast a stone at her." . . .

> As she continued tears welled up in her eyes. . . . And we both wept.
>
> "Don't you see," said Mother, "how human He was; like all of us, He too suffered doubt."[6]

Hannah's formal baptism ceremony took place on January 10, 1898, eight days before Charlie's discharge. Unlike infant baptism, the believer's baptism she underwent was reserved for children and adults who wished to evince their deep and abiding faith in Christ as their saviour.

In view of his mother's desperate religious conversion, it's not surprising that when Chaplin released *The Kid* in 1921 he opened the film with a still shot of Christ on the Cross, which he intercut with shots of his film's heroine: an unwed mother cradling her newborn (and soon to be lost/stolen) infant as she is discharged from a maternity ward into a cold, unfeeling world by passing through the gates of a charity hospital (which clearly resemble surviving photographs of the gates of the Lambeth poorhouse-infirmary). The title card introducing this sequence reads: "The woman whose sin was motherhood."

And in the shot that follows — which Chaplin wisely omitted when he reedited this slightly flawed masterpiece fifty years later — his heroine's head is illuminated from behind by a stained-glass window in order to create a Madonna-like halo effect. His childhood image of his mother's self-sacrificing ordeal was such that Chaplin later said:

> I loved my mother almost more when she went out of her mind. She had been so poor and so hungry — I believe it was starving herself for us that affected her brain.[7]

Describing one of Chaplin's chronically psychotic mother's post-traumatic flashbacks to her harrowing experience of near starvation, Harry Crocker wrote:

While he loved her, it was impossible for him to see her in her ill condition and not be mentally wracked. Though she was living in the most comfortable circumstances, she could never put her mind from the severe poverty of her earlier days and the fear of hunger. "Here," she would say when with Charlie, meanwhile stuffing his pockets with little pieces of bread and cake or perhaps a bit of fruit "Take this; you never can tell when you need it." Memories of his early London days depressed Chaplin terribly, and his mother's visits left him in a despondent mood for several days.[8]

Reprising those hilarious starvation gags early in that film, the character Charlie later entertains the dance hall prostitute Georgia by playing with his food in his equally brilliant "Dance of the Rolls."

While her religious conversion in 1895 could not prevent her from becoming psychotic in 1898, her decision to join Christ Church did protect her from a much worse fate than she would have otherwise suffered during this economically disastrous period in her life. As a result of her theatrical but heartfelt religious conversion, she and her two sons instantly became members of the "deserving poor." That critically important designation was determined informally by the ministers, social workers, and mission Bible readers who handed out tickets for free soup, bread, and relief parcels to deserving members of their congregation who listened to their sermons with sincerity and sang their hymns with conviction. Of more lasting importance than those mission handouts, the "deserving poor" also received valuable endorsements from influential clergymen, which made a critical difference with local charity relief boards in determining how their children lived and where they went to school.

Despite his profound antipathy toward the rigid authoritarian system at Hanwell, Chaplin was well aware that selective admission into that institution was highly sought after and that the sanctuary it provided could make a crucial difference in a pauper child's life, as the Mundella Committee pointed out.[9] Instead of experiencing an unchecked free fall into the depths of poverty like the godless poor, the deserving poor and their offspring were provided with a safety net. But depending on the sanctimoniousness of their benefactors, the charity might be received at the expense of their dignity.

Though neither insincere in professing her faith nor sycophantic in petitioning for charity, Hannah Chaplin sometimes "sounded like a Cockney barmaid." On one occasion several years later, when she felt belittled by the hoity-toity daughter of a fellow churchgoer whose mother also happened to be her landlady-benefactress, Hannah demanded: "Who do you think you are? Lady Shit?" The young woman replied: "That's nice language coming from a Christian!" Hannah shot back: "Don't worry. It's in the Bible, my dear: Deuteronomy, twenty-eighth chapter, thirty-seventh verse, only there's another word for it. However, shit will suit you."[10] She and the boys moved out the next day.

Alluding to this memory of his quick-witted, proud Cockney mother's pungent repartee when patronized by her so-called betters, the elderly Chaplin summed her up with great affection and dignity in *My Autobiography*:

> Although religious, she loved sinners and always identified with them. Not an atom of vulgarity was in her nature. Whatever Rabelaisian expression she used, it was always rhetorically appropriate.[11]

Another incident that Chaplin never forgot occurred six weeks before her first nervous breakdown. On that occasion she removed the boys from Norwood, the charity institution to which they had just been admitted one week earlier. Unable to face the pain of another extended separation from Charlie and Syd, she told the authorities that she was back on her feet and was ready, willing, and able to look after them once more.

Well aware that they would actually be back in the poorhouse by nightfall, the three Chaplins picnicked on ninepence worth of cherries and cake in Kennington Park and savored their final outing together before returning in time for the preadmission delousing routine and afternoon tea. For the rest of their lives, Hannah's sons shared the memory of the fierce love that impelled their softly weeping but defiant mother to make that final symbolic protest against "the system." (Visits to parks after that always left Chaplin with bittersweet nostalgia and low-grade depression that lingered for days.)

Three days after their Norwood discharge, the boys were forced to return there. Four weeks later, after a ten-day period of mental observation in the Lambeth Infirmary, Hannah was in Cane Hill. And twelve days after that, the Norwood bakery van rolled up to Charlie Chaplin Sr.'s two-room flat on Kennington Road and unceremoniously deposited Charlie and Sydney into the care of their father and his common-law wife, Louise.

If the civic authorities had taken the time and trouble to make a preliminary home visit before shipping the boys to Kennington Road to punish their father, they would have been forced to admit the dubious nature of the District Relief Committee's earlier conclusion that Charlie Chaplin Sr. was an "ablebodied" parent.[12] Weaving, reeling, staggering, and stumbling his way home from drinking bouts at the Queen's Head almost every night of the week, sometimes decked out in the formal evening dress of his bibulous stage character, he was nothing if not an alcoholic.

For an evocative "long shot" of what his father was like, see *One A.M.*, the film in which Chaplin nailed, letter perfect, a satirical imitation of a drunken swell's attempt to get in the front door of his home and put himself to bed after a night on the town. There is every reason to believe that this two-reeler, which ends with the elegant swell curling up in a bathtub, was inspired by Chaplin's childhood memories of his hard-drinking father's late-night mishaps.

Not the least bit interested in the issues of paternal fitness and chronic alcoholism, however, the civic authorities were concerned only with the thirty-five-year-old actor's refusal to provide child support. In a running series of skirmishes with the law over the previous three years — from 1895 to 1898 — Charlie Sr. had used every tactic he could to avoid paying his court-ordered fifteen shillings per week. By November 1897 he was forty-four pounds, eight shillings in arrears.

His brother Spencer, the landlord of the Queen's Head, bailed him out after a warrant was issued for Charlie Sr.'s arrest with the added offer of a one-pound reward for information leading to his capture.

By the time Spencer stepped in, his younger brother was a fugitive from justice, yet he was neither unemployed nor impoverished. He was earning a decent living but still felt bitter about Lily's adultery and resentful over the unfair legal judgment he felt she had managed to finagle. Moreover, he lacked the cash to come up with the child support he owed.

A few years earlier, at the peak of his fame, he would have been able to retire that entire debt with a single week's work. If Chaplin's account of his father's career in *My Autobiography* is accurate, Charlie Sr. was then capable of earning as much as seventy-five pounds a week for a theatrical engagement.

But even if, out of filial pride, Chaplin exaggerated his father's earning power, Charlie Sr. never set aside any portion of his income for child support. The pressures and temptations of his professional identity were such that he ostentatiously drank up and threw around his cash with reckless abandon and indifference to his own future financial security, or his two sons' immediate welfare. He merged his professional life with his private life until the two were indistinguishable: his stage character's lifestyle became his star image.

Young Charlie would not repeat that mistake. He would play his drunks sober. And if his impersonations brought him more lasting recognition than his briefly famous father enjoyed, it should be said on Charlie Sr.'s behalf that his eagle-eyed son had the distinct advantage of learning from a real pro.[13]

Estimating the peak period of Chaplin's father's popularity on the basis of six surviving portraits of him from the covers of sheet music for popular tunes of the day, his stardom was brief, lasting from 1890 to 1896. He never was a superstar like his romantic rival Leo Dryden, whose smash hit "The Miner's Dream of Home"[14] — that enormously successful number in which Lily had sung backup — became a classic and earned a record sum. But Charlie Chaplin Sr. was sufficiently famous that his man-about-town star image, in a variety of resplendent character costumes, was used to commercially plug "Eh! Boys?" "Everyday Life," "As the Church Bells Chime," "Oui! Tray Bong!" "She Must Be Witty," and "The Girl Was Young and Pretty." In the first of those song sheets, "Eh! Boys?" he is depicted as an affably smiling, elegant swell casually decked out in the top hat, tails, and striped pants that were the standard props of his distinctive theatrical persona.

When Charlie and Syd arrived on his doorstep, Charlie Sr. was two years past his prime. But mentions of him in the *Era* as late as 1899 are still sufficiently numerous to explain how he continued to afford the steep rent on his posh flat on Kennington Road. From 1896 to 1898, however, his popularity had gradually slipped. And at the time the boys showed up, his career was spiraling downward.

By the end of September 1900 he would be out of work. Shortly after that, his eleven-year-old son Charles Chaplin would be one of the many music hall professionals who performed gratis at his father's farewell benefit: a benevolent tradition among members of the music hall fraternity. No longer living in the limelight — or Kennington Road, for that matter — Charles Sr. was entering the sad twilight of his life, dodging creditors by moving from one shabby hovel to another in the back streets. One year later, he would be dead from cirrhosis of the liver.

But back in 1898, in nine-year-old Charlie Chaplin's impressionable eyes, his father's flush life must have seemed like a millionaire's compared to the grubby lifestyle and cramped quarters he and Syd had recently experienced with his malnourished, bedraggled mother. Although Charlie sorely missed his mother, he was thrilled to have the opportunity to finally meet this debonair music hall star whose name he bore and whose elegant mannerisms he immediately began to cultivate with an expert eye and hero-worshipping intensity:

> He fascinated me. At meals I watched every move he made, the way he ate and the way he held his knife as though it were a pen when cutting his meat. And for years I copied him.[15]

Chaplin's father must have been aware of his stagestruck son's hunger for affection and approval, but he was never demonstrative with the boy until the last time they ever saw each other, three years later and only three weeks before his death, in the barroom of the Three Stags pub. Both inebriated and air hungry as he drowned in his own secretions from liver failure, Charlie Sr. would hug and kiss his twelve-year-old son for the first and only time in their lives.

His common-law wife, Louise, openly resented the fact that the offspring of Charlie Sr.'s estranged wife had turned up on her doorstep, unannounced and uninvited. An alcoholic herself, she was frequently "morose and disagreeable." When drunk, she would grumble "quite audibly . . . of the injustice imposed upon her" by "having to look after Sydney and me." She never hit Charlie. But her hostility toward Syd "held me in fear and dread," Chaplin recalled.[16]

Thirteen-year-old Syd dealt with her hostility by giving her a wide berth. He left the flat early in the morning and stayed away till midnight, when he returned famished, raided the larder, and went straight to bed if he was lucky enough to avoid running into her. Syd's absence intensified Charlie's loneliness and left him feeling emotionally vulnerable and apprehensive: "This reviling of Sydney frightened and depressed me and I would go unhappily to bed and lie fretfully awake. . . . those days were the longest and saddest of my life."[17]

His unpredictable father's increasingly frequent absences made things worse for everyone in what amounted to a vicious alcohol-fueled cycle. The more hurt and rejected Louise felt by his neglect, the more unpleasant she became, and the more he stayed away.

Charlie Sr.'s most self-destructive moods and their heaviest drinking and ugliest rows as a codependent alcoholic couple were triggered, or aggravated, by the increasing frequency with which he was experiencing holes in his bookings. Based on Chaplin's insightful portrayal of the painful relationship between Calvero's slipping popularity and self-medicating alcoholism in *Limelight*, it's likely that a similar scene was taking place with his father during this two-month period when they lived together in close quarters and young Charlie studied him "like a hawk."[18]

If so, Charlie Sr.'s downwardly spiraling career ran in tandem with his on-again, off-again relationship with Louise. The more worthless and rejected Chaplin's father felt by his formerly adoring public, the more he rejected Louise, whose love he undoubtedly felt he did not deserve. As Calvero puts it in *Limelight*: "that's the trouble with the world, we all despise ourselves." Understandably, he was most affectionate with her on nights when he still had a booking. To fortify himself on those occasions, he would swallow six raw eggs in a glass of port before leaving for the theater. And the blackout-prone actor could be equally charming and tender on the day after a successful theatrical performance, provided he was not suffering from one of those groggy hungover amnesias of the morning after:

> She loved Father. Even though very young I could see it in her glance. . . . And I am sure he loved her. I saw many occasions of it. There were times when he was charming and tender and would kiss her good night before leaving for the theatre. And on a Sunday morning, when he had not been drinking, he would breakfast with us and tell Louise about the vaudeville acts that were working with him, and have us all enthralled. I would watch him like a hawk, absorbing every action. In a playful mood, he once wrapped a towel round his head and chased his little son[19] around the table, saying, "I'm King Turkey Rhubarb."[20]

Resentfully dependent on this impaired alcoholic with whom she was still deeply in love, Louise would revenge herself, whenever she felt neglected by their father, by locking one or both boys out of the house in a tipsy fit of spiteful pique.

A typical example of their dysfunctional alcoholic relationship began early one Saturday afternoon with Louise abandoning young Charlie in order to get back at Charlie Sr. for abandoning her earlier that day. Returning to the flat after his customary Saturday morning half-day at the Kennington Road School, Charlie found it deserted, the larder empty and no note telling him where to go or what to do. He waited and waited until he could wait no more. "I could stand the gaping emptiness no longer, so in desolation I went out, spending the afternoon visiting nearby marketplaces. I wandered through Lambeth Walk. . . . The distraction soothed me and for a while I forgot my plight and hunger. When I returned it was night."[21]

Lambeth Walk, a two-hundred-yard strip of roadway hemmed in on both sides by barrows with costers hawking carrots and turnips to haggling customers, meat stalls with leather-lunged Cockney butchers shouting the price of prime joints for Sunday afternoon dinner to passersby, and gaming stalls with roll-or-bowl a-ball-a-penny pitchmen offering tempting prizes to lucky winners; Lambeth Walk, with the London railway arches framing it from behind, softly illuminated from end to end with the comforting glow of naptha flares and oil lamps; Lambeth Walk, main market street and social hub of the district, teeming with humanity on a Saturday night — it was the logical place for Charlie to go to cheer himself up.

Charlie also recalled one particular melody whose haunting refrain soothed his soul while waiting for his father or Syd to come to the rescue:

> Suddenly there was music. Rapturous! It came from the vestibule of the White Hart corner pub, and resounded brilliantly in the empty square. The tune was "The Honeysuckle and the Bee," played with radiant virtuosity on a harmonium and clarinet. I had never been conscious of melody before, but this one was beautiful and lyrical, so blithe and gay, so warm and reassuring. I forgot my despair and crossed the road to where the musicians were. The harmonium player was blind, with scarred sockets where the eyes had been; and a besotted, embittered face played the clarinet.[22]

Charlie returned home and saw lopsided Louise, three sheets to the wind, fumbling with the front door. When he tried to sneak in after waiting for her to go to bed, she confronted him and demanded: "Where the hell do you think you're going? This is not your home." Charlie then wandered the streets until in the wee hours he finally found his father, who took him back to the house and, after a boozy row, slugged Louise on the side of the head with a clothes brush and knocked her out cold.

*　　*　　*

Living together in close quarters for two barely endurable months as a court-mandated family inevitably led to more nocturnal evictions for the boys. The more Charlie Sr. stayed away, the more Louise threw his two sons out on the street, until the civic authorities finally put a stop to it. The Society for the Prevention of Cruelty to Children stepped in after a policeman, returning Charlie and Syd to their drunken stepmother, reported that she was reluctant to readmit them at three o'clock in the morning after they had been found sleeping on the street by a watchman's fire.

There were even times, Syd later recalled, when he and Charlie "actually had to eat from garbage pails."[23] Chaplin would later depict those foraging experiences in comic long shot by transposing them into his Little Tramp's habit of picking up castoff cigar butts with fastidious elegance. A true connoisseur of other people's leavings, his debonair Little Fellow picks up discarded stogies and panatelas from the street, genteelly rolls them between his shabbily gloved fingers, delicately sniffs them as if they were fresh from his own personal humidor, and lights up with all the expansive self-satisfaction of a J. P. Morgan, before shuffling off with his Rummy Binks gait to his next comic adventure.

What in real life was the two-month childhood ordeal of being inappropriately placed in the custody of his father by bungling civic officials during his mother's psychiatric hospitalization became, in art, a sustained comic long shot in the masterpiece *City Lights*.

The film opens with an establishing shot that instantly pegs Charlie as a social outsider and consummate urban outdoorsman. A disruptive nuisance and offensive eyesore, he is peacefully snoozing on a statue of Peace and Prosperity which is being un-veiled in a public ceremony in a park, much to the annoyance of pompous civic officials and an irate policeman, who shake their fists and try to oust him from his snug perch with the stated in-tention of tossing him in jail.

While scrambling down from the statue, which he has de-filed accidentally, he tries to beat a hasty retreat. In the act of escaping from the authorities, he compounds the insult. Inad-vertently hoisted on the sword of Peace, he responds by thumb-ing his nose at authority in a brilliant slapstick sequence in which Chaplin the filmmaker cleverly employs different elements of the statue to question the dubious virtues of civic pride and progress with ironic visual wit worthy of the sardonic verbal wit of his fellow sentimental radical Charles Dickens.

In this opening scene of *City Lights*, the hypocritical manner in which a windbag politician and a sanctimonious ladies' club officer take offense at this unsightly spectacle of homelessness is as relevant to Chaplin's late-nineteenth-century London boy-hood as it is to the modern 1930s era of the Great Depression in which this film is ostensibly taking place.[24]

In fact, the Los Angeles shooting location for the statue scene in *City Lights* bears a striking resemblance to a photograph of St. Mark's on Kennington Park Road, which was not very far from Charlie Sr.'s flat.[25] It would not be surprising if St. Mark's was one of the places where Charlie bedded down for the night when booted out of the house by Louise.

As a holdover silent-era film with a state-of-the-art sound-track, *City Lights* substitutes kazoos for human voices in order to satirize the bloviating insincerity of those would-be do-gooders deeply offended by the sight of this penniless, homeless street person, who clearly fails to make the grade as a member of the "deserving poor."

Waddling away from his close encounter with official repre-sentatives of "the system" and taking his daily constitutional as an elegant if shabby man-about-town, Charlie encounters an equally marginal flower girl, whom he promptly falls in love with, a blind young woman who inspires feelings of chivalry in him without the slightest hint of erotic interest. Gazing at Charlie but obviously unable to see him, she envisions him instead as a wealthy, debonair millionaire capable of rescuing her from blindness and homelessness (she could not pay the rent). For his part, Charlie becomes so caught up in love for this beautiful, blind young woman that she effortlessly winds him around her little finger, in a running series of metaphorical sight gags, to the point that he willingly gives her the shirt off his back. He sets out to raise money to cover her overdue rent and to finance a trip to Europe where, a newspaper article has announced, a Viennese surgeon has just invented a free miracle cure for blindness for anyone with the price of a ticket. Personally lacking the funds to rescue this damsel in distress, Charlie finds a wealthy patron to sponsor his philanthropy, an elegantly dressed man-about-town in formal evening clothes who, whenever he is blind drunk, carelessly throws around large sums of money that could easily save the girl. Charlie is preparing to bed down for the night on a park bench when they meet by chance at a visually familiar quayside, which Chaplin, while shooting this film, kept referring to as the Thames Embankment. Interrupting his customary bedtime routine, Charlie, the good Samaritan, prevents this stewed-to-the gills playboy from committing suicide by throwing himself into the river and, later, by attempting to blow his brains out, not once but twice.

It rapidly becomes clear that, when drunk, this blackout-prone millionaire alternates between states of free-spending generosity and suicidal depression. When cold sober, on the mornings after the night before, he suffers from hungover amnesia, which prevents him from recognizing anyone he has met or remembering anything he has done during his boozy nights on the town.

Unaware of the drowning man's wealth or social status at the time he first risks his own life, Charlie ends up in the "Thames" while rescuing him. He and the drunken swell instantly bond. Grateful to this altruistic Little Tramp for saving his life and giving him a reason to live, the elegant swell hugs and kisses his rescuer profusely before bringing him back to his mansion to dry off and share a nightcap.

Later in the film, as their on-again drunk, off-again sober attachment progresses, Charlie will be the one to hug and kiss his benefactor profusely for generously providing him with a thousand dollars to rescue the blind girl, whom the millionaire has never met. Unfortunately for Charlie, the Jekyll-Hyde disconnect between his friend's states of sobriety and inebriation is so complete that Charlie will eventually end up in the clink, unfairly accused by his amnesic benefactor of stealing the dough he was freely given. But not before he bestows his buddy's bounty on the blind girl, altering her life. As Charlie gives her the gift that will restore her sight, it's likely he recognizes but then immediately dismisses the thought that this sightless young woman would reject him in a heartbeat if she could see who he really is.

The film ends with the formerly blind flower girl and the Little Tramp encountering each other by chance after her Viennese miracle cure and his discharge from prison. No longer a street person, she is now managing a prosperous flower shop while expectantly waiting for her former benefactor to return. Her sight restored, her eyes now glaze over only when she wistfully daydreams of finally meeting the handsome millionaire once more.

More threadbare and penniless than ever, Charlie passes the flower shop window and the moment of truth arrives. They gaze at each other. Unaware of this derelict's identity but touched by his shy attention and shabby appearance, she offers him first a rose, then a coin.

Afraid of being recognized, Charlie starts to scurry away. Coaxing him back by extending the rose and then pressing the coin into the palm of his hand, her eyes glaze over as she instantly realizes, through her highly developed sense of touch memory, that the Little Tramp is her benefactor.

"It is enough to shrivel the heart to see, and it is the greatest piece of acting and the highest moment in movies," the film critic James Agee wrote about the final scene that follows.[26]

Chaplin chose someone with no previous acting experience to play the part of the flower girl: Virginia Cherrill. He saw her at a prize fight and immediately asked her to audition for the part. What struck him at once was the fact that this very nearsighted but beautiful young woman was so vain that she refused to wear glasses, and because she was so myopic she appeared to be gazing into space when she tried to focus. As her screen test confirmed, her ability to project effortlessly that out-of-focus look made her a natural to play the part.

Blindness was in some sense an intuitive substitute for madness in Chaplin's creative imagination. Losing contact with reality by staring into space and going out of focus was how nine-year-old Charlie had imagined Lily when Syd came off the soccer field at Norwood and tried to explain what a nervous breakdown meant in terms his kid brother could understand. "In my despair I had visions of her looking pathetically at me, drifting away into a void," was how he understood why she could no longer look after him.[27]

Restoring his mother's sanity was as important to Charlie the child as restoring the blind girl's vision was to Charlie the screen character in *City Lights*. Needleworking and flower selling were equivalently marginal trades in late-nineteenth-century London. And Charlie's feelings of umbilical attachment to the girl were very much like Charlie's feelings of attachment to his mother. Despite the fact that Charlie was painfully aware of his mother's drastically altered looks in the six months leading up to her first psychotic episode, he undoubtedly continued to think of her as the divine Lily whenever he yearned for her during the Cane

Hill separation, just as he had done earlier during their Hanwell separation.

Charlie's increasingly miserable ordeal of being caught in the alcoholic crossfire between his father and Louise prompted an increasingly desperate wish to be reunited with Lily. As everyday life deteriorated for everyone living in that Kennington Road flat, Charlie's double-edged fantasy — of rescuing his mother from madness and being rescued by her from the daily abuse he was experiencing — became more and more urgent. Doubtless there were nights when Charlie soothed himself to sleep, both indoors and out, by dreaming wistfully of being reunited with his miraculously recovered and once more beautiful actress-mother — assuming, that is, she would still find him lovable despite his own increasing unkempt physical appearance as a result of the gross neglect he was experiencing from his father and Louise. Thirty years later, Chaplin's childhood rescue fantasies helped shape the plot of *City Lights* and supplied the emotions for that final reunion scene between his down-and-out screen character and the delicate flower girl.

Dostoyevsky once said that the best things you write come out of a place you don't understand; the way Chaplin arrived at the plot for *City Lights* supports that observation. But as Dostoyevsky's remark also suggests, there is no reason to assume automatically that Chaplin thought of this highly autobiographical film as autobiographical just because it turned out to be.[28]

Did Chaplin connect the flower girl's blindness with Lily's madness? Did the alcoholic millionaire remind him of hard-drinking, self-destructive Charlie Sr. as he threaded his way through his plot labyrinth, filming this autobiographical story in a free-associative fashion over a three-year period from 1928 to 1930? Was he aware of how he inched his way forward in the comic love story with a bittersweet ending by tunneling his way backward into his own tragic life story?

Surviving production records, story conference notes, and gag session notes (recorded and typed by studio secretaries) make it possible to reconstruct chronologically some of the salient points in the circuitous creative route leading to the final version of *City Lights*. Chaplin did not begin at the beginning or find his way to the end of this tale in linear fashion.

The climax of the film, the bittersweet reunion scene, was actually the starting point for his love story. As Robinson put it, that final scene was "the very *raison d'être* of *City Lights*."[29] Typed studio records indicate Chaplin the storyteller relied on this original germ of an idea to launch his narrative and then worked backward by trial and error.[30]

This said, any handwritten notes he jotted down containing personal insights and painful references to the highly autobiographical experiences disguised in *City Lights* are apparently missing or unavailable. We know, from an interview with Richard Meryman in 1966, how Chaplin dealt with autobiographical material:

> if I have a scene that's poetic and has emotional content I have to do that alone. And write in pencil. . . . If it's something too personal that I have to do in long hand, it's not very much, maybe a couple hundred words at most. . . . Anything very personal, poetic, which I think is emotional, I write myself and then I dictate it, because I'm the only one who can decipher what I've written. I dictate in the very cold language, and that's done.[31]

The "very cold language" he employed for privacy purposes resulted in sanitized typewritten records containing a disguised backstory completely stripped of any emotionally charged imagery. That transcription process let Chaplin collaborate on *City*

Lights with assistant directors like Harry Crocker in story conferences and brainstorming gag sessions, secure in the knowledge his privacy was protected. At the same time, the cryptic wording of those typescripts obliquely referred to highly charged personal memories whose encrypted significance only he could understand. Crocker wrote:

> The comedian was extremely reticent about his early youth. There were two major reasons for this. Most of his memories of his extreme youth were extremely unpleasant and he resolutely kept from dwelling on them. The more important reason was a professional one. In the great majority of his early screen appearances, Charlie, as the little waif, drifted into the scene, an anonymous character from nowhere, going nowhere . . . he made audiences laugh, he made them cry; then he walked away into the sunset. Charlie felt that it would be a great mistake to give out to the public his personal history. . . . let the public see only the vague, shadowy figure on the screen: let that figure give them amusement and pathos: let them see only Charlie Chaplin the mime.[32]

From a creative perspective, embedding his life story in his film story was like doing a striptease in public, which no one else but Sydney Chaplin could recognize. As Chaplin once said about acting and filmmaking in general, if the audience can see how it's done, it loses all its magic. And he of course would have lost his privacy.

Chaplin was so confident in the final scene for *City Lights* that almost exclusively on the strength of that scene he began launching extremely expensive, time-consuming preproduction studio preparations months in advance of knowing where the story was going. As an established filmmaker with fifteen years' experience and a proven track record, Chaplin had good reason to put his own checkbook at risk by placing his faith in this germ of an idea for what would eventually become his crowning artistic achievement.

While by no means an identical ending, that final scene was very much like a bittersweet comic ending he had debuted in the past to universal acclaim. Ten years earlier, there had scarcely been a dry eye in the house during the final scene of *The Kid*. It was an equally autobiographical "rescue" film, which Chaplin himself described as "a picture with a smile, perhaps a tear."

As Agee's remark about the final scene between the tramp and the flower girl implies, Chaplin outdid himself and every other filmmaker when he made *City Lights*. The immediate artistic impetus for *The Kid* had been the death of his three-day-old firstborn son; with *City Lights* it was Chaplin's mother, who had died four months before he began shooting the picture.

As a writer working backward from the climax and trying to flesh out the rest of his story, Chaplin's next major plot problem was to create a plausible and sympathetic character who could provide his penniless tramp character with the necessary funds to restore the blind girl's vision and thus set the stage for the final scene he had envisioned. He didn't have far to go:

> I remember one Saturday night when Louise and Father had been drinking, and for some reason we were all sitting with the landlady and her husband in their front-room parlor on the ground floor. Under the incandescent light Father looked ghastly pale, and in an ugly mood was mumbling to himself. Suddenly he reached into his pocket, pulled out a handful of money and threw it violently to the floor, scattering gold and silver coins in all directions. The effect was surrealistic. No one moved. The landlady sat glum, but I caught her roving eye following a golden sovereign rolling to a far corner under a chair; my eye also followed it. Still no one moved, so I thought I'd better start picking it up; the landlady and the others followed suit, picking up the rest of the money, careful to make their actions overt before Father's menacing eyes.[33]

If that wide-eyed little child had dared to act on his feelings, Charlie's borrowing or stealing some of that carelessly strewn money from his well-off actor father in order to provide his seamstress mother with the food, shelter, and medical care she so sorely needed would have been a thoroughly understandable impulse. Had he attempted to do so, it would have been very much like Charlie's fund-raising experiences with the flower girl and the eccentric millionaire in *City Lights*.

More generally, the Little Tramp's heroic efforts to save the blind girl and rescue the suicidal millionaire undoubtedly expressed Chaplin's original childhood wish to come to the aid of each of his parents — both for their benefit and for his. Alternating between rescuing the flower girl from blindness and preventing the depressed millionaire from destroying himself was the fictional counterpart of Chaplin's original childhood wish to restore his beautiful young mother's sanity and to stop his debonair *lion comique* father from drinking himself to death.

While those two parental rescue fantasies can be viewed and understood as entirely separate from one another, they also were interdependent, in life and art.

In life, Chaplin's childhood rescue fantasy of helping his father overcome his self-destructive behavior seemed also a way to help his mentally ill mother. His father had the means to help his mother but lacked the inclination. He still held a grudge against her for betraying and abandoning him not once but twice. His bitterness aggravated his depression and worsened his alcoholism. In theory, Charlie's reconciling his parents could have given them the opportunity to deal more effectively with their emotional problems by helping each other.

In art, Charlie's selfless rescue of the angrily depressed man-about-town from drowning, and later from blowing his brains out, ultimately does facilitate the tramp's subsequent rescue of the blind flower girl. "I'm cured. You're my friend for life!" is the alcoholic millionaire's overly optimistic and premature conclusion as he and Charlie pull each other out of the "Thames."

When the two return to the millionaire's mansion for a nightcap (and a relapse), Charlie and the audience discover the source of his depression: obviously, his wife has threatened to leave him. Enquiring about her now, he is told by the butler that she has just had her bags picked up and has left, presumably forever. Feigning supreme indifference, the millionaire immediately heads for the liquor cabinet to get a drink for himself and his diminutive boon companion. On top of the cabinet sits a glamorously posed photograph of a strikingly beautiful woman. The millionaire casually tosses it away and proceeds to pour the drinks for himself and his guest. A few minutes later, and further into his cups, he suddenly experiences a delayed emotional reaction and impulsively puts a pistol to his head. Charlie rushes to his rescue and saves his life a second time. At one point in the film, this allegorical father-son duo even end up bedding down for the night together as Charlie provides his buddy with comic substitute companionship, metaphorically replacing the missing wife.

City Lights allowed forty-year-old Chaplin the storyteller a second chance to accomplish in celluloid what he had been unable to accomplish in real life as a nine-year-old. With unprecedented artistic success, he set out to make whole the image of a family sundered long before.

In accordance with the loss-restitution hypothesis of creativity, the death of Chaplin's mother on August 28, 1928, was the stimulus for *City Lights*. While hard evidence cannot be found in studio notes, it was the mourning and grieving process triggered by his mother's death that was, to borrow the words of David Robinson, "the very *raison d'être* of *City Lights*."

If we employ the psychoanalytic tactic of using a life to read a film and a film to read a life, *City Lights* enriches our under-standing of Charlie Chaplin's childhood. The picture ends with the momentous question that nine-year-old Charlie posed to himself with great trepidation: what would it be like to be finally reunited with his mother after her two-month stay in Cane Hill?

Child Prodigy

So enthralled was I with Dickens' characters that I would imitate . . . them. It was inevitable that such budding talent could not be concealed for long. Thus it was that one day Mr. Jackson saw me entertaining the other boys with an imitation of the old man of *The Old Curiosity Shop*. Then and there I was proclaimed a genius, and Mr. Jackson was determined to let the world know it. . . .

After our clog dance Mr. Jackson walked onstage with the earnestness of one about to announce the coming of a young Messiah, stating that he had discovered a child genius among his boys.

— Chaplin[1]

O N THE DAY OF HER HOSPITAL DISCHARGE, Hannah Chaplin found a cheap top-floor room in a tenement next to a slaughterhouse, persuaded "someone to trust her for the rent of a sewing machine" and "someone else to trust her for material" to sew shirts, "and by night she . . . [had] a dozen . . . ready to sell."[2]

When she picked up the boys the next day, they leapt into her arms "and the thought that she had been ill never entered our heads."[3] Lucid and optimistic, she had managed a rental at 39 Methley Street, a few streets away from Charlie Sr.'s Kennington Road digs. Although it was shabby, it was a home. Moreover, Syd and Charlie were profoundly relieved to be leaving their stepmother.

While Hannah made a brave show of starting life again, under the surface her family's finances were as precarious as her underlying physical health. Working fifty-four hours a week as a sewing machine operator, she earned somewhere between six shillings ninepence and seven shillings sixpence a week. According to late-nineteenth-century London sociologist Charles Booth, the poverty line at this time was between eighteen and twenty-one shillings per week. Families whose incomes went below this level were considered abjectly poor and lived in substandard, if not subhuman, conditions.

The mathematics of Hannah's situation were such that she, Charlie, and Sydney — plus her estranged husband — all needed to pitch in for them to stay afloat. "Father's payments of ten shillings a week were almost regular," Charlie recalled.[4]

Whether Charlie Sr. decided to meet his weekly child support obligations with regularity because he had gotten to know and love his two sons or had finally learned to fear the court is unclear. Until his recent two-month, court-enforced custodial experience with Charlie and Sydney, neither of these two equally plausible causes for his dramatically reformed behavior had been put to the test.

Given Charlie Sr.'s regular contributions, it was inevitable that some form of regular commerce with Hannah or the boys took place, if for no other reason than to deliver the weekly ten shillings. In any case, within two weeks of Hannah's psychiatric discharge, the Chaplin parents met to discuss Charlie's future. It was the first time since the original breakup of their marriage eight years earlier that the two former teenage sweethearts had conferred civilly and cooperated mutually as concerned parents with a common goal.

Charlie's mother was now thirty-three, his father thirty-five. While there still were residual feelings of hurt and disappointment on both sides, they were no longer confronting each other as adversaries. Overcoming their earlier legal conflicts, they now tried to focus on the best interests of their children.

For Charlie, his parents' new spirit of cooperation would result in one of the most formative experiences of his life: an introduction into stage performance technique and the rich heritage of British music hall. He was about to join an elite troupe of eight professional child dancers, who tapped out a perfectly synchronized series of complex clog dance steps with lightning speed and perfect coordination, night after night, from London to Scotland to Ireland to Wales and the Midlands. While he would be paid a pittance for this theatrical apprenticeship, it would also furnish him with a priceless education. But before he could join the Eight Lancashire Lads for their next major booking in Manchester on Christmas Day 1898, he needed the personal and legal permission of the two people whose stage careers were the source of his own ambition.

Selling churchgoing Hannah Chaplin on the idea of launching nine-year-old Charlie's stage career as a Lancashire Lad proved a much more daunting task than it would have been to persuade the free-spirited adventuress Lily Harley. But having recently rekindled his namesake son's already well-developed interest in becoming a music hall performer, Charlie Sr. used all his powers of persuasion to convince the boy's mother.

In light of his own occasional difficulties in meeting his weekly child support payments, because of the unpredictable nature of show business bookings, which as Hannah well knew were beyond his control, coupled with her own limited earning capacity, Charlie Sr. proposed that the two shillings sixpence per week (plus room and board) their son could earn as a child performer would go a long way toward making ends meet.[5] Although the troupe was based in London and played the provinces less frequently, Hannah Chaplin was unswayed by her estranged husband's shillings-and-pence logic. What won her over in the end was the fact that William Jackson, the company's founder and manager, was a devoutly religious family man. Not only did the good-natured, middle-aged ex-schoolteacher from Lancashire run the troupe with the help of his warmhearted and motherly wife, but four of their own children performed as well. Proud of the fact that his Lads had a reputation for rosy-cheeked radiance achieved without benefit of greasepaint, Jackson conveniently neglected to mention those occasionally exhausting but financially rewarding three-music-halls-a-night stints in London when nature's fading glow required the artificial stimulus of cheek pinching, applied by the boys themselves, of course. Focusing instead on spiritually idyllic Sunday mornings and the fact that he and his family were strict Catholics who attended church regularly, he undoubtedly allayed Hannah's reservations about exposing her impressionable young son to the glamorous but godless world of music hall, whose pitfalls and pratfalls she knew all too well.

During his two-and-a-half-year stint with the Lads, Charlie spent two-thirds of his time in London. When the Lads had holes in their bookings, he lived with Hannah and Syd on Methley Street, but when the Lads were working he stayed at the Jacksons', just around the corner on Kennington Road, a few houses down from Charlie Sr. Approximately nine months were spent touring the British Isles from Land's End to John o'Groats.

Lancashire clog dancing (like the Irish step dancing of the modern Riverdance Company) was a complex type of precision folk dancing performed in wooden-soled clogs with metal tips. It is said to have originated in the cotton mills of Lancashire, where the men sitting at their weaving machines would tap their feet to the rhythms of the factory equipment in order to keep warm. Evolving from an informal workplace amusement into a popular working-class entertainment, and from there into a formal folk art form, it rapidly became part of the class-conscious theatrical traditions that marked the proletarian origins of British music hall.

Gussied up in their white linen blouses with lace collars, plush knickerbocker trousers, and red dancing shoes, this appealing group of youngsters beat out their lightning-speed taps with perfect coordination. It took Charlie six weeks to conquer his stagefright and master their complex steps before opening with the Lads at the Theatre Royal in Manchester in a 1898 Christmas pantomime production entitled, appropriately enough, *Babes in the Wood*. Working that show, the Lads probably played in front of the curtain as an act to entertain and distract the audience while elaborate backstage scenery changes were being made, and then appeared within the pantomime tale itself as costumed child supernumeraries — forest animals, elves, fairies, dwarfs.

Joining this troupe of preadolescent dancers, whose educations were circumscribed by their stage lives, Charlie would remain functionally illiterate to the point that when he eventually got his first speaking part in a play as a budding teenage actor, Syd would be obliged to read the entire script to him out loud in order for him to learn his lines. However, even late in life, in his sixties, Chaplin could still recite an entire play from this period — not just his own part — from memory. Not only was he a perfectionist workaholic from early childhood into old age, he was also endowed with a phenomenal memory, whose vast storehouse of information would furnish much of the raw material for his creative imagination throughout his career.

Although Charlie's professional acting experience as a supernumerary in pantomime was extremely limited, the stagestruck prodigy thoughtfully analyzed and memorized the nuanced moves of the principal players in all three of the traditional Christmas-season productions in which he appeared as a Lancashire Lad between 1898 and 1901: *Babes in the Wood*, *Sinbad the Sailor*, and *Cinderella*. Chaplin told a reporter two decades later in 1917:

> Every move they made registered on my young brain like a photograph. I used to try it all when I got home. . . . My earliest study of the clowns in the London pantomimes has been of tremendous value to me.[6]

Paying tribute to those thoroughly mesmerizing childhood experiences, sixty-three-year-old Chaplin would sum up his artistic debt by playing the part of a principal clown in *The Death of Columbine*, the pantomime ballet he choreographed for *Limelight*.

The sophisticated sight gags and complex performance techniques encompassed in the more than two hundred years of British pantomime traditions were the academic equivalent of a crash course in basic slapstick. Watching from the wings, it was possible for Charlie to observe and begin to appreciate the clown, the audience, and the complex relationship between them. While the intellectual ability to deconstruct and understand first-rate physical comedy performance technique was a far cry from the ability to execute the same before live audiences, it was a critical first step in the professional education of the future slapstick comedian.

The study of wily clown tricksters in slapshoes as they gracefully impersonated clumsiness while stealthily filching sausages from unsuspecting shopkeepers and shrewdly outwitted irate comic policemen in chase scenes while conspiratorially engaging their audience of kids and adults in sly complicity, was a first-rate educational preparation for a future Keystone film comedian. In addition to providing Charlie with an introduction into the acrobatic physical comedy techniques of kicks, blows, slips, slides, skids, and somersaults, it enabled him to observe the stage fundamentals for such visually sophisticated gambits as playing a chicken (*The Gold Rush*) or a tree (*Shoulder Arms*), and the improvisational basics for transforming everyday physical objects like dinner rolls into ballet slippers (*The Gold Rush*) or a loaf of bread into a concertina (*A Jitney Elopement*), or the mechanical use of hidden ropes and pulleys for magical transformation scenes in which a slum street resembling Methley Street could metamorphose into a heavenly Garden of Eden populated with soaring angels (*The Kid*).

Spending Christmas Day 1898 onstage and backstage in his first day ever as a paid show-business professional at the Theatre Royal in Manchester must have been a thrilling experience compared to the pervasive sadness and loneliness of his last two Christmases spent in the orphanage. Swapping his regimented Hanwell uniform for a distinctive Lad's costume instantly made nine-year-old Charlie one of eight talented wage earners rather than one of a thousand-plus indigent wards of the state. Chaplin later claimed that the inmates at Hanwell were assigned numbers and his had been 151.[7]

While his claim of being assigned an inmate number may have been a form of self-pitying exaggeration, there is no doubt that Chaplin did suffer from lifelong Christmas Day depressions, which he attributed to an emotionally traumatic experience that occurred two years earlier, on Christmas Day 1896 at Hanwell. It was a memory of his bitter disappointment at being unfairly punished for an accident in bed, which was still on his mind more than sixty years later while raising his own children. Having grown up in material comfort, some of Chaplin's children found their father's annual Yuletide grumblings about his Dickensian boyhood and a Christmas Day orange he never received difficult to fathom. He undoubtedly had such painful experiences in mind when he told a reporter "my childhood ended at the age of seven."[8]

In any event, while nine-year-old Charlie was now spending yet another Christmas apart from Hannah and Syd — this time they were 185 miles away in London — he was not entirely alone even if it felt that way. In addition to the Jacksons, his father was in Manchester at the time. Charlie Chaplin Sr. opened at the Manchester Tivoli on Boxing Day and would therefore have been theoretically available to celebrate the momentous occasion of his son's professional show-business debut at the nearby Theatre Royal. That is, assuming he was not too busy celebrating the Yuletide spirit in his customary fashion.

Babes in the Wood closed in mid-February 1899. The Lads did not play London until early April, when they opened at the palatial Oxford Music Hall where many of the greatest stars in the business played.

For Charlie, the experience of going through the exact same dance steps night after night, with unvarying precision and no room for self-expression, did little if anything to develop his talents or contribute to his fund of knowledge. To relieve the monotony of his own routine, he studied other peoples'. While waiting in the wings, Charlie observed the greats and near-greats perform throughout his two and a half years as a Lancashire Lad. Employing his photographic memory and remarkable powers of imitation, he amused himself and entertained some of the other Lads when they returned home to the Jackson flat by endlessly practicing his impersonations and satirical takeoffs of other acts on the bill, until he got them dead-on by using all of the tricks Lily had taught him in those earlier tutorials during her work breaks.

In this way the fast learner and clever copycat advanced his understanding of basic acting technique and geometrically expanded what eventually became his mental filing cabinet of comedy ideas, sight gags, and stage business. A mind "like an attic," the collecting habits of a "magpie," an "encyclopedia of comedy" — these would be some of the epithets his Hollywood collaborators later used to describe Chaplin's prodigious memory.

As modern clinical research in human development has demonstrated, childhood genius comes in more than one flavor, or what Howard Gardner refers to as "multiple intelligences."

While Charlie Chaplin was a semiliterate child with the equivalent of a fourth-grade education, who suffered from a lifelong reading disability,[9] he nonetheless merited the term "child genius" that William Jackson originally bestowed on him as a precocious ten-year-old, regardless of how well or poorly he might have performed on standardized IQ tests, had they been available at that time.

As to the well-known tendency of creative geniuses to deconstruct, cannibalize, and resynthesize their artistic predecessors, while steadfastly refusing to acknowledge their debt to them as the expression of an intergenerational competitive process which the critic Harold Bloom has aptly termed "the anxiety of influence," Chaplin was understandably reluctant to detract from the impression of his own originality by paying tribute to the artists who influenced him.

Two music hall greats whose performances the seventy-five-year-old Chaplin casually mentioned having seen in passing while working the halls as a Lancashire Lad — without acknowledging his creative debt to either — were Marie Lloyd and Dan Leno. For at least the length of a one-week booking, on separate occasions, Lloyd and Leno each appeared on the same bill as the Lancashire Lads at the Tivoli in London. A week of backstage study was all it would have taken for precocious Charlie to get them both down pat.

Magically radiating her intimate vitality to the twopenny "gods" on high as she serenaded them with her first hit and permanent signature song, "The Boy I Love Is Up in the Gallery," sixteen-year-old Marie Lloyd, a Cockney girl, got her start in the halls playing the bottom of the bill beneath, among others, Lily Harley. And throughout her thirty-six-year career as the greatest comedienne of her time, Our Marie, as she was known to her admirers, took great pains to perpetually renew her art by never breaking faith with her original working-class audience, even after gaining recognition and praise from the likes of T. S. Eliot. Recalling Lloyd shortly after her death in 1922, Eliot wrote:

> The lower class still exists; but perhaps it will not exist for long. In the Music Hall comedians they find the expression and dignity of their own lives. . . . the working man who went to the Music Hall and saw Marie Lloyd and joined in the chorus was himself performing part of the act; he was engaged in that collaboration of the audience with the artist which is necessary in all art and most obviously in dramatic art.[10]

Songs like "My Old Man Said to Follow the Van and Don't Dilly Dally on the Way" celebrated and glorified her working-class audience's familiarity with the everyday experience of skipping out on the landlord when the rent was due.

Delivering her comic character songs with a conspiratorial wink-and-nod patter while broadly aspirating 'er aitches instantly lessened the formal proscenium distance between Lloyd and the audience. Leaning forward to whisper some juicy off-color confidence in the private code of Cockney street slang to the blighters in the balcony, so as not to be overheard by some prissy busybody in the stalls, was a surefire way of disarming the entire house.

No one was a greater mistress of the time-honored conventions and bawdy devices of low comedy than Our Marie. Neither overtly lewd nor obscene, Lloyd exuded a subtle but suggestive working-class frankness about the facts of life with her provocative walk, naughty nod, and impudent smile. While sufficiently ladylike to appease her most prim and censorious critics in the dress circle, she also managed to satisfy her earthiest admirers in the gallery. Waging a one-woman war on hypocritical Victorian respectability, she was able — as was Chaplin later on — to tread tastefully the fine line between comedy and filth.

Her saucy innuendoes playfully added covert meanings to her most innocent comments. It was precisely because of her rapid-fire, nonverbal mode of comic delivery that the Lord Chamberlain declined to censor her as obscene. Her timing was perfect and her acting technique impeccable. In the wink of an eye, she could effortlessly alternate between a lady of quality and a Cockney bawd. Her comic characterizations would serve as a generic role model for Chaplin's future screen character's split-second, split-personality shifts between an immaculately mannered swell and a vulgar ne'er-do-well.

Well schooled in that great music hall tradition of cheeky double meaning by Lloyd, Leno, and the like, Chaplin would import it to Hollywood, where he slipped his bawdiest working-class gags past the censors with a flair that was clearly the match of Our Marie. Picking up a glass of beer and quietly secreting it in his trousers, Charlie delicately jiggles a few spilt drops down his pants leg with all the gentility of an ale-quaffing pub patron discreetly informing the barman that his horse may be developing diabetes (*The Property Man*). Looking up from his dinner plate in search of the passing bird who has just plopped down his lunch, Charlie leaves no doubt as to what he thinks of prison food (*Modern Times*). Restoring circulation by rubbing his rump instead of his hands, after belting down a stiff drink in the Monte Carlo Dance Hall, he decorously informs us exactly what part of his anatomy has been frozen off by the cruel Arctic winter raging outside (*The Gold Rush*).

As Marie Lloyd put it in her well-known song "Ev'ry Little Movement Has a Meaning of Its Own," it was entirely a matter of delivery. And just as ladylike Lloyd played some of her coarsest comedy against the counterpoint of la-di-da refinement, so Chaplin would invest in his Little Tramp such expressions of crude funny business as delicately wiping his nose on the train of a lady's flowing garment whose hem he is in the process of kissing in a courtly manner (*His New Job*).

*   *   *

As a status-conscious septuagenarian, who was beset by anxiety over how his creative genius would be judged by posterity as he traced out his early artistic development in his autobiography, Chaplin refused explicitly to acknowledge the crucial formative influence that Lloyd, Leno, and others of their ilk had played in shaping his professional development, starting with his boyhood days as a Lancashire Lad. But as a world-famous movie star in his early forties who was untroubled by the anxiety of influence, Charlie was much less dodgy when it came to freely acknowledging his boyhood debt to his music hall predecessors.

In the privacy of his Los Angeles living room, Chaplin delighted in conjuring up devastatingly accurate and ingenious leftover childhood impressions of the music hall giants from his Lancashire Lad days, which he performed gratis for the amusement of his friends and admirers. Spellbound during a colorful series of nostalgic conversations with his slightly homesick countryman, British journalist Alistair Cooke later wrote that Chaplin

> fell into reminiscences of the old music-hall songs, and, cued by my mention of some of the great gone names, he went off into a bout of marvelous total recall, ballooning before my eyes into the bosomy swagger of Marie Lloyd and bawling out "A Little of What You Fancy Does Y' Good," then shrinking into the exquisite shape of Vesta Tilley [a great male impersonator] . . . and singing "I'm Colonel Coldfeet of the Coldstream Guards."[11]

It also would be a grave mistake to dismiss Lloyd and Leno as lowbrow comedians. They were talented Cockney-born character actors who earned their daily bread by beguiling working-class audiences with moving comic portraits and gentle satirical parodies of themselves. British music hall was a hodgepodge of variety entertainment with trained seals, comic jugglers, magic acts, knife throwers, fortune-tellers, acrobats, and the like. But it also was — when practiced in its highest form by serious thespians like Leno and Lloyd — a sophisticated proletarian art form whose historical origins were a direct outgrowth of the Industrial Revolution. Many of its comic character songs and love ballads were a spoken and sung idiomatic form of Cockney folk poetry set to music and performed by first-rate actors who, like Chaplin, came from the working class, whose lives they sang and joked about.

It could be argued that Lloyd's and Leno's art was verbal and vocal while Chaplin's was not. But the pantomime techniques they employed to advance their performance narratives were some of the nonverbal nuggets young Charlie unconsciously imitated or consciously copied to enrich and inform his own future technique as a pantomime character actor.

Intellectuals like the great Russian director Vsevolod Meyerhold were quick to point out — as was Sarah Bernhardt — that the polished performance skills employed by these gifted working-class actors, who broke down the traditional "fourth wall" convention of classical theater by intimately addressing their audiences, were as technically sophisticated as the most elegant stage work of the finest actors of the much more culturally prestigious legitimate theater.

Summing up the hallmark essence of her fellow artist Dan Leno, Marie Lloyd said:

Ever seen his eyes? The saddest eyes in the whole world. That's why we all laughed at Danny. Because if we hadn't laughed, we should have cried ourselves sick. I believe that's what real comedy is, you know, it's almost like crying.[12]

Summing up the essence of his fellow artist Charlie Chaplin, Stan Laurel said:

He had those eyes that absolutely forced you to look at them. He had the damnedest way of looking at an audience. He had the damnedest way of looking at *you*, on stage. I don't think anyone has ever written about those eyes of his. . . . That's a part of the secret of his great success — eyes that make you believe him in whatever he does.[13]

Chaplin's tendency to acknowledge or overlook Leno's influence varied over time. During a sentimental visit to London in 1921, he openly referred to Dan as a boyhood "idol of mine" and gratefully accepted the gift of a pair of the deceased actor's shoes from members of his family. Receiving that nostalgic memento of the great comedian whose artistic shoes he had symbolically filled was thirty-two-year-old Chaplin's tribute to the first actor who had ever demonstrated to him by example how his own soulful gaze could be used to enrich slapstick and make it funnier by making it sadder.

At the time of that gift presentation, Chaplin probably considered it a compliment to be praised as "Lenoesque." In fact, in 1915 the film magazine *Bioscope* had already paid him that compliment by describing him as "the Dan Leno of the screen."[14]

Fifty years later, however, when he sat down to pen his memoirs, the term "Chaplinesque" had officially entered the English language thanks to a poem with that title by Hart Crane and — much more important — thanks to that heart-stopping final close-up of Charlie's heavily mascaraed and deeply soulful eyes in the last scene of *City Lights*. For seventy-five-year-old Chaplin to have described one of the signature features of his own performance style as Lenoesque would have served no purpose for his readers.

There was only one music hall star from this earliest phase of his professional life whose formative influence Chaplin fully acknowledged in his autobiography. That man, a famous Dickens delineator named Bransby Williams, was remembered more for the subject matter of his performances than for his stagecraft. As usual, Chaplin the child prodigy effortlessly performed letter-perfect imitation of Bransby Williams doing his death-of-Little-Nell soliloquy as the grandfather in *The Old Curiosity Shop*.

It was Charlie's elegant and polished private rendition of Bransby Williams that amazed William Jackson and inspired him to declare Chaplin a child genius. But Chaplin's onstage debut as Nell's grandfather, still dressed in his clog-dancing outfit and sporting an old man's fright-wig, proved extremely mortifying because he lacked both confidence and technical expertise in performing solo. Amazing his fellow clog dancers with his brilliant improv sketches of an entire rogues' gallery of Dickens characters taken from Bransby Williams's stage repertoire — performed in intimate settings for his roommates — was a far cry from projecting himself in public before unpredictable and unforgiving live audiences in music halls that held anywhere from five hundred to three thousand people. There was the queasy question of stagefright.

It would be several years before the red-faced boy would once again run the risk of performing solo in a speaking part before a music hall audience, after his humiliating one-night flop as a squeaky-voiced ten-year-old grandfather. Although he was not jeered, insulted, or baited as Lily was at Aldershot five years earlier, Charlie was already beginning to develop an anxiety about playing interactively before live audiences that would dog him the rest of his life. Ironically, he would eventually master his fear of the audience's potential sadism by personifying one of them onstage in a devastating satire.

The most significant debt that functionally illiterate ten-year-old Charlie Chaplin owed to Bransby Williams was the enthralling canvas of Dickens characters that Williams brought to life for him, at a time when Chaplin was not yet able to read the books that housed them. The two memorable individuals with whom Charlie identified most closely were secretly highborn Oliver

Twist and his working-class trickster pal Jack Dawkins, both of whom would later inform Chaplin's shabby-genteel tramp character's trickster psychology. The streetwise Artful Dodger and the orphanage waif Oliver were two boys his own age whose "real-life" experiences immediately rang true to Charlie based on his own recent childhood experiences as an urban outdoorsman and Hanwell inmate. Not surprisingly, when he finally taught himself to read, *Oliver Twist* would become Chaplin's favorite novel, which he read over and over again for relaxation and pleasure, even into extreme old age, in part because its rags-to-riches theme resonated with the remarkably similar outcome of his own life.

Chaplin's eldest son, Charlie Chaplin Jr., wrote: *"Oliver Twist* was a favorite of Dad's because young Oliver's experiences in the orphanage so closely approximated his own. . . . Dad repeated the story often, but I don't recall his ever telling it in the same way. Each time he would add fresh embellishments from his own imagination, so that Syd and I never knew exactly what to expect. But we could always count on its being exciting."[15]

Commenting on Chaplin's identification with Dickens, Alistair Cooke wrote:

> He talked in a touching and rambling way about his childhood, but neither then nor ever later did he moon over his poverty or sentimentalize the groveling times. . . . As he went on, acting out with great spirit and delicacy his early attempts at shabby gentility . . . and then went further back to miming a wealth of characters fixed forever in his boyhood . . . I had the odd feeling that I had heard and seen all this before. Charles Chaplin was Charles Dickens reborn. . . . there is an eerie similiarity between *Oliver Twist* and the first sixty pages . . . of Chaplin's *Autobiography*. But as a reincarnation of everything spry and inquisitive and Cockney-shrewd and invincibly alive and cunning, Chaplin was the young Dickens in the flesh.[16]

To offset his one day of ignominious vocal failure playing Little Nell's grandfather, ten-year-old Charlie also enjoyed one day of dizzying success as a self-styled panto comedian. Discouraged but by no means defeated by his Dickens debacle, he was not content to return to the chorus line with his tail between his legs. Still hungering for the limelight, he rose to the occasion when the opportunity to show off in a nonspeaking part presented itself.

Playing the fabulous London Hippodrome as part of a grand ensemble in a spectacular ballet pantomime, *Cinderella*, the Eight Lancashire Lads were hired to portray costumed cats and dogs as supporting cast in a scene featuring Marceline. It was Charlie's job, dressed as a cat, to be the stationary prop object over which the famous clown tripped backward as part of his funny business.

Performing in the first matinee, Charlie wasted no time upstaging the star by sniffing the rear end of one of the dogs in a most "uncatlike" way and breaking up the audience. Then, having captured their undivided attention, he proceeded to sniff out a spot on the stage and mock-urinate, doggie fashion, one leg poised high in the air. For good measure, he turned his cat mask full face to the house and, by "pulling a string which winked a staring eye," flirted with his audience, letting them in on the gag before he "capered off to great applause."[17]

Although he was not allowed to repeat the gag a second time, he had had his first exhilarating taste of voiceless comic improvisation. Even more important was his discovery that by winking at a live audience — a trick Chaplin would later repeat over and over again by turning full face to the camera and peeking into the lens — he could break down all formal barriers between viewer and performer and establish instant intimacy.

Having stumbled onto that time-honored crowd-pleaser the comic aside, whose lineage could be traced from the comedies of Aristophanes to the gambols of Harlequin and frolics of Shakespeare and into the confidential patter of Lloyd and Leno in the music halls, Chaplin would carry it with him to Hollywood in the lens-flirting, peekaboo antics of his Little Tramp. He would — so film critics claim — be the first to perfect that well-timed peek into the camera, a surefire way to create for his sympathetic viewers the illusion that he had just stepped off the screen and curled up in their laps, while all the time holding them in the palm of his hand.

While it is not hard to identify the connection between Charlie's discomfort with live vocal performances and Lily's Aldershot experience, there is room to wonder what role, if any, his *lion comique* father's disastrous descent down the career ladder played in Charlie's subsequent affinity for voiceless performances. Not very long after young Charlie's onstage debacle as a Dickens delineator, Charlie Chaplin Sr. finally met his Waterloo. September 1900 marked Charlie Sr.'s last recorded engagement at the Granville Theatre of Varieties, Walham Green. By then he was also living in shabby quarters in one of the mean streets off Kennington Road.

Washed up as a singer, he now dwelt in a drunken twilight haze of "febrile hilarity" at the Queen's Head where, remaining a celebrity of sorts, he nostalgically lived in the past by rubbing elbows with old show business cronies who had known him in happier days. A scant few months later, shortly before leaving the Lancashire Lads, young Charlie clogged with his troupe as one of the many acts playing the benefit performance for his dying father who "appeared on the stage breathing with difficulty" as he made his farewell speech to the audience. Shortly after that, Charlie saw his father alive for the last time, sitting in the corner of a pub, sunken-eyed and ill, his body swollen to enormous proportions by the dropsy of alcoholic cirrhosis. After inquiring warmly about Hannah and Syd, he took his son in his arms and kissed him for what Chaplin later claimed was the first and only time. Charlie would never forgot his parting glimpse of his father resting with "one hand, Napoleon-like, in his waist-coat, as if to ease his breathing."[18]

Around the time he was saying goodbye to his father, Charlie was forced reluctantly to bid the Eight Lancashire Lads farewell. Concerned that her son "looked pale and thin" and that their hectic schedule of nightly performances might be adversely affecting his lungs, Hannah Chaplin wrote such an alarmed and fretful note to Mr. Jackson that the usually easygoing impresario indignantly dispatched Charlie home, sputtering and fuming that he "was not worth the bother of such a worrying mother."[19]

A little later, Charlie became acutely short of breath. Terri-fied that her son was developing TB, Hannah sped Charlie off to Brompton Hospital where, after prescribing symptomatic treat-ment for the air-hungry child, a hospital physician reassured the anxious mother that her son was not tubercular.

Apparently no one considered the possibility that the twelve-year-old boy's sudden symptoms of suffocation might be con-nected to his dying father's shortness of breath. Recalling his miserable illness during this dismal period of his life, Chaplin wrote:

> Nothing was found wrong with my lungs, but I did have asthma. For months I went through agony, unable to breathe. At times wanted to jump out of the window. Inhaling herbs with a blanket over my head gave little relief. But, as the doctor said I would, I eventually outgrew it.[20]

One can only wonder how much the oppressive heaviness on Charlie's chest might better have been released by weeping than by any herbal prescription the Brompton pharmacy had to offer.

*   *   *

It was on their way home from that hospital that Hannah and Charlie encountered a grim spectacle: some boys were hounding a shaven-headed derelict woman in rags "like a stag at bay." After dispatching the "smirking and giggling" youngsters, Hannah approached their victim and was taken aback when she feebly croaked: "Lil, don't you know me?" Peering into the sick woman's dirty face and searching her memory, Hannah was stunned to discover that the crone was none other than Dashing Eva Lester, an old vaudeville friend with whom she had once shared the bill. It seemed like only yesterday that the *Era* reviewer had praised Eva as "one of the prettiest and most fascinating serio-comic songstresses we have."[21]

After taking Eva in for a few days — feeding and cleaning her up — Hannah "gave her what clothes she could spare and loaned her a couple of bob" before she vanished back into the night, and a life of "sleeping under arches." It was lives like Eva's, as well as her own and Charlie Sr.'s, that roused Hannah "almost into a fury at the idea" of granting her importuning son's request for permission "to go back to the music halls." Years later, Chaplin still vividly recalled how his irate mother "passionately made me promise never to act in one."[22]

In the last few weeks before his death, Charlie Sr. and Lily had an opportunity to say goodbye to each other. No longer holed up in his lair at the Queen's Head — a domain Hannah Chaplin refused to enter — Charlie Sr. had been gotten sufficiently drunk by his concerned friends that he could be docilely led into the sanctuary of St. Thomas's Hospital — a domain *he* feared to enter.

As the alcohol began to wear off and the thirty-seven-year-old realized where he had been taken, he "fought wildly" like a caged animal, but to no avail. To ease their reluctant patient's painful swelling, his doctors tapped sixteen quarts of fluid from his waterlogged body. And to ease her ex-husband's spiritual agony, Hannah visited him several times at the hospital and humored him whenever "he spoke of wanting to go back to her and start life anew in Africa." Upon hearing that news, young Charlie brightened visibly, until his mother set him straight as to where things really stood.[23]

On May 9, 1901, Charlie Chaplin Sr. died. Hannah and twelve-year-old Charlie were among the handful of mourners that included a few members of the Chaplin family and some old show-business friends. The elaborate funeral — wreathes, satin-lined casket, horse-drawn carriages, preacher, and all the threnodic trimmings — was supplied courtesy of the Variety Artists' Benevolent Fund and a well-to-do Chaplin relative. But unfortunately, Charlie Sr.'s farewell show did not have enough backers, and as the pomp and ceremony drew to a close, his final remains were consigned to plot 577 B3 com. in the Tooting Cemetery — a common pauper's grave.[24] Standing in a driving rain, young Charlie began to weep as "the grave-diggers threw down clods of earth on the coffin which resounded with a brutal thud."[25]

On May 9, 1903 — exactly two years after her estranged husband's death — Hannah Chaplin was again admitted raving mad into the Cane Hill Lunatic Asylum. Her commitment papers read:

> Charles Chaplin, son . . . states she keeps on mentioning a lot of people who are dead and fancies she can see them looking out of the window.[26]

Having never actually seen his mother psychotic before, Charlie at fourteen, was "shocked" and filled with "ineffable sadness" as he stood by helplessly and witnessed Hannah's formerly animated window-gazing progressively degenerate into vacant-eyed window-staring for days on end before making its final

grotesque descent into the netherworld of hallucinatory improvisation.[27]

Although Hannah Chaplin's commitment certificate does
not mention precisely who the revenants in the window were, it
seems a safe bet that her good-time Charlie and dear friend Eva
were among them. Confiding to the admitting physician her anxiety over being unable to cross the River Jordan, she at once
made it clear just how desperately she yearned to see her old
friends and loved ones once more.

Woman in the Window

I learned from her everything I know. She was the most astounding mimic I ever saw. She would stay at the window for hours, gazing at the street and reproducing with her hands, eyes and expression all that was going on down there, and never stopped. It was in watching and observing her that I learned not only to translate motions with my hands and features, but also to study mankind.

— Chaplin[1]

LONG AFTER HER SHOW BUSINESS DAYS WERE OVER and that three-room flat in the Westminster Bridge Road was nothing more than a memory, Hannah Chaplin, despite her demoralizing circumstances, still remained an actress at heart. As an unskilled sweatshop pieceworker in her late thirties attempting to raise two children, struggling to keep her head above water and her family above the poverty line, she earned so little that her substandard diet undoubtedly compromised her already impaired mental faculties. The single most important compensatory mechanism she had at her disposal was her creative imagination. Hannah Hill may have failed to accomplish her romantic plan for escaping working-class poverty, but Hannah Chaplin's persistent love of the theater helped her transcend the misery and squalor of her immediate surroundings and made life more bearable. She could still magically transform her unromantic working-class world into a romantic stage set for herself and her sons with her amusing improv takes and takeoffs of the foibles and mannerisms of their friends and neighbors, which she delivered with pungent running commentaries and invented stories that broke Charlie up. They were poor, but they still had fun.

Even after her first mental breakdown in 1898, looking out of her full-size top-floor tenement flat window at 39 Methley Street and later out of a tinier garret window in an even more tightly cramped and dilapidated attic room with a foreshortened, sloping ceiling at 3 Pownall Terrace until the last few weeks before her second Cane Hill admission, Hannah amused Charlie by engaging in imaginative window-gazing games that he never forgot. Their zany games taught him wickedly funny improv tricks that he would use for the rest of his life and pass on to his own children.[2]

Not only would Chaplin later credit those moments with his mother as the most influential experience in his own artistic development, he would also take the time, trouble, and considerable expense to have his studio art director, Danny Hall, build for *The Kid* an interior film set replicating their Pownall Terrace garret and an even more elaborate exterior set of their old Methley Street neighborhood. He would use that Methley Street set not only in *The Kid* but also in *A Dog's Life, Easy Street, The Immigrant, Pay Day, Modern Times*, and *City Lights*. To jump-start his creative imagination before threading his way blindly through plot labyrinths on Methley Street, Charlie sometimes warmed up with a few clog-dance steps. Afterward, he liked to stroll casually around the old neighborhood — dressed in his Tramp costume, sometimes humming old music hall tunes to himself — while mulling his next creative move as he drank in nostalgic memories from his South London boyhood.

Chaplin would even relocate Methley Street in Nazi Germany, where it served for the last time in his filmmaking career as the metropolitan backdrop for his political satire *The Great Dictator*. Still drawing heavily on the games with Hannah when she taught him how to zero in on the distinctive foibles of mannerism, dress, gait, posture, facial expression, and body language of passersby with dead-on accuracy and mordant wit, Charlie would focus his powers on Adolf Hitler after meticulously observing his oddball subject's quirks, insecurities, and trademark gestures in Leni Riefenstahl's *Triumph of the Will* in a private screening at the Museum of Modern Art in New York City.

But the creative legacy of those childhood games with his storytelling mother went far beyond acting. The formative influence of Chaplin's Kennington boyhood on his subsequent artistic development as a writer — not an actor — was very much like Sherwood Anderson's relationship to Winesburg, Ohio, William Faulkner's connection to Yoknapatawpha County, and of course, most important of all, Charles Dickens's love affair with London. Drawing from intimate personal experiences — whether their medium was film or the printed page — all these storytellers' greatest works derived their richly textured meanings from a deeply personal sense of place, which in turn furnished each of them with an authentic and distinctive narrative voice. For Chaplin, the only one of these storytellers to write without words, the authorial sense of place would always be in the streets where he and his mother lived, as well as other childhood locales that served as visually evocative backdrops for his deeply personal films. One of Chaplin's fellow Hanwell alumni, the South London–born Cockney writer Thomas Burke, wrote:

> In all his films he is living in the past, recapturing the atmosphere of the streets. . . . In every film of his I can see the touch of the daily round of Kennington that I knew as he knew. The core of every film is some personal recollection, and I never see a new

Chaplin film without recognising the origin of at least two incidents.[3]

Acknowledging Burke's unique qualifications to make that judgment, Chaplin described him as "the one man who sees London through the same glasses as myself."[4] Burke and others easily spotted the Thames Embankment, the gates of Kennington Park, St. Mark's, and the Lambeth workhouse as well as South London church missions, food stalls, and pawnshops in the films Chaplin made from 1916.

Estimating conservatively, there were more than twenty separate places within a one- or two-mile radius in a ten-year span where Hannah and her sons lived between the height of her prosperity in 1893 and the depths of her poverty in 1903. As Chaplin later realized, to his own dismay: "Within three months we must have lived in 4, 5 or 6 places. . . . Suddenly the pity of it [and] this poor woman with two children [moving] from one room to another room" struck him profoundly.[5]

Sorting out those childhood memories in *My Autobiography*, there were only three places — each of which had felt like a home — that stood out vividly in his mind's eye: 39 Methley Street, Chester Street, and 3 Pownall Terrace. Strung together in a daisy chain, they marked the ups and downs of an economically unstable roller-coaster existence best described, by Dickens, as "the battle of life." Methley Street was their longest-lasting home, Chester Street the most promising, and Pownall Terrace the most devastating.

Not only did it take everyone in the family to make ends meet during their two and a half years at Methley Street, but they had also been constantly obliged to live a life of deficit spending by relying on their local pawnshop to get through each week and put food on the table. Unlike some of their slightly better-off neighbors, who used one or two of their valuable personal possessions as collateral for their cash flow needs, Hannah's weekly security deposit was a shabby blue serge suit, pawned every Monday when Syd donned his telegraph uniform and dutifully redeemed every payday so he had something to wear on weekends. She was devastated when one day the pawnbroker thrust out his hand to show her why the threadbare bottom of Syd's trousers made them no longer acceptable as a pledge for her weekly loan.

Twenty years later, after asking Danny Hall to build a South London pawnshop that would allow him to revisit "the less than good old days — the seamy side of my life,"[6] Chaplin proceeded in *The Pawnshop* to bring moviegoers to helpless tears of laughter by playing a conscientious pawnbroker's assistant who heartlessly demolishes an anxious customer's sole valuable possession, an alarm clock, in the course of meticulously authenticating its worth and — having rendered it worthless — auscultates it with a stethoscope and with a clinically impartial shrug declares its bum ticker unacceptable for pawn.

In view of his mother's remarkable talent for finding humor in the midst of squalor, it would not be surprising if she too, once she got over the initial shock, had later been able to laugh at their hard-pressed family's loan shop mishap. The ability to laugh in the face of tragedy was a highly prized virtue in the Cockney worldview and the music hall culture that idealized it. As Chaplin later put it: "Cruelty . . . is an integral part of comedy. We laugh . . . in order not to weep."[7]

Apart from his mother's sense of humor, which she retained until she became floridly psychotic, Hannah Chaplin's other major device for dealing with the increasing adversity in her life was her deepening faith. That is, until her religious fundamentalism also reached delusional proportions, largely as a result of her progressively degenerative central nervous system disease.

As economic times grew more perilous, she turned away from orthodox Anglicanism and began attending born-again revival meetings conducted by charismatic preachers in local neighborhood missions in order to bolster her flagging spirits. Sometimes she took Charlie with her. When she did, he tried his best to please:

> I was about nine at the time and I have always been a bit shy about the episode because, to tell the truth, I was a flop. But I was so moved that I wanted to give Testimony in front of all the people about to be saved. But when the moment came all I could stutter was "I am so happy, so happy." The crowd burst out laughing at me and I felt so ashamed.[8]

While his mother's faith was no laughing matter, Chaplin's certainly did become one. After getting Danny Hall to build a replica interior set of a South London mission for *Easy Street* in 1916, he did a tongue-in-cheek satire of this childhood experience by playing the part of a godless homeless person who undergoes a heartfelt religious conversion under the sweet loving influence of a buxom mission worker. After miraculously seeing the light, the Little Tramp sheepishly returns the mission's hefty collection box, which he had previously stowed in his baggy trousers, trickster-style, as part of his streetwise survival tactics. Imbued with his new faith and deep love of this maternal mission worker, Charlie joins the police and single-handedly cleans up the old neighborhood of crime, violence, poverty, and all of the other social ills that had beset Methley Street and environs during his South London boyhood.

While their family's stay at Chester Street, which consisted of two rooms above a barber shop, was much shorter than at Methley Street, it was by far the most comfortable and hopeful of the three principal homes they lived in. The move there took place in April 1901, one month before Charlie Sr.'s death. He had not been working for the last year because of his end-stage alcoholism, and the impact of his death on the family's fragile finances was lessened by sixteen-year-old Syd's stepping up to become the main breadwinner and man of the family. Hannah still operated a rented sewing machine, and Charlie would soon become a regular member of the labor force, but it was Syd's substantial financial contribution that kept them afloat.

Adding three years to his age on his seaman's papers, handsome, stocky Syd Chaplin found a job as ship's steward on a series of well-paid but sometimes unpredictably long sea voyages back and forth to South Africa and, later, to New York. Every time his ship docked in Southampton, he would hurry home with his pockets bulging with waiter's tips, and the three Chester Street residents would feast on glorious luxuries during what Charlie later referred to as the all-too-brief "cake-and-ice-cream period" that preceded his mother's ordeal with starvation and malnutrition at 3 Pownall Terrace.[9] After a few months, unforeseeable delays kept Syd from making it back to London in time to keep the cash flowing, and as a result Hannah and Charlie were obliged to move to that shabby attic room at 3 Pownall Terrace. By then thirteen-year-old Charlie had become a full-time laborer.

Shortly after Charlie Sr.'s death, Hannah had nabbed little Charlie in the act of peddling narcissus floral arrangements to sympathetic ladies in the saloons and barrooms of Kennington wearing a prominently displayed mourner's armband and theatrically whispering of his recent paternal bereavement in the most hushed and dulcet tones his nasal Cockney accent permitted. In no uncertain terms, she let him know how much he "offended her Christian scruples." "Drink killed your father, and money from such a source will only bring us bad luck" was her message.[10]

While she could not force the enterprising thirteen-year-old to tread the straight and narrow, she was determined to prevent him from treading the boards like his dad, whose memory and stage career he had begun to idealize. Their poverty obliged her to let Charlie permanently interrupt his already minimal education in order to help support the family. But it was jobs like selling newspapers or working as a page boy for a wealthy family that won Hannah's endorsement. Given the disillusioning outcome of her own career and Charlie Sr.'s and poor Eva Lester's, young Charlie's returning to the halls was out of the question no matter how much he pleaded.

On Sundays, however, while Hannah sought spiritual relief from fundamentalist preachers in open-air meetings and Kennington tabernacles, Charlie engaged in pagan worship services of his own farther up the Kennington Road, at the Tankard, where the well-known music hall artistes of South London congregated on Sunday mornings to exchange gossip and swagger in their checkered suits and gray bowlers, their diamond rings and stickpins sparkling in the noonday sun.

It was there that Charlie Chaplin Sr.'s son came to stargaze and hero worship that Cockney pantheon of greats who had made it to the top of the bill. After pub closing and his vaudeville gods' departures for their afternoon dinners, Charlie trudged back to his attic garret and the mortifying poverty that set his family apart from the downstairs neighbors, who at least could afford to cook their own Sunday roast instead of dining on greasy scraps from the neighborhood slop shop.

Determined to better his family's condition, Charlie set his sights on higher wages than any newsboy or page boy might hope for. Fibbing about his age as his big brother had done, he lasted barely a few hours at a South London glassblowing factory where, overcome by the heat, he "was carried out unconscious and laid on a sand pile."[11] Like his future comic creation, the mishap-prone, baggy-trousered Little Fellow who waddles in oversized boots like a pint-sized toddler trying to fill his father's shoes, Charlie set out determined to do grown men's jobs.

His most memorable experience was a three-week stint feeding paper sheets to a gigantic, twenty-foot-long Wharfedale printing machine. Awed by the scale of "the beast," the small boy "thought it was going to devour me" until he was made "a nervous wreck from the hungry brute wanting to get ahead of me"[12] — incidents that would of course be reechoed in the infernal comic machinery of *Modern Times.*

More generally, the resemblance between Chaplin's hardworking childhood and the Little Tramp's enterprising adventures was hardly coincidental. A "veteran of many occupations,"[13] Charlie also saw duty as a doctor's boy, barber's helper, and retail shop assistant, in addition to hawking old clothes, peddling flowers, and giving dancing lessons — all in the two short years since leaving the Eight Lancashire Lads. Nothing if not industrious, Chaplin's Little Tramp would find temporary employment in such diverse occupations as dentist's assistant, baker's helper, factory worker, paperhanger, street cleaner, waiter, janitor, floorwalker, and propman — to name but a few of his fleeting encounters with life's lowly realities while in transit to his castle-building reveries of the finer things it has to offer.

Traumatic as they undoubtedly were, only a handful of Charlie Chaplin's childhood days were ever spent foraging for food and sleeping on the streets. Faithful to his creator's biography, the vast majority of his screen character's days would be spent gainfully employed at a series of transient but definite occupations, not as an unemployed drifter struggling to survive.

A crucial tension in Chaplin's future one- and two-reel farcical etudes on manual labor would arise from the apparent ease with which his screen character flipped between the two opposite poles of his boyhood ambivalence toward work. In the wink of an eye, Charlie could oscillate between characterizations of an earnest would-be glassblower and a street-smart narcissus-peddling hustler. The former gets ahead by the sweat of his brow, the latter furrows his, cocks an eyebrow, and looks for an angle.

If, on the one hand, the Little Fellow is a hardworking, accident-prone victim whose brokenhearted comic predicaments unfold while in valiant pursuit of his Horatio Alger–like dreams, the Little Tramp, on the other hand, is a shabbily dressed dandy, would-be aristocrat, and gentleman of parts who is only passing through the working-class world and amusing himself by taking temporary engagements while waiting for his ship to come in. The trials of each are sources of humor in their own right, but it is the ineffable blend and split-second alternation between the two that gives Chaplin's comedy of work its distinctive flavor.

While our sympathies go out for the kicked-in-the-pants dilemmas of the plucky Little Fellow who plays by the rules, it is the vagabond insouciance with which he shrugs off the practical and moral constraints that confine the rest of us nine-to-fivers and with which he kicks back at life that makes the audience egg him on with such good humor. Whimsically toying with his work and playfully dallying with those he is meant to serve, with an air that suggests he has yet to arrive at his true station in life, the Little Tramp tips his topper and twirls his cane with the confidence of someone who knows that a nobler destiny and more prosperous days are just around the corner.

For the now fourteen-year-old Charlie, that destiny would arrive in the form of a postcard from Blackmore's Theatrical Agency in the Strand, inviting him to audition for a play — but not before he paid the tragic price of losing his mother once again. Paradoxically, the madness that released Hannah Chaplin from her grim existence mercifully freed Charlie Chaplin from a prospective lifetime of menial labor and allowed him to return to his interrupted theatrical career as a child performer. Within weeks of Hannah's second hospitalization, he would be back on the stage after more than two years of a maternally enforced absence. Technically faithful to his earlier promise to his mother — at least for the moment — this time he would choose the legitimate theater, not the raucous music halls that Hannah so strongly disapproved of and damned as the cause of Charlie Sr.'s untimely death.

An Actor's Life for Me

Every morning, lying luxuriously in bed in my lodgings, I pored over the London journals, seizing eagerly on every comment on my acting, reading and rereading it. I was the "most promising young actor on the English stage," . . . "the best Billy London has seen yet." To me, as I gazed at these notices, William Gillette was merely "also mentioned." I felt that I alone was making the play a success and I walked afterward up and down the Strand in a glow of pride and self-confidence, dressed in all the splendor money could buy, swinging my cane, nodding carelessly to the men I knew and picturing them saying to each other after I had passed, "He is the great actor at the Duke of York's Theater. I knew him once."

— Chaplin[1]

HAD ANYONE WARNED SYDNEY CHAPLIN that his mother's stability hung in a delicate balance and his brother's security rested on such a precarious foundation, he would have never shipped out for South Africa. As it was, he set sail for the Cape of Good Hope in March of 1903 with the hope of a fair voyage and expectations of a prosperous return. Secure in the knowledge that the twenty pounds he saved from this voyage would be enough to support his family and also permit him to spend the next four or five months in London trying to break into show business, eighteen-year-old Sydney was filled with daydreams of becoming a professional actor. While he was not a child prodigy like Charlie, he had, in the old days, also learned technique and performance fundamentals from their mother.

Justifiably proud of his accomplishment as the family's principal breadwinner, he was looking forward to lavishing more "cake-and-ice-cream" treats on Hannah and Charlie. They would be astonished by the immense crate of bananas he had lugged all the way from South Africa. Unaware of a family emergency, he took his sweet time coming home, savoring images of the reception he would receive as the conquering hero who had reversed the family's fortunes for months to come.

Had he known that Hannah was being committed to Cane Hill on the same day the *Kinfairns Castle* docked at Southampton on May 9, 1903, he would have sped down the gangplank and hurried home to rescue his kid brother instead of dawdling like some gentleman of leisure. For Charlie, who was hungry, grimy, tattered, and leading the desperate hand-to-mouth existence of a fugitive from the Kennington magistrates (who would have taken him into protective custody and sent him to the orphanage), those few days between his mother's hospitalization and his brother's return seemed an eternity. "If Sydney had not returned to London I might have become a thief in the London streets. . . . I might have been buried in a pauper's grave," Chaplin later remarked.[2]

Years afterward, in *The Gold Rush* with its crazily balanced cliff-top home, starvation-induced hallucinations, wanderings in the wilderness, seesawing fortunes, buckling foundations, and yawning abysses, Chaplin would transform this nightmarish ordeal into the zany comic predicaments of the Little Tramp and Big Jim, his rescuer, sidekick, and boon companion. But as fourteen-year-old Charlie mounted the rickety stairs that led to the third-floor garret at 3 Pownall Terrace where he lived with his mother, there was nothing comic about his sick feeling that the universe was falling apart.

The first sign that something was drastically amiss had been the apathetic resignation with which the usually animated ex-actress accepted the factory foreman's decision to repossess the rented sewing machine, her sole means of support. Shortly thereafter she began neglecting her physical appearance. Their once snug attic room with its quaint sloping ceiling gradually degenerated into squalor, with foul air, filthy dishes, and a depressing atmosphere that made Charlie jump at the slightest excuse to get out. Worse by far was the way Hannah sat "listlessly looking out of the window,"[3] quiet and motionless for days on end. When he could no longer blind himself to the fact that her mind had cracked and he could not mend it, Charlie broke down. Falling on his knees and burying his head in his mother's lap, he sobbed uncontrollably while she vacantly stroked his hair and they waited for the parish doctor to arrive, perform his examination, and fill out the necessary papers.

Accompanying her to the Lambeth Infirmary, the red-eyed boy blinked in the harsh glare of a "stark afternoon sun" whose rays "seemed to ruthlessly expose our misery to a gathering crowd of curious onlookers,"[4] who mistook Hannah's staggering, veering gait for drunkenness rather than the weakness of malnutrition and, perhaps, a mild case of early tabes dorsalis.[5]

The only thing that spared Charlie pain and mortification at their lack of privacy was his defensive disengagement from himself. It felt like a dream. When he returned to the empty tenement room, he again broke down and wept. Over the next few days, scenes of his mother's madness and his inability to save her were played and replayed in flashback after flashback.

And over the years to come, his alter-ego screen character's rescue of physically stricken or socially fallen or oppressed women would become the recurrent theme, echoed and re-echoed in his films. He played the glazier-mender of broken hearts and windows who adopts the lost kid and later restores him to his grief-stricken mother; he played the rescuer who restores sight to the blind flower girl, hope to the stranded dance-hall prostitute, the dream of a home of her own to a starving and recently orphaned gamine, the courage to perform before a live audience to a psychosomatically paralyzed ballet dancer, the courage to resist fascism to a Jewish woman (by the name of Hannah) who has become one of Hitler's victims — and always the basic theme of the rescue and repair of wistful women would be the same.

As the train from Southampton pulled into Waterloo Station, Syd arrived just in time to yank Charlie from the brink of his nightmare. That is, once he recognized him. Initially mistaking him for a slum urchin who was trying to help carry his luggage in the hope of earning a couple bob, Sydney was shocked when the filthy, tattered street arab said: "Sydney, don't you know me? I'm Charlie."[6]

After feeding him and scrubbing him clean, Syd went shopping for "warm underwear and a Norfolk suit and new shoes . . . and a bright silk tie" for his kid brother.[7] Commenting on the critical importance of Sydney Chaplin's protective relationship to Charlie, Hannah's younger sister Kate, who also was a part-time showgirl and part-time demimondaine, wrote in 1916:

> It seems strange to me that anyone can write about Charlie Chaplin without mentioning his brother Sydney. They have been inseparable all their lives, except when fate intervened at intervals. Syd, of quiet manner, clever brain and steady nerve, has been fa-

ther and mother to Charlie. Charlie always looked up to Syd, and Sydney would suffer anything to spare Charlie.[8]

Once Charlie was presentable, the two Chaplin brothers began making the rounds of the London theatrical agencies together in the hope of landing a part in a play. Given the fact that Syd had initially taken Charlie for a typical Cockney slum urchin, it's scarcely surprising that professional casting agents came to the same conclusion.

After a few weeks of canvassing, Charlie received a postcard from Blackmore's Theatrical Agency in the Strand asking him to come in for an audition. It was Mr. Blackmore himself who took one look at Charlie and decided he would do nicely for two juvenile roles one of his clients was trying to fill. Referred for two tryouts that consisted of little more than brief conversations, Charlie was lucky enough to be given both parts without ever being asked to read from a script, a task that his borderline literacy would have rendered impossible at the time.

Sharp veterans with years of theatrical experience, Chaplin's interviewers needed only a few minutes to size him up and decide he was a natural for both roles. A newsboy and a page boy — each a resourceful street urchin with a Cockney accent — were parts he had already played in life. Doing them on stage was right up his alley.

It took barely three days of Syd's feeding Charlie the lines and coaching him before he was word perfect in the first play. Before Charlie left for rehearsal, they agreed there was no harm in Syd's dropping by the producer's office just to see if he could "raise the ante."[9]

Although this did not work, the two sharpers happily algebraized that Charlie's handsome salary of two pounds ten shillings per week would allow them to bank sixty quid a year — a tidy sum for two lads from the slums anxious to bid farewell to deficit spending and life in a pawnshop economy. The only sad note in the otherwise heady affair had come when the two brothers talked with "filmy" eyes of how much it would have meant to Lily to share their joy with them.[10]

Rehearsals went well — so well, in fact, that the astonished director asked Chaplin if he had ever acted before. Accepting his praise along with the admiration of the other cast members as if it were his "natural birthright" (which in a sense it was) Charlie took their flattery in stride. Nonetheless, such things as "stage-craft — timing, pausing, a cue to turn, to sit," were entirely new to him. He eagerly added them to his bag of tricks.[11]

If the traditions of the British legitimate theater can be described as the oldest and finest in the English-speaking world, it could be said that the Cockney youngster had just been accepted into an elite finishing school — a first-rate provincial touring company. As with any boarding school experience, an education away from home could be lonely. And for Charlie, all but some six or seven scattered months of the next two and a half years would be spent on the road.

The first play, *Jim, A Romance of Cockayne*, opened at the Royal Court Theatre in Kingston-upon-Thames and closed two weeks later to a series of negative notices. The only exception in an otherwise lukewarm review by the *Era* critic read:

> Master Charles Chaplin is a broth of a boy as Sam the newspaper boy, giving a most realistic picture of the cheeky, honest, loyal, self-reliant, philosophic street Arab who haunts the regions of Cockayne [Cockney land].[12]

An even more sanguine reviewer wrote: "I have never heard of the boy before, but I hope to hear great things of him in the near future."[13] Fortunately for Charlie, who could not dine on his notices, the second play was a warhorse that would please 'em from Land's End to John o'Groats. Bidding farewell to Syd, who took a job as a bartender while awaiting his first show business break, Charlie set out for Newcastle with the company of *Sherlock Holmes*.

Evenings and matinees were spent as Billy, the famous detective's loyal page boy. Between performances, there was nothing but time to kill for this grammar school dropout. Living alone in a drab series of provincial lodgings, Charlie bought a pet rabbit for companionship and invested five shillings in a camera.

To earn extra cash and stave off boredom, he canvassed the streets of working-class neighborhoods, hawking photographic portraits to passersby, which he developed and printed in the closets and darkened spare rooms of the boardinghouses where he stayed. Occasionally, on market days, he sang and clog-danced in local pubs and passed the hat to visiting farmers.

Life on the road was proving to be lucrative but lonely when, midway through the first tour, he was able to persuade the company manager to give the part of Count Von Stalberg, which was about to become vacant, to Syd. Overnight capitalists by South Kennington standards, the Chaplin brothers were raking in four pounds five shillings a week and reveling in each other's company.

The only obstacle to their bliss was the absence of their mother and, within weeks of their own reunion, her two boys were able to remedy that as well. After eight long months in the asylum, sometimes in a padded cell, their mother had recovered sufficiently to join them in Reading, where they were touring with *Holmes*.

Prepared to celebrate the joyful occasion by lavishing her with the results of their industry, her two worshipful admirers commissioned a de luxe apartment complete with two bedrooms, a parlor, and a pianoforte. Filling her boudoir with flowers in January, the two swells "arranged an elaborate dinner to boot."[14] But as when the Little Tramp had a New Year's Eve rendezvous with the dance hall girl in *The Gold Rush*, the guest of honor never showed up. For it was Hannah Chaplin, not Lily Harley, who got off the train in Reading.

"I'm just happy to be alive," she said with a hollow chipperness that left Charlie "fighting back a depression." No longer suffering from malnutrition or forced to contend with the severe chronic stress of sweatshop piecework, Hannah had "aged . . . and gained weight" and "appeared rather dowdy." Residually depressed, with coarsened features, thicker limbs, and a stockier torso, their mother bore not the faintest physical or emotional resemblance to the vivacious, violet-eyed songstress-actress of her two sons' loving memories. And Hannah's wooden manner was even more upsetting to Charlie than her drastically altered physical looks. As they sat there in "uncomfortable" silence, fishing awkwardly like strangers for something to say, the boy was crushed by his mother's indifference to the fine meal and fancy lodgings they'd gone out of their way to arrange.[15]

Though not yet the theatrical star of his dreams, the fourteen-year-old boy had, by successfully establishing himself as a well-paid child actor, accomplished the very real, and very remarkable, feat of temporarily surpassing Syd as their family's principal breadwinner. Not only had he helped make it possible for his mother to be discharged from the madhouse, he had also demonstrated that he now had the earning power to feed and shelter her and protect her from ever having to submit to demeaning and grueling sweatshop piecework again.

To Charlie's boyishly exuberant way of thinking, that called for a victory celebration and, perhaps, some special token of his mother's love. But as would be the case with so many of those brokenhearted "happy" endings in Chaplin's comedies, where the industrious Little Fellow endures hardships and tribulations in the rescue or pursuit of a heroine's love which he never can truly possess no matter how he tries, the fruits of Charlie's labor were bittersweet.

Like the Little Tramp in *City Lights*, whose fundraising ordeals help restore the blind flower girl's lost sight, only to result in his being separated from her by the transparent but even more formidable social barrier of her florist shop window, Charlie found himself completely isolated from Hannah by the very tangible but completely invisible bell-jar bubble of her chronic mental illness. Behaving "more like a guest" than a mother, she moved with a "quiet and reserved . . . detachment" that "saddened" Charlie.[16]

During those lonely months on the road before their Reading reunion, he had longed to "show her off to the company" of *Sherlock Holmes*. But it was Lily, not Hannah, he had described so proudly to the other members of the cast. And now Charlie was filled with "misgivings" about introducing that drab, prematurely aged, and emotionally unresponsive shell of a woman to Moriarty, Watson, Holmes, and the rest of his colorful show business friends. Devastated by how little remained of the mother he knew, even though she had just been discharged as recovered by the hospital authorities, Charlie was thoroughly ashamed of himself for being so disappointed in her and did his "best to hide the fact."[17]

Dutifully keeping house for her sons, Hannah shopped for groceries and went through the motions, but her heart was not in it. Dismayed by the recognition that they had "outgrown the intimacy" between them, all parties politely agreed that "it would be less costly" for Hannah to return to London rather than tour with them.[18] Within a month, she was back in South Kennington, where the boys installed her in that comfortable two-room flat on Chester Street and sent her one pound five shillings a week living allowance.

When they were in town, they sometimes stayed with her. But the easygoing familiarity of the old days was a thing of the past. Financially secure for the rest of her life, Hannah would never again be driven mad by the hunger or malnutrition of dire poverty. Nonetheless, barely a year after her Reading reunion with the boys, she was again "found wandering and incoherent in the streets" of Kennington and returned to the Cane Hill Asylum.[19]

At the time of her final relapse on March 6, 1905, Charlie was touring the Midlands with a second company of *Sherlock Holmes*.

Retreating from a reality she could no longer manage into a madhouse home that she sometimes referred to as Cain Hill (on those rare days when a spark of her old sense of humor returned), Hannah would spend the rest of her days in institutional or custodial care. Over the years that followed, no matter how diligently he worked, how phenomenally wealthy or successful he became, Charlie could never restore that sweet gift of lucidity to the mind of the woman who had loved him most deeply. And if bittersweet experiences like Charlie's Reading reunion with Lily Harley served as prototypes for every brokenhearted love story he ever filmed, it was Hannah's fate that supplied their premise.

Chaplin visited the attic at 3 Pownall Terrace in 1921. He did not write about it at the time. But he described that visit to a reporter in 1936:

> We went through streets that I remember as you remember a nightmare. I saw myself, a scared, undersized, skinny kid, leading my mother by the hand, dragging her through the fog and the smells and the cold toward our miserable home, while other kids yelled and jeered at her. . . . I was living that nightmare over again, but I wanted to do it. I had to do it. It was like going back to visit a grave where someone you have loved lies buried.[20]

Chaplin's reference to that attic as the place where his mother lay buried spoke volumes about his feelings that it was at 3 Pownall Terrace that he had last seen the woman he adored. Hannah Chaplin physically survived for another twenty-five years and was buried in a Hollywood cemetery in 1928. But in truth she "died" on March 9, 1903, the second anniversary of her former husband's death, the date on which she became chronically psychotic for the rest of her life.

Clowning Around

In the two years I was with *Casey's Circus* I gradually gave up my idea of playing great parts on the dramatic stage. I grew to like the comedy work, to enjoy hearing the bursts of laughter from the audience, and getting the crowd in good humor and keeping it so was a nightly frolic for me. Then, too, by degrees all my old self-confidence and pride came back, with the difference, indeed, that I did not take them too seriously, as before, but merely felt them like a pleasant inner warmth as I walked on the Strand and saw the envious looks of other actors not so fortunate.

— Chaplin[1]

O N OCTOBER 17, 1905, AFTER TOURING the British Isles in three consecutive road companies of *Sherlock Holmes*, Chaplin finally "arrived." He opened as Billy in a West End production of *Sherlock Holmes* at the Duke of York's Theatre. Having played the same part night after night for nearly two years, he had paid his dues and merited the flattering notices he received from the London critics.

"Every celebrity in London seemed to be flocking to see the production."[2] The young star would soon advertise himself as Master Charles Chaplin in a paid announcement he placed in the Professional Cards columns of the *Stage*, a show business trade paper. Far more impressive than any purchased publicity was an unsolicited professional endorsement he received by being included in the first edition of *The Green Room Book; or, Who's Who on the Stage*:

> **CHAPLIN, Charles,** impersonator, mimic, and sand dancer; b. London, April 16th, 1889; s. of Charles Chaplin; brother of Sidney Chaplin; cradled in the profession, made first appearance at the Oxford, as a specialty turn, when ten years of age; has fulfilled engagements with several of Charles Frohman's companies (playing Billy in "Sherlock Holmes", &c.) and at many of the leading variety theatres in London and provinces.[3]

"My brain was spinning with the thrill of every incident," Chaplin wrote with wry amusement ten years later as he recalled his reaction to his first magical moment of near stardom.[4] The sixteen-year-old actor's dizzy feelings of success must have seemed light years away from the fourteen-year-old boy's feelings of powerless vertigo when he mounted those rickety stairs at 3 Pownall Terrace only two years earlier. He had come a long way in a short time by amassing an impressive string of professional credits, and he was justifiably proud.

In addition to appearing in a gala performance of *Sherlock Holmes* hosted by the British royal family in honor of the king of Greece and Prince Christian of Denmark, the obscure Cockney boy from the other side of the river enjoyed an almost unheard-of privilege in being awarded a ticket to the exclusive Westminster Abbey funeral of Sir Henry Irving, the first-ever actor-knight. Even more thrilling was going to work night after night and seeing his own name on the same bill as William Gillette, the great American playwright-actor who cowrote the stage play *Sherlock Holmes* with Arthur Conan Doyle and was currently appearing in the title role, which he had made famous.

All of these were portents of the theatrical greatness that awaited him. He had originally vowed and prophesied that fame when he was an eight-year-old orphanage nobody. Given his remarkable string of recent professional achievements, it's easy to see why the young Charlie was conceitedly and affectedly strutting the Strand, cane in hand, dressed to the nines and casually tipping his topper to his fellow actors with a cheeky air of superiority. Chaplin the boy hero of his own dreams may have been heading for a fall. But if he was, he didn't see it coming.

What he did see was that Master Charles Chaplin had miraculously escaped a social-class life sentence of poverty and drudgery by making it into the West End and the culturally prestigious world of the legitimate theater. For Charlie, the elitist Duke of York's Theatre in St. Martin's Lane was far more illustrious than the populist Canterbury Music Hall across the river on the Westminster Bridge Road where Lily had first taken him to see Charlie Sr. perform. By making a big splash in the West End, the epicenter of the English-speaking theatrical world, he was redeeming his famous father's faded reputation and also fulfilling his actress mother's thwarted dreams of professional success. In their respective heydays as aspiring music hall greats, Charlie Sr. and Lily had ostentatiously advertised their immense successes by parading up and down Kennington Road dressed to the nines for the edification of their fans and admirers. Now it was their son's turn to play the top. But this time a flashily dressed member of the Chaplin clan was strutting the Strand in the West End with Cockney pride.

His father lay in a common pauper's grave. His mother had recently joined the living dead, now residing in an institution for the medically indigent, which Charlie found so upsetting he could barely tolerate visiting her. The humiliation of those two devastating losses goes far to explaining the compensatory grandiosity with which Master Charles preened and strutted. His painfully self-conscious adolescent affectations were a matter of family honor and personal pride. He was following in his misbegotten parents' professional footsteps. But he was also hoping to escape their ultimate fate by succeeding as a serious dramatic actor in the staid legitimate theater rather than attempting to earn his living as a popular entertainer in the much more rambunctious and rowdy music halls.

Having just become by his own estimate "England's greatest boy actor,"[5] it now behooved him to be highly selective in accepting his next theatrical engagement, both in terms of his choice of dramatic roles and his selection of theatrical companies, a fact that he took pains to make clear to no less a theatrical personage than Madge Kendal, a leading actress of the day. A fortnight before the completion of the London run of *Sherlock Holmes*, Charlie was summoned for an interview and audition with "stalwart, imperious" Mrs. K, who first kept him waiting and then informed him that he would have to return the next morning for his official tryout. Smarting from her rudeness, and dismayed to learn that her company would be touring the provinces, Charlie coolly informed "Madam" that he was not accepting out-of-town engagements. "And with that I raised my hat, walked out of the foyer, hailed a passing cab — and was out of work for ten months."[6]

While it was actually no more than three months before Chaplin found steady work in a fresh part,[7] his flamboyant description of this incident accurately captures the cheeky insouciance that led to a critical turning point in his career. As a result of that impetuous gesture, the promising teenage actor soon found himself making his reluctant debut as a slapstick comedian ignominiously consigned to playing what he once referred to as "low vulgar comedy in dirty fourth-rate houses."[8] While those venues were neither filthy nor fourth-rate, in Charlie's mind they were a universe apart from his beloved Duke of York's Theatre, to which he hoped to triumphantly return in the very near future.

Chaplin's disdainful reaction to the formidable Madge Kendal was not based exclusively on his fine notices or his having made it into *Who's Who*. Charlie thought he had an ace up his sleeve when he walked out that door.

With two weeks left in the London run of *Holmes*, he was absolutely certain that William Gillette was planning to invite him to accompany him to New York, where they would then begin a fruitful mentor-protégé (or father-son) collaboration, which would ultimately lead to his own stardom. It was not until the final curtain, as he watched Gillette's Japanese manservant carrying out the great actor's bags and no last-minute knock came on his dressing room door, that it began to sink in. As if "in a bad dream," Charlie finally realized that he was completely on his own.[9]

Over the months that followed, he made the rounds of the agents — first with cane but later with hat in hand. Initially he was received warmly on the basis of the fine reputation he had earned for his role as Billy. But as time wore on, the reception became more chillingly familiar as he was greeted with that demoralizing old refrain: nothing for you today.

"While Sydney was working in the provinces I stayed in London and played around poolrooms," he recalled. "Through this haze and confusion I lived alone. Whores, sluts and an occasional drinking bout weaved in and out of this period, but neither wine, women nor song held my interest for long."[10]

It came as a rude awakening, but for all his airs Charlie was forced to consider the possibility that his recent triumph on the legitimate stage had been more a matter of fortuitous typecasting than he cared to admit. The plain fact was that night after night the past two and a half years of his life as a theatrical juvenile had been spent serving as a loyal but lowly page to the great Sherlock 'Olmes. Given his working-class dialect, delicate physical features, and boyish stature, his grandiose dream of playing a handsome leading man on the legitimate West End stage simply lay beyond the scope of his natural endowments.

South London he had been born and South London he had been bred. Cockney to the bone, he was perhaps better suited to play for commoners than kings. And their theater was the rowdy, boisterous music hall that spoke and sang to them in "kerracter," using their own lingo and taking royalty with a grain of salt:

> Father's going to change his socks and Auntie have a bath,
> On the day King Edward gets his crown on.
> With a brick we'll hit the landlord to make the baby laugh,
> On the day King Edward gets his crown on.
> The lodger's going to get blind drunk, as soon as day begins,
> Sister's wearing bloomers fixed up with safety-pins,
> To celebrate the great event mother will have twins,
> On the day King Edward gets his crown on.
>
> Parading up and down the Strand, all of us you'll see,
> On the day King Edward gets his crown on.
> We'll all buy penny ticklers, and won't we have a lark?
> All the policemen mother meets she'll cuddle in the dark,
> Father's going to smack 'em on their vaccination mark,
> On the day King Edward gets his crown on.[11]

Although it was Charlie Chaplin who eventually mined that mother lode of cosmopolitan proletarian comedy for the jackpot prize, it was Sydney Chaplin who first discovered the fool's gold that could be earned playing bawdy slapstick in the less splendid working-class music halls that were the Cockney performer's entrée into the palatially elegant, brilliantly illuminated, ornamental splendor of the Edwardian variety halls. And it was only with the greatest reluctance that Master Charles first consented to stoop to prospecting in such a crude comic vein, by joining Syd, who was then playing the lead in *Repairs* — one of those broad farcical sketches with clumsy paperhangers, inept plumbers, and sloppy housepainters, whose klutzy slapstick doings were choreographed to the delicate strains of ballet music played softly in the background. See Chaplin's two-reeler *Work* for an early example of this farcical handyman genre and *Limelight* for examples of how such musical accompaniments were used to heighten slapstick effects in music hall routines.

Influenced by "my old patronizing attitude toward Sydney, who had never been considered the clever one of the family," Charlie had earlier "promised him large returns for all he had done for me as soon as I should become a famous actor."[12] But now the tables were turned and, driven by necessity, Charlie reluctantly joined Syd, who was actively pursuing his chosen profession of music hall comedian.

It was only two years earlier, during one of his tours to South Africa as a steward on the *Kinfairns Castle*, that Syd Chaplin had first tried his hand playing comedy for the ship's passengers. That first taste of farce was to his own and his audience's liking and was enough to point Syd toward a music hall career. In a class-conscious society where rank and station at birth sealed most people's fate for life, making it to the top of the music hall bill was, for Cockney lads from the slums, one of the few routes up the social ladder — to the point of royal command performances by 1912, and knighthoods by the mid-twentieth century.

From their inception in the early 1800s as rowdy song and supper clubs — the Coal Hole in the Strand, Cyder Cellars in Maiden Lane, Evan's in Covent Gardens — the primitive forerunners of the British music hall served as stepping-stones to stardom based on glorifying rather than concealing a performer's humble social origins. Sam Collins, one of the great early singers and eventually the proprietor of his own famous hall, Collins's Music Hall on Islington Green, was a former chimney sweep who made a career singing comic Irish songs in full dialect and regalia. Slum ballads like "The Rat-Catcher's Daughter" and "Paddy's Wedding" swelled an audience's heart with Cockney pride as they listened to members of their own class robustly celebrating their own way of life.

But of all those early songs, it is the powerful character ballad "Sam Hall," one of the smash hits of the early nineteenth century, that best exemplifies the means by which revolutionary social forces coalesced and eventually emerged in a new genre of working-class art as British music hall:

> My name it is Sam Hall, Sam Hall,
> My name it is Sam Hall.
> I robs both great and small.
> But they makes me pay for all,
> Goddam their eyes.

A bitter psalm parody that was popularized by W. G. Ross dressed in the grimy and battered garb of a chimney sweep, "Sam Hall" recounts the dismal tale of the condemned prisoner's death-cart ride up spectator-lined Holborn Hill and his hanging at Tyburn.

As the grisly realism of that ballad recalls, public executions by hanging had until recently been one of the most popular forms of entertainment among London's lower classes. And the average song and supper club audience's emotional reactions bore an uncanny resemblance to Sam's description of those of the original Tyburn mob. Some found it hilarious, while others shuddered in horrified fascination as actual scenes from working-class life were being transformed into art for a working-class audience by working-class performers, with all the vividness of a Hogarth print or a scene out of *The Beggar's Opera*.

From the days of Elizabeth through the reign of Victoria, London had always had its street singers, those balladmongers and broadsiders whose songs depicted, even romanticized, life among the lower classes for their own amusement and edification, including the ever-popular gallows ballads. But what was new was the establishment of a proletarian theater in the form of the music halls — a development directly traceable to both the democratizing influence of the French and the urbanizing influence of the Industrial Revolution.

It was by no means the first time that profound social upheaval and intellectual ferment had conspired to spawn a new form of people's theater, with its own unique conventions and yet drawing its performers and traditions from the itinerant street art that preceded it. A remarkably similar process had occurred when the great humanistic revolution of sixteenth-century Renaissance Italy overwhelmed the austere religious drama of the Middle Ages and replaced it with the bawdy, improvisational commedia dell'arte, whose slapstick Arlecchinos and Pantalones had apprenticed as the wandering jongleurs, acrobats, and jesters of the medieval fairs and villages.

Nor of course was the spirit of artistic revolution in early-nineteenth-century England located only among the lower classes. In their bold literary manifesto, the preface to *Lyrical Ballads*, Wordsworth and Coleridge declared their rebellion against the aristocratic traditions of English literature, with its flowery imagery and elitist, artificial diction, stating their intention to write about ordinary people using the everyday language they spoke. But while the ballads of the Romantic poets and the ballads of the British music halls may have each derived their separate inspiration from this dawn of the Age of the Common Man, it would not be until Charles Dickens that a mainstream, middle-class English writer would so famously capture that salty patter and twang of working-class stiffs that was such a standard feature of the social realism of the emerging proletarian music halls, which Dickens attended with relish and drew upon for his portraiture.

From their earliest days as song pubs and supper clubs, those crude precursors of the halls had turned their makeshift physical arrangements and informal social settings to theatrical advantage by creating a remarkable audience-performer intimacy that would remain forever the hallmark of that venerable institution. There were no stages or proscenium arches at first, not even platforms to set singer and listener apart. In every sense — physical proximity and social class — the performer was one of the audience. In fact, many a gifted music hall artist was known to have begun his career by winning first prize in one of those weekly amateur-night "free and easies" that were held in the song rooms of working-class neighborhood pubs.

Later, in the heyday of the palatial halls, when surrounded by respectable ladies and gents comfortably ensconced in the red plush orchestra seats that separated the artistes from the ruddy-bloody blokes on the backless benches of the balcony, the veteran performer knew better than to turn his back on his original constituency. As the twopenny-seat hoi polloi were prepared to remind him, with physical and vocal immediacy, his success would always remain dependent on his ability to project himself intimately and convincingly to the lower classes in the upper tiers, direct descendants of those lowly groundlings of Shakespeare's day whose connoisseur tastes and robust appetite for low comedy had proved such a crucial shaping influence in the Elizabethan theater.

If for the audience the intimacy and immediacy of the music hall engaged them in compelling people's theater, for the performers those same circumstances engendered a certain amount of anxiety and tension that some found energizing and others debilitating. One theatrical device actors relied on to manage the insecurities that intimate audience exposure could provoke was to maintain a distance between themselves and the spectators by erecting an imaginary "fourth wall." The fourth wall is an established convention of classical theater, in which the audience and the actors share the tacit assumption that an invisible barrier exists between them. Whenever an actor gazes in the direction of the audience, who are gazing at him, he pretends to be seeing and looking at whatever there is in the physical and emotional reality of the scene he is playing. The presence of the audience is ignored. The fourth wall convention precludes him from acknowledging or addressing them directly. The technical performance skills employed are known as "representational acting."

In contrast, "presentational acting" occurs when the fourth wall convention is abolished and the artificial separation between the audience and the actor is dissolved. The audience's presence is openly acknowledged, leaving the actor free to communicate — verbally and nonverbally — with the people seated directly in front of him, who in the case of the music hall are of course (for better or worse) free to take the same liberty with him.

For great live-performance presentational actors like Dan Leno or Marie Lloyd, the distinctive audience-performer relationship that resulted from the abolishment of the fourth wall, originating with the earliest beginnings of British music hall in taverns and taprooms, constituted a professional opportunity to showcase their unique gifts. They both possessed (or skillfully employed their presentational acting skills to create the illusion of possessing) a completely natural and easygoing manner that allowed them to reach out across the footlights and intimately converse with working-class audiences by taking them into their confidence. They each had what seventy-five-year-old Chaplin called "that intimate come-hither faculty with an audience,"[13] which, by his own admission, he sorely lacked. Or to put this slightly oversimplified self-assessment into perspective, they possessed the intimate live-audience vocal performance skills he lacked. His presentational skills as a silent film actor were of course world class.

Already trained as a music hall pantomimist, he would arrive in Hollywood at the dawn of an emerging technology and teach himself to exploit the new recording medium of cinema by finding a deeply personal but completely protected way to communicate and share his innermost self with film audiences without ever being threatened with direct reciprocal communication. Attempting to exploit another new recording medium, the early phonograph, in order to preserve his performances for posterity, Dan Leno lamented: "How the hell can I be funny into a funnel?"[14] He was energized by that same feedback from live audiences that Chaplin, except as a pantomimist, found so frightening.

Ever since Aldershot, where the horrified five-year-old had personally witnessed his actress-mother's degrading experience at the hands of a rowdy mob of drunken hecklers, Charlie had been wary of the cruel treatment and coarse ridicule that unruly working-class audiences sometimes dished out for their own amusement. Speaking through Calvero, his alter ego in *Limelight*, Chaplin described the mob psychology of the music hall audience as "a monster without a head that never knows which way it's going to turn . . . [and] can be prodded in any direction."

Considering this background, it's easy to see why sixteen-year-old Charlie dreaded the prospect of playing the halls and dreamed of success in the refined legitimate theater with its polite audiences and secure fourth wall. Rationalizing those fears as artistic preferences, he snobbishly looked down on the proletarian world of music hall as culturally inferior to the Duke of York's Theatre.

"Burning with shame and resentment"[15] as impecunious circumstances forced him to lower his artistic standards and play East End lowbrow rather than West End highbrow, young Charlie would reluctantly learn how to cater to the English working-class public's insatiable appetite for the pungent social comedy of the music halls. Like their so-called betters, who delighted in the elegant repartee of the likes of Congreve, Sheridan, and

Wilde, those lowborn Cockneys took equal pleasure in their own homespun comedy of manners, which tweaked all forms of social pretense.

It would take two full years of touring and training as a music hall performer before Chaplin, at age eighteen a successfully apprenticed slapstick comedian, would be able to self-contentedly stroll rather than self-consciously strut along the Strand. The maturational process he was about to undergo, by making peace with his inability to succeed as a dramatic actor and mastering the tricks of the trade as a comic actor, would lay the foundations for all of the great art he would produce for the next fifty years.

Basic Training

I, the guardian of Charles Chaplin, agree for him to appear in Casey's Court wherever it may be booked in the British Isles only, the agreement to commence May 14th, 1906, at a salary weekly of £2.5.0 (two pounds five shillings) increasing to £2.10.0 the week commencing July 1906.

— (signed) Sydney Chaplin[1]

WHILE HE WAS RELIEVED TO BE WORKING, the sixteen-year-old former dramatic actor was mortified to find himself playing a buffoon part in dumb show as a bungling plumber's assistant whose klutzy pratfalls and slow-witted, blank-faced reactions were enhanced by clownish white face paint and a Bardolphian red nose. The crass indignity of England's greatest boy actor hiding his features beneath a fool's mask was almost unbearable. In every provincial city and town along the route of that seedy slapstick company's itinerary, it felt as if he was being dragged further and further away from the West End and his beloved Duke of York's.

Having fallen from grace, Chaplin soon discovered that his show business comeback depended on his learning how to fall with grace. Just as classical ballet had entrechats, pirouettes, and arabesques for beginners to master, so basic clownship had its standard repertoire of glissades, flip-flops, and *sauts périlleux* (somersaults.) On encountering the proverbial banana peel of the music hall comedy stage, a first-rate slapstick comedian had to be able to execute backslides, nosedives, fanny flops, and alley-oops on cue — in deadpan or in double take — deploying his body in space with the soaring ease and apparent weightlessness of a prima ballerina.

While the superbly coordinated teenager placed little immediate importance on the felicitous discovery that he possessed all of the natural acrobatic gifts required to play lowbrow slapstick, Chaplin the film star would later be enormously flattered by the lavish praise and admiration he received from the likes of Pavlova and Nijinsky, who placed his art on an equal footing with theirs. Or, as W. C. Fields remarked somewhat more pungently, "That sonofabitch is a goddam ballet dancer . . . and if I get a good chance, I'll kill him with my bare hands!"[2]

For any serious student of comedy new to the slapstick game, touring the provinces had advantages over performing in as many as three separate music halls a night in London. Between shows, there was ample time to sharpen skills by tirelessly practicing the fine art of trapping one's foot in the paste bucket or unleashing mayhem with the carpenter's ladder, both standard property items of the *Repairs* company sketch.

And there were even opportunities to engage in industrial espionage by carefully studying other comedy acts on the bill in their nascent state of rehearsal undress, freshly deconstructed as they were at the start of each new workweek. Monday morning band rehearsal, with cues and songs for all acts, generally ended before midafternoon, leaving performers free to while away the hours before first curtain, in dalliance or in drink for the young and carefree, but making last-minute changes, trying out material from other comics' routines, or putting finishing touches on one's own act for the more ambitiously inclined.

Seven years earlier, as a newcomer to the halls, determined to execute the steps and routines of the Eight Lancashire Lads with flawless precision but beset by a stage fright so great that "I could hardly move my legs," Charlie had struggled diligently to master his steps.[3] One false move, much less a fall, had posed the mortifying prospect of being pelted with jeers if not with rotten fruits and vegetables by boisterous music hall crowds. It took six weeks of constant practice before the perfectionist nine-year-old felt confident enough to go on. As a fourteen-year-old, he had rehearsed with equally methodical precision until he could enter, exit, and move with a graceful command of stage space through Holmes's Baker Street digs. But now everything was topsy-turvy. He was being asked to impersonate awkwardness. Skill and timing were required to syncopate a slip or coordinate a crash to the rhythm and beat of a pit band's cues with metronomic precision.

From the standpoint of physical technique, there was a correct way to walk unsuspectingly, nose first, into a wall, with a turn of the head in order for it to appear funny. Not until he had the fundamentals down pat could a clown expect to embellish and improvise by adding distinctive topping gags of his own invention, such as reflexively tipping his hat. And while the Little Tramp's quirky mannerism of absentmindedly tipping his topper to trees he encounters, as if to so many passing acquaintances, may or may not have originated on the Keystone Film Studio lot (*Twenty Minutes of Love*), the foundation on which it was built came straight out of British music hall.

After eight brief weeks apprenticing as a minor player in *Repairs*, Chaplin auditioned for his first major comedy role. Responding to an ad in the *Era* announcing auditions for boy comedians between the ages of fourteen and nineteen, Charlie arrived to discover more than a hundred hungry juveniles packing the staircase to the theatrical office and spilling out onto the street below, as they nervously awaited their tryouts. Finally, after three hours' delay, his turn came.

> I straightened my hat, squared my shoulders and marched in, determined to be very haughty and dignified. . . . a fat red-faced man, with his waistcoat unbuttoned, sat by a desk chewing a big cigar.
> "Mr. Dailey," I said, "I ——" I don't know how it happened. My foot slipped. I tried to straighten up, slipped again, fell on all fours over a chair, which fell over on me, and sat up on the floor with the chair in my lap. "—— want a part," I finished, furious.[4]

Although Chaplin claimed he landed the part solely on the basis of this unplanned seat-of-the-pants entrance, one of his interviewers recalled there had been more to it than that:

> I put him through his paces. He sang, danced, and did a little of practically everything in the entertaining line. He had the makings of a "star" in him, and I promptly took him on salary, 30s per week.[5]

Conceived as a sequel to an earlier show, *Casey's Court*, which had enjoyed a successful run, *Casey's Court Circus* consisted of a series of topical parodies of music hall and circus acts seen from the point of view of working-class teenagers all of whom lived in the same slum alley, or court. Apart from Will Murray, a mature comedian in his late twenties who played Mrs. Casey in drag, the cast consisted of fifteen colorful "street urchins." Played by actors at that awkward stage between boyhood and manhood, they were a motley crew of East End juveniles who might best be described as a Cockney version of the Dead End Kids, well along their way to blossoming into the Bowery Boys.

As a minor, it was illegal for Charlie to enter into a contract on his own, and Syd signed as his guardian.

Although they regretted moving in separate directions, each of the brothers was advancing in his career at a rapid rate. While joining the *Casey's* troupe provided seventeen-year-old Charlie with his first major experience as a comic juvenile, Sydney was about to achieve a much more prestigious success by signing a fabulous one-year contract with "the Guv'nor," Fred Karno, England's foremost producer of music hall comedy sketches. By fall, Syd would be touring the United States and enjoying featured billing in one of the empire-building Karno's globe-trotting comedy troupes upon which, like Britannia itself, the sun never seemed to set.

One of Charlie's two turns in the *Casey's* review was a parody of the romantic outlaw Dick Turpin's ride to York on his faithful mare, Black Bess. It was a comedy chase scene, in which Chaplin first developed one of the Little Tramp's most distinctive mannerisms. Will Murray recalled:

The climax was the flight after the death of "Bonnie Black Bess."

You can imagine the position of poor Mr. Turpin. He had to run, hide, do anything to get out of the way of the runners, and yet he had nowhere to go except round the circus track.

Nevertheless, Charlie started to run — and run — and run. He had to turn innumerable corners, and as he raised one foot and hopped along a little way on the other in getting round a nasty "bend," the audience simply howled.

I think I can justly say that I am the man who taught Charlie how to turn corners. . . . It took many, many weary hours of monotonous rehearsals, but I am sure Charlie Chaplin, in looking back over those hours of rehearsals, will thank me for being so persistent in my instructions as to how I wanted the thing done.[6]

In a technical sense, Murray may have taught Chaplin that famous one-legged skid turn, which later became one of his Little

Tramp's signature movements, like the Rummy Binks shuffle. But the funny business did not begin with Murray. Just as Coleridge described poetic truth as a "divine ventriloquist" whose utterances passed through the lips of every poet, so the comic muse spoke through each generation of its wandering jongleurs, clowns, and jesters. Viewed from the perspective of theatrical history, that same stylized skid turn had probably had audiences howling three hundred years earlier in St. Mark's Square, Venice, when the original mountebank Harlequins mounted their banks, or narrow trestle stages if you will, and confronted the same technical problem of comically conveying rapid motion in a tightly confined space.

Like an obedient pupil going through rote Latin and Greek drills he would never forget for the rest of his life, Charlie went through his rehearsal exercises over and over again until an entire repertoire of classic comic moves was permanently etched into those neuronal templates where skilled, automatic acts finally become stored. No wonder a debonair but aging Chaplin could still tumble from a sofa without spilling a drop of tea from his cup in *Monsieur Verdoux* with much the same alacrity and grace as a youthful Buster Keaton could flip-flop without spilling a drop of coffee from his cup in *College*. Both men received their classical slapstick comedy educations in the vaudeville houses and music halls of their respective countries.

The great Tommaso Visentini, one of the foremost Harlequins of his day, was reputed to execute that same maneuver with a glass of wine. And if more complete accounts survived, there is little doubt that Visentini would have been found in debt for that tumbling gag to some ancient Roman acrobatic comedian who had done the same thing with a flask of olive oil. As James Agee put it in his description of Keystone's Mack Sennett, "He took his comics out of music halls, burlesque, vaudeville, circuses and limbo, and through them he tapped in on that great pipeline of horsing and miming which runs back unbroken through the fairs of the Middle Ages at least to Ancient Greece."[7]

Chaplin's second turn in *Casey's Court Circus* was a parody of Dr. Walford Bodie, one of the best known and most sensational music hall acts of the day. A "Mesmerist and Electrical Wizard" whose "lightning cures" of the infirm were based on a combination of fantastical hypnotism and "bloodless surgery" accomplished by means of electricity, Bodie had no scientific credentials beyond a brief apprenticeship as an electrician with the National Telephone Company. Hounded by an irate medical community, which unwittingly provided him with endless amounts of free publicity as they vehemently denounced his patently false claims of medical cures, Bodie laughed all the way to the bank. He reputedly earned four hundred pounds per week for his music hall turn. When challenged, he freely admitted that the initials M.D. which he sometimes placed after his name stood for Merry Devil. A third-rate charlatan, he was nonetheless a first-rate showman who broke box-office records.

Having planted confederates in the audience, Bodie — sporting a silk top hat, cane, and opera cape — would ask for volunteers. Seating the subject in his famous Electric Chair, which he ceremoniously placed directly in front of the footlights for the delight of his audience, the Great Bodie would make an impressive series of hypnotic gestures and spellbinding flourishes complete with penetrating glances and sonorous suggestions delivered in an appropriately soothing voice that emanated resonantly from beneath a flowing waxed moustache of villainous proportions.

When his accomplice fell into a deep trance, Bodie would step back triumphantly, offering the cloth-capped Cockneys in the gallery an unobstructed view of his first astounding feat of legerdemain. Then, after a pause to heighten the moment, the

Wizard would point dramatically in the direction of his somnolent stooge, who convincingly "jumped sharply upwards as though he had received an electric shock."[8] When the subject, by then fully aroused and on his feet, looked suspiciously at the chair, the good doctor held it up for his inspection to reassure him that it was unwired and free of all devices before inviting him to sit down again.

With hypnotic mastery established over this first "patient," Dr. Bodie set the stage for an elaborate running gag, which could serve as a comic counterpoint to the spectacular medical marvels that awaited his audience. While proceeding with the serious Aesculapian business of curing the crippled, paralyzed, and infirm, whose crutches and canes were displayed in front of the theaters wherever he played, the venerable healer would periodically convulse his audience with laughter by playfully nipping his first subject's fanny with little "electric" jolts by means of posthypnotic suggestion.

Chaplin prepared to "do" Bodie with gusto. He saw the role as a vehicle that could help reestablish his credibility as a dramatic actor in the legitimate theater:

> I would put on such a marvelous character delineation that even the lowest music-hall audience would recognize it as great acting and I would be rescued by some good manager and brought back to a West End theater.
>
> The idea grew upon me. Despising with all my heart the cheap, clap-trap burlesque which the manager [Will Murray] tried to drill into me, I paid only enough attention to it to get through rehearsals somehow, hurrying out afterward to watch Doctor Body [*sic*] and to practise before the mirror in our lodgings my own idea of the part.[9]

Murray confirmed that Chaplin mastered that Bodie impersonation by practicing in front of a mirror — much as Dickens's daughter Mamey recalled watching her father do when he wanted to capture and consolidate his impressions of real-life characters he encountered, so he could to use them as the basis for his fictional portraits. But Murray and his erstwhile protégé were in disagreement as to whether Chaplin learned to "do" Bodie by studying him in person. Murray claimed that Chaplin "had never seen Bodie's turn, but I endeavoured to give him an idea of the Doctor's little mannerisms."[10]

Whatever the case, Chaplin did have at least one opportunity to size up the great charlatan and study his mannerisms and quirks from an intimately close-up, offstage vantage point. At Westminster Abbey, at Sir Henry Irving's funeral, the two actors had been seated — or, to put it more precisely, placed — next to each other. For while the well-behaved boy actor kept his seat and displayed his best manners in spite of his obstructed view, Charlie had been amazed by the outrageousness way Bodie, in order to obtain a better view of Irving's ashes being lowered into the crypt, stepped on top of the prostrate body of a duke who had passed out.

Their encounter occurred seven months earlier. It might seem farfetched, even under such a memorable circumstance as Irving's funeral, to assume that an hour or two spent in another's presence could result in such vivid impressions of that person's quirks and mannerisms that a seventeen-year-old boy could reproduce them faithfully after so many months. But there was nothing ordinary about Charlie Chaplin's visual memory or his powers of impersonation. He observed his subject's traits firsthand even if he did rely on Murray to supply some details of Bodie's music hall act.

For Charlie, opening night arrived with a mixture of anxiety and excitement. Backstage, painting his "face stealthily among the uproar and quarrels of the other fourteen boys, who were all in the same dressing-room fighting over the mirrors and hurling epithets and make-up boxes," he heard hoots and whistles coming from the raucous crowd out front. An earlier act on the bill of the "cheap East End music-hall" had already been driven offstage, pelted with rotten fruit. But it scarcely seemed safer backstage among the familiar maze of scene-shifting property men, gossiping chorus girls, and acrobats doing their warm-up exercises. He avoided Murray by milling purposely with the others "in the darkest part of the wings," as he waited to make his entrance. Having determined to "make up as the real Doctor Body" instead of painting his face in the grotesque caricature mask his director had dictated, Charlie felt like "a boy committing his first burglary" as he prepared to dash past Murray and "get on the stage before I was caught."[11] For an inexperienced teenage comedian playing his first big part, it was a supreme act of willful disobedience.

After slipping past Murray "quick as an eel," the elegantly attired young Dr. Bodie applied his brakes and slowed to a more stately paced, ceremonious entrance, as befitted his fame and station:

> I advanced slowly, impressively, feeling the gaze of the crowd, and with a carefully studied gesture, hung my cane — I held it by the wrong end! Instead of hanging on my arm, as I expected, it clattered on the stage. Startled, I stooped to pick it up, and my high silk hat fell from my head. I grasped it, put it on quickly, and, paper wadding falling out, I found my whole head buried in its black depths.
>
> A great burst of laughter came from the audience. When, pushing the hat back, I went seriously on with my serious lines, the crowd roared, held its sides, shrieked with mirth till it gasped. The more serious I was, the funnier it struck the audience. I came off at last, pursued by howls of laughter and wild applause, which called me back again. I had made the hit of the evening.[12]

A review in the *Era* of *Casey's Court Circus* confirms Chaplin's claim, declaring that, "the fun reaches its height when a burlesque of 'lightning cures on a poor working man' is given."[13] But much to Charlie's dismay, despite the roaring applause and good notices he received, no West End talent scout appeared to whisk him back to the legitimate stage, and the *Era* reviewer had not even seen fit to mention him by name.

Nonetheless, he was beginning to be known in music hall circles as a talented young entertainer and, more important, he was starting to make peace with the idea of becoming a professional comedian and relinquishing his cherished dream of succeeding as a dramatic actor. Percy Honri, an established headliner whose act *Concordia* occasionally played the same bill as *Casey's Court Circus* during this period, came away with the very distinct impression that Chaplin stood out from all of the other juvenile actors in the company as "a very earnest lad who went through his paces as tho his life was dependent on it."[14]

Not only was Chaplin mastering the basics of slapstick and learning how seriocomic counterpoint could be used to soften its crudeness, he was also learning the crucial tactical strategy of immediately engaging an audience when he made his entrance. In the course of learning to "do" Bodie, he discovered the felicitous use of theatrical "moes" or character props. Moes were used to instantly establish nonverbal rapport with an audience by giving the performer readily identifiable physical characteristics that defined his stage character even before he began to speak.[15]

No doubt the real Dr. Bodie originally selected his luxuriously flowing waxed moustache so that its dazzling elegance could be as easily beheld by the boys in the balcony as the swells in the stalls. Likewise, Bodie's other signature character props — his elegant cane, silk hat, and cape — all helped to reinforce his iconography as a spellbinder. And as Charlie was learning, like generations of comics before him, those very same moes could as easily be turned to trademark comic advantage if one bobbled the cane, tripped over the cape, and made the hat ill-fitting.

But for all the theatrical tricks of the trade and performance skills Chaplin picked up during his fifteen-month stint in the *Casey's* troupe, his most important gain was a major conceptual breakthrough:

> I had stumbled on the secret of being funny — unexpectedly. An idea, going in one direction, meets an opposite idea suddenly. "Ha! Ha!" you shriek. It works every time.
>
> I walk on to the stage, serious, dignified, solemn, pause before an easy chair, spread my coat-tails with an elegant gesture — and sit on the cat. Nothing funny about it, really, especially if you consider the feelings of the cat. But you laugh. You laugh because it is unexpected. Those little nervous shocks make you laugh; you can't help it.[16]

Now, obviously, Charlie Chaplin knew how to be funny long before *Casey's Court Circus*. As a veteran Lancashire Lad playing panto in *Cinderella*, he had disobeyed stage directions and defiantly improvised his first gag as the boy in the cat suit doing two typical canine routines (sniffing and peeing) that startled the audience. And over the years that followed, much of Chaplin's time appears to have been devoted to being instinctively funny, offstage and on.

But what Charlie never understood conceptually until his *Casey's* days was the element of audience surprise in humor — that is, what makes a gag funny. For it was one thing to be funny by instinct, on a strictly hit-or-miss basis, and quite another to have a firm technical appreciation of how gags are constructed, what their trip-wire mechanism consists of and why they work. While such "clicks" of insight were no substitute for natural acting ability or creative imagination, this structural understanding of comic performance technique would permit Chaplin to experiment more freely in pairing two-step gag images and vary the timing of their comic delivery. For the first time in his career, even though he had in fact been "gagging" for years, he was beginning to understand comedy in a structural sense.

Consisting of two incongruously mismatched images, the unexpected collision of which leads to surprise and the emotional release of laughter, a gag's success depended on its ability to catch the audience off guard. While a mature comic might achieve that element of surprise by the sheer wackiness with which he could spin off fantastical pairs of mismated images, a newcomer like Charlie was better advised to stick to the basics by using standard, time-honored gags and concentrating on perfecting the timing of his delivery as his major means of getting a laugh. The fancy funny business could come later.

Classic comedy's "rule of three" taught that the second mismated image, whether visual or verbal, should be delivered after a pause of two beats — that is, on the third beat — as in Burns and Allen's famous: "Say goodnight, Gracie" . . . (one) . . . (two) . . . "Goodnight Gracie." Deliver it too soon and there is no time to prepare the audience for a surprise. Present it too late and they have lost all interest. Timing is everything.

But like any rule worth its salt, comedy's rule of three was nothing more than a principle to be honored as much in the breach as in the observance. The important point was to master the structural build-and-kill rhythms of comic delivery by learning to count lines or beats silently in order to maximize a laugh by presenting the punch line at the optimum moment. Only after those basics had been mastered could a comedian begin to evolve his own style of delivery and sharpen his powers of invention in a distinctively personal manner. And eighteen-year-old Charlie was still a far cry from such sophisticated developments by the time he left *Casey's Court Circus.*

While he had passed from late adolescence to early manhood, he had by no means reached his comic majority. Still, the time had now come for him to leave behind that slum alley with

its troupe of boy comics. Either too old or too uninterested to remain one of the gang, Charlie did not join them in their next great
adventure on that July morning in 1907 when they marched off to
a full-scale invasion of the provinces as *Casey's Army.*

His fifteen months in *Casey's Court Circus* had been well
spent. In the course of learning the fundamentals of music hall
slapstick, burlesque, and satire, Chaplin had become steeped in
time-honored theatrical traditions and techniques of classic comedy. Barely able to read and write, Cockney Charlie had not the
remotest inkling of the classical foundation upon which his solid
comic education rested. Nor was he aware that the type of low
comedy he played was considered highbrow in some intellectual
circles. As he later put it, "the word 'art' never entered my head
or my vocabulary."[17]

Nonetheless, he was an ambitious young man filled with
dreams of self-betterment and big plans to succeed. Having finally made peace with his failed adolescent dream of becoming
England's greatest juvenile actor, his sights were now set on a
more realistically attainable form of greatness. This time it was

> Top of the bill in a West End music-hall. That was all I wanted.
> That was the limit — the maddest dream — the most hopeless
> goal.[18]

The Greenhorn and the Guv'nor

Syd arrived, accompanied by a young lad, very puny, pale and sad looking. He seemed undernourished and frightened, as though he expected me to raise my hand to hit him. Even his clothes were too small for him! I must say that at that first moment he seemed much too timid to do anything good on the stage, especially in the knockabout comedy shows that were my specialty. Still, I didn't want to disappoint Sydney, so I took him on.

— Fred Karno[1]

N O LONGER BITTER OVER HIS FAILURE TO SUCCEED as a dramatic actor, the resilient Cockney teenager set his sights on becoming a famous West End comedian. Top of the bill at the Oxford was his latest plan. Like everyone else in the business, he considered the Oxford "the most important music hall in London."[2] Dan Leno and Marie Lloyd both played there to adoring audiences, who came from all strata of society, not just the working class. Their salaries were enormous, their fame immense. Unprecedented wealth and celebrity awaited the happy few who were talented and lucky enough to win the public's love and climb to the top of the bill.

In the world of music hall comedy, the East End was a time-tested route to the West End. Leno and Lloyd had both traveled that path as struggling young actors on the way up. The line between failure and success was so thin that there had even been one brief moment in 1886 when Marie Lloyd, aged sixteen, had played the bottom of the bill beneath twenty-one-year-old Lily Harley.

And so in the early fall of 1906, having had no luck finding a job in a new comedy troupe during the four months since leaving *Casey's Circus*, resourceful, optimistic, and industrious eighteen-year-old Charlie Chaplin elected to make his own luck as a self-employed solo act. He would freelance gratis by playing the bottom of the bill before working-class audiences in one of those same East End venues he had looked down on so disparagingly in his Duke of York days. During this current period of unemployment, he had been forced to rely on his older brother to cover the expense of his meals and lodging in a Kennington rooming house that catered to young theatrical professionals.

Once he had graduated to the official status of a principal comedian in Fred Karno's repertory company, twenty-one-year-old Sydney Chaplin's salary increase and renewed contract placed him in an ideal position to help his kid brother through this rough patch.[3] Syd also tried to capitalize on his standing with Karno by lobbying him to give Charlie an audition. But the Guv'nor wasn't interested, at least for the time being.

Having previously succeeded before an East End audience at Foresters in Bethnal Green, Charlie decided it was a logical starting place to launch his new venture as a stand-up comic. Dan Leno had played that venue on his way up. Located off the Mile End Road in a heavily Irish and Jewish immigrant working-class neighborhood, Foresters had been a good luck house for his *Casey's* troupe. The basic plot device and the slum urchin characters of *Casey's Court Circus* were explicitly Irish, and the troupe's warm welcome from neighborhood audiences had been virtually guaranteed by their Gaelic ethnicity. The Foresters management remembered Chaplin as talented, and were willing to give his new act a one-week unpaid tryout on their regular bill on a sight-unseen basis. New acts were usually required to perform at "trial turn" matinees before they were given a regular booking.

Unlike mammoth music halls like the Oxford, Foresters afforded novice and nervous solo performers a unique physical and acoustical environment in which to communicate intimately with their audience, that time-honored principle of music hall comedy whose critical importance Charlie had learned backstage during his two and a half years as a Lancashire Lad.

But if the place to showcase his talent was carefully thought out, the comedy role Chaplin chose was more hastily selected. The use of an ethnic stereotype for comedy material was a well-established tradition in British music hall. But the idea of a non-Jewish actor adopting Sam Cohen as his stage name and trying to "do" a comic Jew for Jewish audiences was a dicey, if not nervy, proposition. It would take a lot of chutzpah and more than a passing acquaintance with Yiddish to pull that off.

"Jewish comedians were all the rage," Chaplin sheepishly recalled many years later. Borrowing two pounds from Sydney, the peach-fuzzed teenage actor "invested in musical arrangements for songs and funny dialogue," as well as some trademark moes, in order to make himself instantly identifiable as Jewish the minute he walked on stage. His plan was to "hide my youth under whiskers" so his audience would not think they were dealing with some greenhorn. Provisioned with this stage costume, Sam Cohen envisioned himself playing all the important circuits in England. If he got the right breaks, he could become "one of vaudeville's biggest headliners" within a year.[4]

On opening night Charlie could barely contain himself. His idea of solving two performance problems with one prop by masquerading as one of the Chosen People and camouflaging his youth beneath a Hassidic beard was a stroke of genius. Had he given it a little more thought, he might have reconsidered in view of the audience he was about to face. Given the absent fourth wall, he would be expected to reach out across the footlights and make that audience feel he was one of them. And they of course were equally free to reach back across the footlights and make their own feelings known. It was an object lesson in audience-performer relations that Chaplin never forgot.

Like his comic stage character, many of the Foresters patrons wore beards. Many of them were unshaven, deeply religious Orthodox Jews, who regarded that practice as a matter of strict religious observance. Almost all of them were refugees from the ghettos and pogroms of Eastern Europe, or draft dodgers or deserters from the Imperial Russian and German armies. Grown men, bone tired after twelve-hour days in the sweatshops, looking forward to forgetting their struggles in an alien land by relaxing with a few good jokes in their neighborhood music hall, they were in no mood to have their religious practices or their ethnicity held up to ridicule by some Cockney *pisher* (pipsqueak), much less to pay for the privilege.

Unlike those rowdy Aldershot soldiers who had reeked of beer and delighted in baiting his mother for the sport of it, these immigrants reeked of pickled herring and garlic sausage. Their sobriety notwithstanding, they could be equally vicious in expressing their ridicule and displeasure.

Their unanimous verdict on the newcomer's tryout was swift: "After the first couple of jokes, the audience started throwing coins and orange peels and stamping their feet and booing." At first Charlie could not comprehend, but then it started to sink in. In what probably was a full-blown panic attack, a terrifying experience he would never forget, Charlie "began to hurry and talk faster as the jeers, the razzberries, and the throwing of coins and orange peels increased." When he came offstage in a daze, he did not wait to hear management's verdict. "I went straight to the dressing room, took off my make-up, left the theatre and never returned, not even to collect my music books."[5]

Looking back on that traumatic experience ten years later, Chaplin told a fellow movie actor: "Back to the stage! I'll never go back to the stage again as long as I live. No. Unless my money leaves me, not ten thousand dollars would tempt me back behind the footlights again."[6]

Recalling that same night fifty years later, in 1964, it still loomed as a "ghastly experience." By then, seventy-five-year-old Chaplin found himself in complete sympathy with the audience. "Although I was innocent of it, my comedy was most anti-Semitic, and my jokes were not only old ones but very poor, like my Jewish accent."[7]

Ironically, by the time of those remarks, he had encountered many years of the reverse experience, of constantly being mistaken for Jewish both by enthusiastic members of that sect and by others as well. Among those others was no less a student of myths and archetypes than a former nickelodeon manager, James Joyce. His reference in *Ulysses* to peripatetic and Jewish Leopold Bloom as "Chase Me, Charley!" (the title of a seven-reel composite of Chaplin's early Essanay shorts) was his way of suggesting parallels between the mythic hero of his novel and the Wandering Jew and Chaplin's nomadic screen character.[8]

Less flattering but equally fulsome in their assessment of Charlie as a quintessentially Jewish screen character, wandering or otherwise, would be the Propaganda Ministry of the Third Reich. Quick to brand Chaplin a "little Jewish acrobat, as disgusting as he is tedious"[9] — even before he made *The Great Dictator* — the Nazis would sneer at the ridiculous comic logic of a puny underdog nebbish and schlepper like Charlie triumphing over *übermensch* heavies twice his size. A subversive comic trickster, whose slapstick victories could conceivably be construed as an implicit mockery of the Third Reich's Aryan philosophy (to say nothing of his uncanny physical resemblance to their toothbrush-moustached national leader), Chaplin's Little Fellow would be officially banned from Nazi Germany's movie screens. But at the time of his mortifying exit from Foresters in a hail of derision from an aggrieved people over his offensive depiction of their race, Chaplin's evolution from crass stereotype to classic archetype lay in the future.

Just as opening night was closing night at Foresters, a similar fate awaited his next entrepreneurial venture, *Twelve Just Men*, a slapstick comedy sketch he wrote about a jury in a breach-of-promise case. That production never made it past the second night of rehearsal after its principal financial backer got cold feet.

Given Charlie's recently heightened rejection sensitivity after Foresters, it's not surprising that he found it too painful to personally reject or disappoint other actors. Unable to break the bad news to the troupe of *Twelve Just Men*, he begged Syd to do it for him. This delegation of responsibility would later become a conflict-avoidance management style that Charlie employed at the Chaplin Studio throughout his film career. He found it impossible to inform actors personally that they were fired or had failed to win an audition.

In addition to looking after his highstrung, flat-broke kid brother during this miserable seven-month period, Syd finally managed to persuade Fred Karno to interview Charlie. That audition — and tryout, if he could get one — was the chance of a lifetime. Karno's troupes were world renowned, his comedy sketches top-of-the-bill.

A brash showman with a flair for publicity and a knack for

slapstick comedy, forty-year-old Fred Karno was an ex-plumber's assistant who had worked his way up from street busking, acrobatic circus performing, and fairground playing to a successful career as a music hall comedian before pursuing an entrepreneurial bent to establish his own comedy empire, with elaborate studio headquarters known as Fred's Fun Factory. He ultimately had two hundred employees, thirty touring companies worldwide, and a repertoire of twenty-plus comedy sketches, the majority of which he wrote and produced himself, with occasional assistance from principal comedians like Fred Kitchen and Syd Chaplin.

Karno's lowly origins gave him an instinctive feel for the working-class audiences who were his original constituency on the way toward developing a more universal comic appeal. Early-twentieth-century humor is not the same as late-twentieth-century humor. But Karno's ensemble sketches enjoyed roughly the same type of mass appeal as the Monty Python or *Saturday Night Live* companies with their verbal-visual slapstick humor and comedy sketches.

By the time of Karno's interview with Chaplin, the renowned impresario already had more than a dozen sketches in his repertoire.[10] His touring companies would eventually play Europe, South America, North America, and Africa as well as the British Isles.

Apart from the enormous prestige of working your way up to principal player in a Karno troupe, there was the immediate economic security of a guaranteed salary. For greenhorns thick-skinned enough to withstand the routinely sarcastic and sometimes sadistic manner in which Karno treated his employees, an apprenticeship as a supporting player offered an education in slapstick comedy ensemble playing second to none.

Each man working for Karno had to have perfect timing and had to know the peculiarities of everyone else in the cast so that we could, collectively, achieve a cast tempo.

It took about a year for an actor to get the repertoire of a dozen shows down pat. Karno required us to know a number of parts so that the players could be interchanged. When one left the company it was like taking a screw or a pin out of a very delicate piece of machinery.[11]

With so much riding on the outcome, Chaplin's first meeting with the Guv'nor proved an intimidating experience for the boyish-looking, scrawny teenage actor, who was then five foot four and weighed 130 pounds. There was a glaring disparity between Syd Chaplin's effusive praise of his younger brother and Charlie's nervous self-presentation, and a skeptical Karno agreed to give the newcomer a tryout in *The Football Match* only as a favor to Syd, whose judgment and talent he respected.

Assigned a supporting role as a slapstick villain who unsuccessfully attempts to bribe a slow-witted soccer goalie into throwing his team's championship match, Chaplin was given one week to read and master his small part.[12] While the Guv'nor billed his companies as "Karno's Speechless Comedians" and described his performers as "pantomimists," few if any of his slapstick sketches could be remotely described as dialogue-free. But it was equally true that wordless slapstick mime figured prominently in every Karno sketch and was usually referred to simply as "business" in the typed script — which is why Karno advised Charlie to pop by Shepherd's Bush Empire and catch *The Football Match* in person. Because of those unwritten improvisational elements in a typical Karno sketch, every member of the cast was expected to invent distinctive funny business of his own — a fact that Charlie was keenly aware of as he set out for Shepherd's Bush.

Determined to succeed at this tryout, which if successful meant a one-year contract, Charlie carefully studied *The Football Match*, employing all the tricks of the trade Lily had taught him. Composed of two main scenes and a finale soccer match, the sketch opened in the makeshift training quarters of the Muddle-ton Piecans, which was located in a pub called The Bull and equipped, gymnasium-style, with punching bags, parallel bars, Indian clubs, dumbbells, and medicine balls — just the kind of props that Karno, himself a former acrobat, specialized in for his "cruel and boisterous . . . low, knockabout comedy."[13] After a grunting chorus of Piecans finished their warm-up exercises and exited, the actor Charlie was to replace made his entrance. As Chaplin carefully noted, there wasn't a laugh in the house until Stiffy the Goalie arrived on the scene to be plied with promises of cash and a special "training oil" made of intoxicating spirits.

Played by the star of the show, Harry Weldon, Stiffy was full of verbal and nonverbal comic invention that kept audiences howling for the rest of the night (and would for thirty years):

> He would lean dolefully against the goalpost, bored with the in-activity, trying to fold his arms which kept slipping through each other. Then there would be a flurry of excitement caused by an impending attack and this would be followed by another period of tedium when he tried to put his hands into his pockets only to find that his shorts had no pockets. It was a classic example of su-perbly timed mime. . . . The odd mannerisms of Harry Weldon, such as a peculiar whistle while he talked, and a catch phrase "'s no use" made a never-to-be forgotten impression.[14]

His "nerves . . . wound tight like a clock,"[15] Charlie prayed to make good as he paced backstage one week later. As he well knew, first impressions could make or break a performer. Capturing an audience on sight, scoring quickly, and never letting down were fundamental attack skills in the tightly compressed time warp that was music hall comedy. And for that crucial interlude — that dull lull he had astutely spotted between the Piecans' exit and Stiffy's entrance — the entire stage and the audience's undivided attention would belong to him and him alone.

On hearing his cue, he exploded like a thoroughbred out of a starting gate. Pulling out all the stops, he used every theatrical artifice he knew to "slay" his audience with laughter and make them his. Having learned from his *Holmes* days the advantage of entering with one's back to the house and provoking the audience into a state of mildly expectant curiosity, Charlie elected that approach. Dressed in a voluminous cape and carrying a cane, Chaplin paused, carefully counting his beats and timing his first gag, before revealing the rest of his moes — a tiny black moustache and Bardolphian red nose — to register his first surprise laugh of the evening.

Moving right along, scoring as he went while pausing just long enough so as not to wipe out the next gag's peak with the receding laughter of the last gag's trough, he worked the house with waves of comic volleys, skillfully milking each individual gag for all it was worth by reinforcing it with facial takes and double takes. After tripping over a dumbbell, he tangled his cane in a punching bag, which punched him right back, creating one of those minor scuffles between man and machine for which he would later become so famous.

Although no one was critically injured in the fracas, it apparently resulted in loss or damage to a crucial trouser button, for the next thing Charlie knew, he was clutching his waist to prevent the imminent descent of his pants to his ankles, while employing his free hand in a desperate search for the missing button. Stooping to pick up what appeared to be a small disc with a klutzy flourish designed to further provoke the audience's expectations of impending undress, Chaplin scrutinized the found object before discarding it with one of those wrinkling asides: "Those confounded rabbits!"[16]

Making his customary nightly entrance, fully prepared to establish his comic dominance, Harry Weldon appeared — only to be immediately undone by Charlie's undoing, foiled by his foil. Before the star could score his first point of the evening, Chaplin grabbed him by the wrist in mock desperation, hoarsely whispering, "Quick! I'm undone! A pin!"[17] This unrehearsed piece of business took Weldon by surprise, as the audience could see, and the unplanned event was made all the more delightful by their uncertainty whether it was an actual mishap or merely feigned.

Now that Charlie had obliged the show's star to grant him a more collegial stage relationship than had been accorded his predecessor, Stiffy and the Villain skillfully partnered and scored off one another for the rest of the evening. While Charlie dutifully returned comic supremacy to its rightful owner, and while the show's principal comedian could not dispute the fact that his own laughs increased significantly as a result of Chaplin's having helped warm up the house, Charlie sensed, as they walked back to the dressing room together after the final curtain, something less than cordial in Weldon's dry acknowledgement of his obviously successful first performance.

But drunk with the afterglow of success and wired with the adrenalin rush of his first-night ordeal, Charlie did not ponder the significance, if any, of Weldon's reserve. Instead he wanted "to weep for joy . . . but no tears would come, I was empty."[18] To unwind, he walked the streets: over Westminster Bridge, past the derelicts bedding down on the Thames Embankment, past an old raspy-voiced, bottle-nosed tomato vendor, to the Elephant and Castle, then to an all-night coffee stall for a cup of tea before heading to Kennington Gate and another cup. Finally at five in the morning, exhausted but exhilarated, he went to bed.

The only disappointment to his otherwise perfect first night was that Sydney was not there to share his joy. He was, after all, the only one who could understand "how much it all meant to me, especially after the Forester's."[19] When Karno came to see how Syd's kid brother was doing two nights later, the anticipatory applause Chaplin received from the audience on his entrance told him everything he needed to know.

By the time Syd returned from playing the provinces, Charlie had signed a handsome one-year contract with Karno for three pounds ten shillings a week, with options to renew for two more years. Having thereby doubled their combined weekly earnings over their previous four-pound-five-shilling coemployment record during their *Holmes* days, and having managed to do so with as much contractual security as was possible in their chosen profession, the Chaplin brothers decided the time had come to pool their salaries and set up housekeeping together. Traveling as much as they did in separate Karno troupes, both at home and abroad, the idea of permanent digs of their own afforded the road-weary troupers the comforting prospect of a safe haven to return to.

In keeping with their advancing years and increasing status, the elaborate furnishings of their four-room bachelor flat at 15 Glenshaw Mansions, Brixton Road, complete with the luxury of a cleaning lady, reflected their evolving tastes. As Charlie put it, "The final décor was a combination of a Moorish cigarette shop and a French whorehouse. But we loved it."[20]

As a budding man of the world, Charlie in his late teens was just beginning to be interested in women. While the only ones he tried to bed were Picadilly tarts and Parisian courtesans (on tour), he could be as romantic as he was randy. During this awkward coming-of-age stage, there were brief encounters with a pair of fifteen-year-olds, whose honor Chaplin serially managed to preserve, by a noble exertion of self-control in the first case and a much more intricate form of neurotic self-sabotage in the second.

First, there was beautiful aquiline-featured Phoebe Fields, with whom he had a running rooming-house flirtation but whose "saintly" virtue he somehow managed to gallantly spare from his own "worst of intentions about girls."[21] That brief mutual attraction occurred during the depths of his despair in the post-*Casey's*, pre-Karno phase of his life.

One year later, during his first dizzying days as a fledgling Karno comedian, came what felt at the time like the great love of his life, an intense infatuation with a young showgirl by the name of Hetty Kelly. On a sultry summer day in 1908, as he stood in the wings of the Streatham Empire, languidly waiting his turn, Charlie's eye was caught by the mischievous smile of a "slim gazelle with a shapely oval face, a bewitching full mouth and beautiful teeth" in the chorus line.[22] Coming offstage, she handed him her mirror to hold, checked her makeup, primped her hair, and walked off with his heart. While it was a clear-cut case of looking-glass love, it soon proved to be a one-sided version of that classic paradigm, unlike the reciprocated backstage romance of his teenage parents' that Charlie had always idealized.

A whirlwind wooing that ended eleven days after it began and, except for one late Sunday afternoon rendezvous, consisted of nothing more than four or five twenty-minute encounters, its memory would linger with Chaplin for years and inspire his 1916 love song, "There's Always One You Can't Forget." Overwhelmed by the impetuous intensity with which Charlie broached the question of marriage after such a brief acquaintance, fifteen-year-old Hetty recoiled at his possessiveness. Rather "bewildered," she understood little of "what it all meant to me." Addressing her as his "nemesis" (the latest vocabulary word he had acquired in what had now become a ceaseless effort to supplement his stunted formal education), Charlie pedantically informed her that "a mystic force had brought us together and that our union was an affinity predetermined by fate."[23]

And while others might take no for an answer, for Charlie an initial refusal was no deterrent to his romantic ardor. For in his case — according to the script of his teenage parents' courtship, as nostalgically passed on in Lily's romantic reminiscences — the immediate rejection of a lover's suit, physical flight to the ends of the earth (or at least South Africa), and even a union with another man and the bearing of his child were not sufficient to deter true love from taking its course. Which helps explain why, even as a grown man, many years and many loves later, Chaplin was never able to put his fantasy of a reunion with Hetty Kelly entirely to rest until he learned, with sad finality, of her death.

By the time his first year of "paid internship" as a speechless comedian drew to a close, Charlie had become familiar with Karno's entire pantomime comedy repertory of slapstick sketches by playing in many and observing all of them in music hall performance or rehearsals at the Fun Factory practice stage. In the case of *The Football Match*, he was still appearing in the supporting role of the Villain and understudying the principal part of Stiffy the Goalie.

While touring the provinces in that show, signs of strain finally began to surface between him and the star. One night onstage in Belfast — where the critics had just panned Weldon and praised Chaplin — Harry slapped Charlie across the face and drew blood. The slap was part of their scripted comic byplay, but Weldon administered it with twice his usual might, leaving his youthful rival stanching the flow of a nosebleed that purposely reduced his spirit of comic invention by half.

Afterward, backstage, the twenty-eight-year-old star and the nineteen-year-old understudy squared off:

> I told him that if he did it again I would brain him with one of the dumbbells on the stage, and added that if he was jealous, not to take it out on me.
>
> "Jealous of you," said he contemptuously, on our way to the dressing room. "Why, I have more talent in my arse than you have in your whole body!"
>
> "That's where your talent lies," I retorted, and quickly closed the dressing-room door.[24]

By now, particularly in the face of the favorable notices he was starting to earn, Charlie could not help resenting the drastic disparity between his weekly salary and Weldon's — four pounds per week versus thirty-four. For the better part of the next year Chaplin lobbied the Guv'nor for the chance to do Stiffy, and ultimately prevailed. For although Charlie, as an experienced pantomimist in his second year, had already played featured parts in a couple of Karno's sketches, even at the Folies Bergère, "those were minor achievements compared to playing the lead in *The Football Match*":

> we were to open at the Oxford, the most important music hall in London. We were to be the main attraction and I was to have my name *for the first time at the top of the bill* [italics added]. This was a considerable step up. If I was a success at the Oxford it would . . . enable me to demand a large salary and eventually branch out with my own sketches; in fact, it would lead to all sorts of wonderful schemes.

In fact, it led to a severe case of laryngitis. So severe that the show's principal comedian could not be heard by the opening-night audience as "anxiety robbed me of all unctuousness and comedy."[25]

Backstage "with an expression of mingled contempt and disappointment," Karno informed Chaplin that he had flopped. Charlie "assured him that my voice would be better the next night." Skeptical, Karno nonetheless restrained himself from giving full vent to his legendary cruelty.[26]

Karno was not known for tact or sympathy in helping jittery performers overcome stage fright. On one legendary occasion, he was said to have greeted an unnerved player — who had just been driven offstage by vicious heckling at Collins's Islington Green and uttered a plaintive "Mr. Karno, I do feel funny" — with the sarcastic retort "Then for goodness sake get out there, quick!"[27]

Chaplin was not facing a particularly ill-mannered house at the Oxford on the momentous occasion of his first night as Stiffy. He was facing inner demons, demons he did not fully understand.

He was poised on the brink of what he equated, consciously or unconsciously, with the fame that had eluded his laryngitic mother and capriciously deserted his alcoholic father. As an impressionable child, he had witnessed each of their humiliating professional debacles, hers at the Aldershot Canteen and his farewell benefit stage appearance at the Horns Assembly Rooms. He knew what it meant for a performer to die onstage by losing his audience. In a nightmare dream sequence in *Limelight* (1952), Chaplin depicts Calvero (an amalgam of himself and his *lion comique* father) in this situation. To die onstage is every performer's worst nightmare. Telescoping memories of Chaplin's failed actor parents, coupled with equally painful memories of his own experiences with "stage death" — as a squeaky-voiced Dickens delineator in a fright wig and a Hassidically bearded Jewish comedian at Foresters — were enough to provoke a massive and disruptive level of performance anxiety on the eve of his long anticipated moment of stardom.

Speaking in clinical terms about the psychology of performance anxiety in acting: a normal, adaptive level of first-night jitters can actually enhance an actor's skills by adding to his mental sharpness; a maladaptive level of performance anxiety (or panic) can destroy it. Instead of getting out there and "slaying" his audience, an overly anxious comedian who has lost his nerve is instead slain by them and dies onstage, largely as a result of his own dread of their thumbs-up, thumbs-down power over his stage life. Foresters was the most conscious source of Charlie's fears. As he recalled, "that night's horror ... left an indelible mark on my confidence."[28]

That night at the Oxford, Chaplin's anticipatory performance anxiety robbed him of the use of his vocal cords — as it had his mother before him. Or else his performance anxiety provoked a physical illness that had the same effect. In either case, Karno's insensitivity made matters worse as Charlie prepared for his second night's try. He was fortunate Syd was by his side:

He rushed Charlie round to a doctor. They called at the chemist's on the way back, bought a gargle and lots of lozenges. Charlie gargled continuously for hours, often with lozenges in his mouth even while gargling. At intervals the voice was listened for. It was returning — or was it? No, the whisper was scarcely audible now. Tears filled Charlie's eyes.

In the dressing room, half an hour before the sketch was due to go on, Charlie was still gargling. Karno came in . . . and decided, after listening to Charlie, that he could not possibly go on like that. The understudy was told to take over. Charlie, looking pathetically from one to the other, broke down and wept bitterly.[29]

Faced with the prospect of a Karno production being mounted at a first-class house with a second-rate cast, the Guv'nor was furious. As for Chaplin, who was under contract and on the payroll whether he worked or not, Karno had no use for his high-strung employee. But before the Guv'nor gave vent to his disgust over being forced to support an actor who could not pull his own weight, Sydney Chaplin stepped in with a better idea.

Instead of permitting Charlie the dubious luxury of remaining idle while recuperating from laryngitis, whatever the cause, Syd proposed that his brother immediately take over the role he himself was playing at the time, as the Drunken Swell in *Mumming Birds*. As Syd reminded Karno, it was a principal role that did not require a speaking voice. Returning Charlie to the fray immediately was far better, both for his own morale and the company's payroll, than waiting three weeks or so till his voice returned and giving him another shot at Stiffy, even if his heart was set on that role. Besides, having already played the Drunken Swell with success, at home and abroad, Charlie knew the part.

The Guv'nor agreed. Syd's suggestion was as astute as it was generous. Not only did it have the merit of returning Charlie to the stage before stage fright could permanently set in, it also was a way to redirect Charlie from his obsessive belief that Stiffy was meant to be the vehicle that established his stardom.

It refocused Charlie on a nonspeaking role for which he was better suited. Or, as Weldon later put it peevishly at a time when his own earnings paled in comparison to his ex-rival's million-dollar salary, "Charlie had undoubtedly a flair for pantomime, but in a speaking part he was rather out of it."[30]

Syd's idea was not just a strategy to avoid the downwardly spiraling vicious cycle of ever-worsening laryngitis that had been Lily's undoing when financial necessity had forced her to continue performing before noisy, unruly audiences with her already failing voice. The part of the Drunken Swell was tailor-made for Charlie for a number of other reasons. As Syd well knew, his brother had been observing alcoholics and practicing their mannerisms and gait ever since Charlie first showcased the Rummy Binks shuffle for Lily in their Methley Street garret ten years earlier.

At an even deeper level, out of that wellspring of personal experience from which method actors dredge and cull raw material to meld and fuse with their stage characters' emotions, the plot of *Mumming Birds* resonated with Chaplin's traumatic childhood experience at Aldershot, where he had personally witnessed a hostile, drunken audience frazzle Lily until she was driven from the stage. The crucial difference was that, instead of assuming his mother's role as the music hall audience's helpless victim, Charlie would play a drunken victimizer with gusto: "I'd sit in a box in the theatre and interfere with everything — all the business going on on the stage. I'd disapprove, disrupt, make noise!"[31]

No less an anarchist-comedy expert on the psychology of audience-performer relations than Groucho Marx (whose tribute to Chaplin sometimes included the perverse trope of signing Charlie's name in his fans' autograph books) recalled his impression of Chaplin's memorable performance as the Drunken Swell:

Chaplin sat . . . and ate soda crackers, one after another. A woman up front was singing all the while, but nobody heard a single note,

I'm sure. They were too intent on Chaplin's every move. A fine stream of cracker dust was slowly coming out of his mouth. He kept that up for exactly fifteen minutes. At the table was a large basket of oranges. Finally, he started to pick up the oranges one by one, and threw them right at the woman. One of them knocked the pianist off his chair. People became hysterical. There never was such continuous laughter.[32]

For Chaplin, the role of the drunken heckler provided an opportunity to score a triumph and settle a score. Audiences loved his comic drunk. But they seemed oblivious to the fact that it was their own behavior he was satirizing. After years of witnessing audiences alternate between drunkenly disrupting and aggressively inserting themselves into performances, Chaplin was at no loss for experiences to draw upon as material for his characterization.

Having been showered with money and applause at Aldershot as a walk-on stand-in for Lily when she was driven offstage by those same drunks, he knew the unpredictable cruelty of music hall audiences. If they sensed any vulnerability or frailty — like a faltering voice — they could attack like a wolf pack. Playing in pantomime, Charlie was secure. Any performance anxiety he felt would not be revealed by his voice cracking. He was immune to attack. Furthermore, by playing the part of a member of the audience, he became an aggressor rather than a victim. Doubly protected, Chaplin embraced with gusto the role of a disruptive lout whose tipsy whims can kill a music hall performer's act.

Torturing the Soprano (a comic soubrette with a fragile voice) is just one among many of the Drunken Swell's nightly activities. He vents his spleen on every act on the bill as a member of the onstage audience in *Mumming Birds*, which is structured as a show within a show.

The house curtain goes up to reveal a stage set of a miniature music hall complete with onstage boxes right and left and a small proscenium arch with a tab curtain at stage center. After the arrival of supernumaries playing background members of the onstage audience, the next to enter and be shown to their box are the Elderly Uncle and his Fat Boy nephew who is armed with a peashooter and a hamper of food. The overture has already begun by the time the last spectator is ushered in, resplendent in formal evening cutaway, silk top hat, and white gloves — the glass of fashion and the mold of form except for a red nose, which suggests a life of excess tippling. Tottering and swaying in spite of a diligent effort to maintain his balance, Chaplin's balletic interpretation of the Drunken Swell was as someone who is desperately trying to appear sober but fighting a losing battle against the powers of the grape.

Shown to his box, across from the Fat Boy and the Elderly Uncle, a very genteel Charlie removes his right glove with élan, tips the usherette with panache, and then proceeds absentmindedly to try and remove the same glove from his now bare right hand until the usherette discreetly points out his error and leaves him to be seated. Oblivious to the mounting crescendo of the overture which suggests the curtain is about to rise, the Drunken Swell suavely removes a cigarette from an elegant case and casually proceeds to light it with a lucifer — an electric bulb located directly outside his box.

Just as he is about to unleash his full fury on the fickle flame that is refusing to yield its fire, he looks up to see the Fat Boy helpfully extending a lit match. Bowing magnanimously, the Swell leans forward to accept the gracious assistance of his new friend (and future partner in mayhem) but, misgauging the distance, instead does a combined nosedive–fanny flop with acrobatic precision and ends up in a drunken sprawl upon the stage he is destined to occupy again and again during the evening — timed exactly on cue as the overture mounts to its finale.

Managing to scramble back to his seat as the curtain rises, Charlie settles down to the funny business of the evening: a running series of pantomimed expressions of disdain, disgust, bore-dom, rage — the entire gamut of contemptuous emotions — accompanied by razzberries, snoring, food throwing, insertion of self into the performance, and just about every other imaginable indignity that a drunken member of the audience is capable of inflicting on a collection of uniformly pathetic music hall acts.

Depending on the particular Karno company and the talents of the individual members of the cast, the specific turns portrayed in *Mumming Birds* (or *A Night in an English Music Hall*, as it was billed in America) varied but were always intentionally terrible in order to justifiably incite the Drunken Swell and his Fat Boy partner to their respective and collective excesses. Separate acts of an unfunny male comic singer and an off-key female vocalist were standard features of the sketch. Sometimes there were bumbling magicians, klutzy acrobats, lackluster actors reciting corny poems, inept jugglers, and others. But inevitably there was the finale with the strong man, Ali the Terrible Turk. Taking on all comers, the scrawny underfed Hercules in droopy drawers is handily bested by none other than Charlie's lopsided drunk, who triumphs by tickling the Turk. He then terminates the evening by leading the entire cast in a comic mayhem climax worthy of the Marx Brothers — which is probably why Charlie's performance warmed Groucho's heart when he caught his act on a cold winter night in Winnipeg in 1911.

The comic sadism in Chaplin's portrayal of audience-performer relations was originally scripted by Karno the author, not Chaplin the actor. But one need only look at the film version that Chaplin later made of that sketch to get some idea of how deeply he resonated with that theme.

Made in 1915, at a time when Chaplin had complete artistic control over every aspect of his films, *A Night at the Show* outdid *Mumming Birds* in giving vent to Charlie's unconscious hostilities. Not content to confine his aggression to the original vehicle of the upper-class swell character, he invented a second character he also played: a guttersnipe rowdy in the gallery. By flipping between these two screen characters he manages to pour beer on himself maliciously while stealing applause from the performers, whom he pelts with tomatoes, ice cream cones, tarts, and everything else under the sun. Not content to confine his aggression to the stage players, he spritzes the entire gallery with a water hose — a fitting outcome that is hardly surprising since, as one film commentator observed without knowing the deep personal sources of Chaplin's hostility, "His real hate is directed towards the audience."[33]

Chaplin's star turn in *Mumming Birds* established him as a principal comedian and earned him a ticket to Hollywood. But it was another Karno sketch, *Jimmy the Fearless*, that actually gave him the chance to go to America, where he was later discovered by the burgeoning film industry. It would be a Canadian-born, ham-fisted ex-boilermaker with an eye for talent, a knack for slapstick, and an infallible instinct for working-class audience tastes who caught the drunk act of the "little limey"[34] at a New York vaudeville house and hired him as an unproven stand-in one year later, when his principal male comedian resigned on short notice. At the time of that original sighting in 1912, Charlie's future employer had come back East to confer with his two business partners, a pair of ex-bookies from the Lower East Side who distributed his films. Known to his employees back in California as the Old Man and the Boss, thirty-two-year-old Mack Sennett was a glib, funny, charismatically charming leader, who ran the Keystone Film Studio in Edendale, California, like a three-ring circus and clown school. Within days of his arrival at Keystone, Charlie would become an insatiably curious student of film directing technique and film editing technology. Bringing to Edendale nineteen years of on- and offstage experience, starting with his first stand-in appearance at Aldershot, he would rapidly become Sennett's principal male comedian and, a mere two years later, arguably the most famous man in the world.

The Immigrant

The *Crainrona* was a cattle boat but it didn't carry any cattle unless you call *us* cattle, and sometimes that's just how we felt. For that matter, the food did mostly taste like fodder; and the weather was pretty rough. But we had fun because we were all in a great business, we were young and we were delighted to be going where we were going. One morning we heard there was land in the distance. I'll never forget the details of what happened next. We were all on deck, sitting, watching the land in the mist. Suddenly Charlie ran to the railing, took off his hat, waved it and shouted, "America, I am coming to conquer you! Every man, woman and child shall have my name on their lips — Charles Spencer Chaplin!" We all booed him affectionately, and he bowed to us very formally and sat down again. Years later whenever I met any of the old [Karno] troupe, that was the one thing about those years we remembered the best, and we used to marvel on how right Charlie had been.

— Stan Laurel[1]

WHETHER THEY PAID FOR THEIR PASSAGE OR STOWED AWAY on passenger ships, cattle boats, or other conveyances during those peak immigration years from 1905 to 1914, ten and a half million equally hopeful and ambitious refugees and adventurers made the same voyage as Chaplin. Like the twenty-one-year-old actor, one or two others may have actually shouted their plans to conquer America from the deck of their ship when it first came in sight of the promised land. But whether they dreamed or screamed it, most came with similar hopes and plans.

Charlie was the third member of the family to make the trip. Charlie Sr. had done so in 1890, and Syd sixteen years later. Both had played New York and returned to London, where they had resumed their music hall careers as well-paid featured performers. While Charlie reassured the Guv'nor that he had no plans to "jump ship" and stay in the States, that was precisely what he hoped to do if he got the chance:

> Since my major setback at the Oxford Music Hall, I was full of the idea of going to America, not alone for the thrill and adventure of it, but because it would mean renewed hope, a new beginning in a new world. . . .
>
> This chance to go to the United States was what I needed. In England I felt I had reached the limit of my prospects; besides, my opportunities there were circumscribed. With scant educational background, if I failed as a music-hall comedian I would have little chance but to do menial work. In the States the prospects were brighter.[2]

Having recently lost a couple of fully trained Karno comedians to the better-paying American vaudeville stage, the Guv'nor had decided to send Charlie to the States and keep Sydney in England. By now Syd Chaplin had four years of experience as a Karno comedian and had in 1909 written his first successful comedy sketch, *Skating*. He was a much more valuable business property and promising star than his highstrung kid brother, who with only two years of seasoning was still learning the ropes. From Karno's perspective, developing a young actor with raw

talent into a full-fledged "speechless comedian" was an elaborate educational and training process that required a great deal of
time and effort. While Karno undoubtedly recognized that Charlie was a motivated fast learner, he regarded venerable old-timers
like thirty-eight-year-old Fred Kitchen as master comedians. In
addition to working the halls as Karno's highest-paid principal
performer, Kitchen wrote sketches with and for the Guv'nor,
coached some of his touring companies, and worked with the
younger actors.

Stan Laurel, Charlie's roommate on the American tour, recalled the Guv'nor's invaluable personal instruction:

> Fred Karno didn't teach Charlie and me all we know about com-
> edy. He just taught us most of it. If I had to pick an adjective to fit
> Karno, it would be supple. . . . He was flexible in just about every-
> thing, and above all he taught us to be supple. Just as importantly
> he taught us to be precise. Out of all that endless rehearsal and
> performance came Charlie, the most supple and precise comedian
> of our time.[3]

For his part, Chaplin remembered Karno more as a manager than
a teacher. When he said, "Karno required us to know a number
of parts so that the players could be interchanged,"[4] Charlie saw
the instruction as secondary to the interchangeability.

Still, as a prospective immigrant, Charlie had a distinct advantage over the average greenhorn. Unlike other young men just
off the boat, he was receiving a first-rate paid education in his
chosen profession, he had a secure job, there was no ostensible
language barrier, and he was free to return to England and his recently established position as a budding music hall star if he
couldn't find a better opportunity in the States. It would take
Chaplin two American tours, lasting twenty-two and fifteen
months respectively between 1910 and 1913, before he finally got
the right offer.

However, as Charlie discovered soon after stepping on American soil, when an irate Jersey City bartender almost knocked him unconscious with a barrel stave upon mistakenly assuming that Chaplin was mocking him, American and British versions of the English language were not the same. Attempting to order a beer, Cockney Charlie had said, "Well, old top, I fancy I should like a mug of mulled ale and a toasted biscuit." Before the offended barkeep could tear his head off, the Karno troupe's actor-manager, Alf Reeves, stepped in and straightened out the misunderstanding.[5]

Reeves, who later served as the general manager of the Chaplin Film Studio from 1918 to 1946, was also responsible for recruiting Charlie and bringing him to America in the first place. Back in London in the winter of 1910, when he was looking for fresh talent for the Karno troupe for its next American touring season, thirty-four-year-old Reeves heard about Charlie and checked out his act at the Holloway Empire, where he was playing the lead role of Jimmy. A sketch whose full title was *Jimmy the Fearless, or The Boy 'Ero*, it was a Cockney comedy about a daydreaming adolescent who is addicted to reading penny dreadfuls (dime novels) and whose escapist yearnings for romance and adventure are forever being shattered by harsh reminders of the realities of his working-class life. (Chaplin would employ this Walter Mitty-like device, punctuated by frustrated awakenings from pipe dreams and sleep dreams, with hilarious results in *His Prehistoric Past*, *The Bank*, *Shoulder Arms*, *The Idle Class*, *The Kid*, *The Gold Rush*, and *Modern Times*.) Alf Reeves never forgot his initial impression of the young Karno comedian: "Just as I popped in he was putting great dramatic fire into the good old speech, 'Another shot rang out, and another redskin bit the dust!' . . .

He looked the typical London street urchin, who knows every inch of the town as he darts through hurrying throngs and dodges in and out of rushing traffic, managing by some miracle to escape with his life. He had a cap on the back of his head and wore a shabby old suit, short in the sleeves and frayed at the cuffs — a suit he had long since outgrown.

But it was not until he did something strikingly characteristic that I realised he was a real find. His father in the skit was ordering him to drop his novel and eat his supper. "Get on with it now, m'lad," and jabbing a loaf of bread at him. Charlie, I noticed, cut the bread without once taking his eyes off his book. But what particularly attracted my attention was that while he absentmindedly kept cutting the bread. . . . The next thing I knew, he had carved that loaf into the shape of a concertina.[6]

Reeves instantly recognized that Chaplin's dreamily transforming a loaf of bread into a concertina, and then "playing" it to drown out the Polonius-like buzz of his father's dinner table conversation, was an unmistakable mark of comic creativity. Not since the days when the legendary Grimaldi had seized on two loaves of bread to serve as a pair of boxing gloves in order to fight with the Vegetable Man, a fantasy monster constructed entirely from vegetables (intended as a parody of Mary Shelley's *Frankenstein*) had the English comedy stage seen such flights of comic imagination achieved with a common penny loaf.

And while Chaplin would later perform an even more dazzling bread routine — the "Dance of the Rolls" in *The Gold Rush* — it was his uncanny ability to surprise audiences by wittily transforming commonplace physical objects into unique creations that marked him a future master clown in Alf Reeves's experienced eye. The highly respected Swiss pantomimist Adrian Wettach (*Grock*), an honorary member of the International Clown Hall of Fame like Chaplin, described the whimsy that kind of comedy required:

Ever since I can remember, all kinds of inanimate objects have had a way of looking at me reproachfully and whispering to me in unguarded moments: "We've been waiting for you . . . at last

you've come . . . take us now, and turn us into something different . . . we've been so bored waiting."[7]

After five years' experience in *Repairs, Casey's Court Circus*,
and several Karno sketches, Chaplin, now twenty-one, was beginning to acquire the requisite acting skills and creative imagination to craft those startling transformation gags for which he
later became famous as a movie actor. In his films, Charlie the
screen character would transform himself into at least six distinct types — the tipsy bumbler, the wily trickster, the streetwise
hustler, the comic misfit, the clever chameleon, and the poet-
magician — and his universe into countless variations. Turning a
cow into a milk machine by pumping its tail; drying teacups and
dinner plates with the laundry wringer of an old-fashioned wash-
ing machine; fashioning an old sock into a change purse and a
handkerchief; storing his lunch in an office safe, and employing a
cuspidor as a baby potty were a few of his comic misfit transformations. As a tipsy bumbler he would transform a cigarette into a door
key, its ashes into a cab driver's tip, and a light bulb into a match.
As a streetwise hustler dodging the bobbies, he could transform
himself into a wall by freezing flat against that structure and pretending to be invisible in order to avoid capture. A wily trickster,
he stuck a lampshade over his head, froze on the spot, and became a standing lamp in order to avoid a confrontation with a romantic rival. Chameleonlike, he could transform himself into an
anesthesiologist who anesthetizes a street bully with a street-
corner gas lamp while conscientiously monitoring his patient's
pulse, or a cardiologist who employs his stethoscope to diagnose
an alarm clock's bum ticker, or an internist who takes his patient's
pulse with clinical aplomb and then orders him to stick out his
tongue to moisten a postage stamp. And the dreamy poet-magician
could, of course, transform dinner rolls into ballet slippers.

Chaplin never specified what he learned from Karno as an
actor. Stan Laurel did:

Wistful. I don't think I even knew what in the hell wistful *meant* at the time. But I gradually got at least part of the idea when Karno used to say it to some of the old-timers in the troupe. I don't remember if he was the one who originated the idea of putting a bit of sentiment right in the midst of a funny music hall turn, but I know he did it all the time. . . . it was a bit touching. Karno encouraged that sort of thing. "Wistful" for him I think meant putting in that serious touch once in a while. . . . you would have to look sorry, really sorry, for a few seconds. . . . Karno would say, "Wistful, please, wistful!" It was only a bit of a look, but somehow it made the whole thing funnier. The audience didn't expect that serious look. Karno really knew how to sharpen comedy in that way.[8]

Stan apparently credited his own trademark gesture of wistfulness, that slow cry and head scratch, to Fred Karno's lessons in seriocomic counterpoint. But Charlie never as generously acknowledged what he had learned from the Guv'nor. Nor did he credit what, if anything, he'd learned from his fellow clowns at the Fun Factory.

Of all the comedy material Chaplin may have unconsciously absorbed or overtly copied from other Karno performers before departing for America, the Little Tramp's signature "ashtray kick" was his single most incontrovertible borrowing, with the most easily traceable source. Fred Kitchen, one of Charlie's Karno mentors, was the person who taught him how to casually toss a lit cigarette over his shoulder and effortlessly back-kick it away without turning his head. When asked by British reporters late in life why he had never toured America, master clown Kitchen claimed it was because everyone would have automatically assumed that he was trying to imitate his former pupil's screen character, since Kitchen's stage character also wore big boots and ambled with a comic gait while tossing lucifers and back-kicking fags.

The origin of Chaplin's ashtray kick has never been disputed by music hall historians, but the big boots are more problematic.

Not only Kitchen but also another music hall droll by the name of Little Tich (Harry Relph) has been credited as the possible source of inspiration for the Little Tramp's big boots — as well as for Chaplin's funny business with his hat and cane. After playing on the bill with him at the Folies Bergère in 1909, Chaplin "came back from Paris inspired by what he had seen Tich doing and soon began duplicating a great many elements of his art," wrote one reputable theatrical historian.[9]

A gracefully coordinated, pint-sized dancer in iconic slap-shoes, whose trademark chapeau ran circles around him while his signature cane also got the better of him, Relph has sometimes been credited with inspiring Chaplin's derby-tipping-and-flipping antics and his comic canesmanship. While Tich's world-class act may or may not have influenced Chaplin's choice of character moes and taught him a thing or two about using those props, it is also the case that "Chaplin was able to put more substance into his walking-stick than there were electrons in the Hiroshima Bomb," in the words of Buster Keaton.[10] In addition to manicuring its owner's fingernails and being put to bed like a baby, Chaplin's cane would trip his rivals, bring girls close, and hoist their skirts — and then get spanked by Charlie for such naughty behavior. His cane would serve as a billiard cue, a toothpick, a conductor's baton, a swagger stick, a golf club, and a dueling sword. All of these transformations were ones his fellow clown Harry Relph couldn't have helped but admire.

Part of the problem in cataloguing most of the borrowed comedy material that twenty-one-year-old Charlie packed in his mental theatrical trunk was his mounting "anxiety of influence" late in life. With an eye on posterity as well as an understandable fear of being consigned to oblivion by the modern filmmaking establishment, Chaplin was careful not to dilute his own claim to genius by frankly acknowledging the influence of music hall greats like Leno, Lloyd, Karno, Kitchen, and Relph. As a home-sick expat in the 1920s and 1930s, on the other hand, he had loved to do those dead-on takeoffs of his former idols, whose acts he remembered catching and studying with photographic precision back in dear old Blighty as a stagestruck youngster and a struggling young actor. By the time he sat down to pen his memoirs, however, the original subjects of those earlier graphic tributes had conveniently slipped his memory.

Even though Chaplin's late-life silence makes it difficult to pinpoint precisely who influenced him most, there is no doubt that by the time he arrived in New York City on a balmy Indian-summer day in 1910, he was well furnished with a bag of bits and shticks, many of which had been lifted wholesale from other comedians' acts and assimilated into his own. In Chaplin's defense, such unacknowledged borrowing from predecessors is a time-honored tradition in the profession. And in the half century since his death, Chaplin's art has continued to receive a similar tribute from a long, distinguished list of contemporary comedians.

In addition to "adopting" gags, Chaplin also refined his own acting technique by studying other people's acting — particularly the nonverbal performances of music hall singers. His knowledge of facial, gestural, and postural expressive acting by the time he left England was prodigious. Equipped with perfect recall for lyrics, tunes, and, most important, the signature delivery for almost every music hall song he ever heard, Chaplin had learned volumes about pantomime acting by observing and copying topical vocalists, despite the fact that he himself was a speechless comedian, not a singer.

No one would disagree with Marcel Marceau's observation that Chaplin "adapted his style of English Music Hall pantomime to cinematography."[11] That remark was meant to include the profound influence of those topical ballads and comic character songs whose plot structure, style of delivery, and philosophical point of view were in Charlie's bones by the time he hit Hollywood. Marceau was not restricting the term "pantomime" to its narrowest sense — his own specialty of dumb show. He was using it in its broader sense to include those complex non-verbal acting skills that music hall vocalists routinely used to get the story lines of their songs across with vivid immediacy to the audience. It was those pantomime aspects of their musical delivery that were filled with carefully crafted bits of stage business: gems of nonverbal invention, gestural inflection, and facial expression that immeasurably advanced the telling of their tales.

Just as these pantomime storytelling skills would prove an enormous asset for Chaplin the actor, so the stories in the ballads would be invaluable as sources for Chaplin the writer, inspiring scenarios and plots for his slapstick film sketches. Again, there is no way to identify and trace systematically the songs from his boyhood and adolescence, whose story lines were transformed into his short films. But there are striking similiarities between the subject matter of Chaplin's early one- and two-reelers and the standard sitcom story lines of typical British music hall comedy ballads. Such themes as the landlady and the lodger, the coy flirt and the would-be masher in the park, the henpecked married man and his battle-ax wife, the tipsy philandering husband and his long-suffering spouse, the constabulary boob and the shady trickster — these are but a few of the typical stock comedy situations in both of these proletarian art forms. Moreover, the slapstick sequencing device of multiplying misfortunes portrayed in musical hall comedy songs is strikingly similar to the cascading calamities so characteristic of Keystone Comedy films.

Although he acknowledged that there had been a relationship between music hall songs and his early one- and two-reelers, Chaplin never identified most of the songs that had shaped those films. He did reveal two examples of that shaping process: his use of "Mrs. Grundy" to set the mood for *The Immigrant*, and of "The Honeysuckle and the Bee" in *The Vagabond*. He also mentioned in passing that one of Charlie Sr.'s signature songs shaped one of his early films, *His Trysting Place*, but he never said which. Given these tantalizing glimpses, there's room to ponder the full extent of the use Chaplin made of his balladic repetoire in shaping his art.

His most striking use of music in silent film was, of course, José Padilla's "La Violetera" in *City Lights*. And his most overt tribute to British music hall songs was "The Animal Trainer" and "The Sardine Song" in his sound film *Limelight*. Harry Crocker described being holed up with Chaplin on a creative brainstorming session in which he was treated to a extensive repertoire of British music hall songs, but he never mentioned the names of the songs and the artistes Charlie did.

It does not require a great stretch of the imagination to recognize the wistful humor and schmaltzy Cockney worldview Chaplin exported with him to America as inherent to those earthy music hall ballads. Delivered in a bawdy comic vernacular, they offered their lowly audiences an elevated view of themselves and their lives by serenading them with the nostalgic trials and tribulations of working-class underdogs like themselves. The hilarious musical misadventures reflected a vicarious spiritual triumph over the poverty, suffering, and class humiliation that was the audience's common lot. Joining in the chorus, and singing along with the stage performer, became a unifying spiritual experience for audiences that almost served as a class-conscious communion. Even more important than the plot of any ballad's story line was that homespun brand of hardboiled sentimentality (often softened by beer suds and gin) with which those tales were colorfully imbued — a crucial stylistic forerunner of the wistful mixture of pathos and slapstick that later became known as Chaplinesque.

Arriving in New York City at ten o'clock that sunny Sunday morning in September, Charlie hopped a trolley to Times Square where "newspapers were blowing about the road and pavement, and Broadway looked seedy, like a slovenly woman just out of bed." Until dusk, that is, when throngs of theatergoers came out and she lit up with a jeweled elegance that hid her stark squalor and made Charlie feel less "homesick."[12]

Charlie's spirits swung in tandem with his perceptions of the urban environment. Stan Laurel recalled:

> He was very moody and often very shabby in appearance. Then suddenly he would astonish us all by getting dressed to kill. It seemed that every once in a while he would get an urge to look very smart. At these times he would wear a derby hat (an expensive one), gloves, smart suit, fancy vest, two-tone side button shoes, and carry a cane.[13]

Since he received a principal's salary of seventy-five dollars per week (of which he regularly banked fifty), Charlie's bouts of sartorial squalor were self-imposed: a mixture of moody indifference, economizing self-discipline, and dreamy absentmindedness. Apart from sightseeing and practicing the violin several hours a day, he was starting to spend his spare time reading ambitiously, a painstaking project that required the constant use of a dictionary. An extension of his earlier plan to improve his vocabulary, his reading program marked the beginning of a lifelong attempt to fill in the massive gaps in his education.

Browsing secondhand bookshops in towns wherever he played, he began reading the classics and would later recall: "in my dressing room between shows I also had the pleasure of meeting Twain, Poe, Hawthorne, Irving and Hazlitt." But his most memorable American discovery would be Emerson's essay "Self-Reliance," whose emphasis on discovering one's own genius rapidly became Chaplin's personal credo. Or, as he put it, "I felt I had been handed a golden birthright."[14] Emerson wrote:

> Insist on yourself; never imitate. Your own gift you can present every moment with the cumulative force of a whole life's cultivation; but of the adopted talent of another you have only an ex-

temporaneous half possession. That which each can do best, none but his Maker can teach him. . . . Where is the master who could have taught Shakspeare? Where is the master who could have instructed Franklin, or Washington, or Bacon, or Newton? Every man is an unique. . . . Shakspeare will never be made by the study of Shakspeare. Do that which is assigned thee, and thou canst not hope too much or dare too much.[15]

Given Charlie's introspective nature, moody temperament, and tendency toward shyness, it's understandable that some members of the troupe mistook his reserve for superiority. The fact that he "lived like a monk and had a horror of drink,"[16] as Karno put it, did not help make him one of the boys. But his monasticism did not exclude female companionship; that shared interest helped him cement ties of masculine friendship with his fellow players. Or, as he put it,

We made many friends with the members of other vaudeville companies. In each town we would get together in the red-light district, six or more of us. Sometimes we won the affection of the madam of a bordel and she would close up the "joint" for the night and we would take over.[17]

Although the logistics of touring — never staying long enough in any one town to meet suitable women and form solid emotional attachments — probably help explain Charlie's youthful whoring, there is a certain aging memoirist's delight with which Chaplin nostalgically recollects his adventures with ladies of the night in Paris, London, Chicago, Butte (Montana), and points west in *My Autobiography*. His account lends credence to his late-life claim that he slept with more than two thousand women: a modest number compared to Wilt Chamberlain's self-claimed record of fifteen thousand, but far in excess of that dapper, lady-killing Frenchman Henri Landru's personal best. (Monsieur Landru would serve as the real-life model for Chaplin's semiautobiographical turn as the compulsive womanizer Monsieur Verdoux in the 1947 film of the same name.)

Mile after mile and town after town, the small band of Karno players made their way across America: "Such cities as Cleveland, St. Louis, Minneapolis, St. Paul, Kansas City, Denver, Butte, Billings, throbbed with the dynamism of the future, and I was imbued with it."[18] After criss-crossing America from New York to California twice in the space of twenty-one months, they returned to England in the late spring of 1912, where Charlie was stunned and dismayed to learn "I was homeless."[19]

Waiting at Waterloo Station, bursting with impatience to share his glad tidings, Syd announced his recent marriage to Minnie Gilbert, a fellow Karno player, and said he had given up their cozy bachelor digs for a honeymoon flat of his own. That news, followed by a depressing Sunday outing to Cane Hill with Syd, where Charlie was unable to bring himself to visit Hannah after being told she was blue in the face from ice water hydrotherapy to control her tendency to belt out rousing Christian marching songs like a music hall trouper, was enough to harden Chaplin's resolve to hurry back to the States and settle there.

Still, there were consolations and nostalgic pleasures to be had during this four-month interlude of combined professional touring and vacationing in England. An invitation from the Guv'nor for a weekend as his personal guest on his Thames houseboat was gratifying proof of the twenty-three-year-old star's rapid rise in his employer's esteem. Yet Karno refused to grant Charlie equal footing professionally by following his advice to modify the American touring company's program for the next season, which only intensified his restless dissatisfaction.

Charlie had dutifully reported how limited was the reception of *The Wow Wows, or A Night in a London Secret Society*, a sketch that was as overly wordy as its title suggests, with talky dialogue and obscure, in-group British humor. But for some reason, Karno remained convinced that his clunker satirizing British upper-class clubmanship was just the thing the American public wanted. Originally, against everyone else's advice, he had insisted that Reeves retain it as the centerpiece for the last tour. (When *Kick In*, an American comedy of college campus life, played London two years later, English audiences required a program containing a glossary of American words and phrases to help them out.)

Having already spiced up *The Wow Wows* by getting every member of the cast to add bits of nonverbal funny business (Charlie showcased his talent for doing drunks by turning his character into a souse), the troupe was not too worried about the adamancy with which Karno insisted on making his pet piece their American centerpiece. Besides, as they had already discovered during the previous season, the touring company was in fact free to play that great crowd-pleaser *A Night in an English Music Hall* just about as often as they and the American theatergoing public agreed they were mutually interested — which was, in fact, far more frequently than the Guv'nor apparently realized.

Returning to the States on the SS *Oceanic* in October 1912, Charlie felt more at home than he had on the first tour. New York was less bewildering and unfriendly than during his earlier sojourn, when he had lived in a brownstone back room above a dry cleaning shop off Forty-third Street. Even its skyscrapers — the forty-one-story Singer Building, the fifty-story Metropolitan Tower, the sixty-story Woolworth Building — which had "seemed ruthlessly arrogant and to care little for... ordinary people,"[20] now struck him as less menacing: "This time I felt at home in the States — a foreigner among foreigners, allied with the rest."[21]

Also, the novelty of travel had worn off. Every place where they played, he had played before. The time between performances hung more heavily on his hands, so Chaplin was able to settle down more seriously to his course of systematic self-improvement by reading with diligence. Like many a foreign-born immigrant before him, Charlie was learning the language of literacy. And in October of 1913, after another full year's touring, he put some of those recently acquired skills into practice by writing a letter to Syd. As it happened, he had some glad tidings of his own to share with his brother.

I have just to sign a contract for <u>150 Dollars a week</u>. 'Now comes the glad news.' Oh Sid I can see you!! Beaming now as you read this, those sparkling eyes of yours scanning this scrible and wondering what coming next. I'll tell you how the land lyes. I have had an offer from a moving picture company . . . the New York Motion Picture Co., a most reliable firm . . . they have about four companies . . . [including] 'Keystone' which I am about to joyne. I am to take Fred Mace place. He is a big man in the movies. So you bet they think a lot of me. . . . I went over to New York and saw them personaly, I had no idea they would pay any money but a pal of mine told me that Fred Mace was getting four hundred a week well I ask them for two hundred . . . Well we hagled for quite a long time and then I had to do all my business by writing them and you bet I put a good business letter together with the help of a dictionary. Finaly we came to this arrangement i.e. A year's contract. Salary for the first three months 150 per week and if I make good after three months 175 per week with no expences at all and in Los Angeles the whole time. I don't know whether you have seen any Keystone pictures but they are very funny, they also have some nice girls ect. Well that's the whole strength of it, so now you know. . . . Just think Sid £35 per week is not to laugh at and I will only want to work for about five years at that and then we are independent for life. I shall save like a son of a gun. . . . And if you know of any little ideas in the way of synaros ect don't forget to let me have them. Hoping you are in good health and Mother improving also I would love her and you to be over hear. Well we may some day when I get in right.
Love to Minnie
And yourself
Your loving Brother,
Charlie[22]

Let's Go to the Movies

Oh the moon shines bright
On Charlie Chaplin,
His boots are crackin',
For want of blackin'.
And his baggy trousers,
They want mendin',
Before they send him
To the Dardenelles.

B Y THE SPRING OF 1915, AS THE GREAT WAR ERUPTED in its first bloody year, endless columns of khaki-clad Aussies, Tommies, and Kiwis streamed along the docks and swept up the gangplanks of the huge Egypt-bound cruise ships and converted luxury liners that were waiting to transport them to the port of Alexandria. There, on the city's outskirts, they would bivouac in hastily erected tent cities while awaiting their final orders. To help keep step, set a lively marching pace, and lend a defiantly holiday mood of vagabond adventure at the outset of what, for many, would be a grim rendezvous with death on the crescent-shaped sands of Gallipoli, they sang that extemporized song whose words evoked the image of their informally adopted regimental mascot.

Back in London, during that 1915 spring, on the streets of Kennington and elsewhere, young children — the boys and girls who had just bid farewell to their fathers, uncles, brothers, friends, cousins, and neighbors as they marched off to the bloody Balkans — played on the pavements, chanting:

> One, two, three, four,
> Charlie Chaplin went to war.
> He taught the nurses how to dance,
> And this is what he taught them:
> Heel, toe, over we go,
> Heel, toe, over we go,
> Salute to the King
> And bow to the Queen
> And turn your back on the Kaiserin.

And when America later changed its tune from "I Didn't Raise My Boy to Be a Soldier" to "Over There," boys and girls on the sidewalks of New York would turn to that street game in which bluff Charlie-boy soldiers showed brave Army nurses how to waddle off to war as they too sought the healing comic solace of play to master the pain and grief of saying goodbye to close friends and family they might never see again.

The strong emotional identification that the children of Kennington and those Balkans-bound foot soldiers formed with Chaplin's early screen hero, the unsteady, flat-footed Little Tramp, was deeply rooted in the ordeals that each group was facing. But it also makes sense, from a broader sociological perspective, to think of their preoccupation with Charlie Chaplin as one reflection of a fashionable craze that was taking the Western world by storm in 1915. In New York, a chorus line of beautiful, tramp-costumed Ziegfeld girls with crepe moustaches pasted on their upper lips were delighting customers nightly with their rendition of "Those Charlie Chaplin Feet"; in Paris everybody who was anybody was learning to dance Le Charlot One-Step.

By 1915, a world already crazed by war was also in the process of finding escape in motion pictures. And after fifteen brief months and forty-one films, the new comedian was all the rage. Everywhere you went, Charlie was there to greet you: there were Chaplin dolls, toys, cartoons, games, comic strips, and books. Chaplin himself remarked that he couldn't even purchase a tube of toothpaste at his local drugstore without encountering the unblinking gaze of his own likeness, in one commercial incarnation or another, staring back at him over the counter.

In the small cities and towns of Middle America, freckle-faced boys — those compulsive collectors of slingshots, squirt rings, and other magical paraphernalia aimed at warding off that age group's sense of vulnerability — mailed off their nickels and dimes for Charlie Chaplin good-luck charms and magic horseshoes just like the one Charlie stuffed in his glove when he kayoed Spike Dugan in *The Champion*. An exemplar of brains over brawn, puny but sly underdog Charlie could outwit menacing hulks twice his size, which made him just the sort of trickster hero the youngsters admired. Undoubtedly their maiden aunts and bachelor uncles, when invited to Sunday dinner, groaned at the prospect of politely enduring yet another postprandial impersonation by their fully costumed nephews, who were all rehearsing for the Charlie Chaplin look-alike contests at the local nickelodeon.

For those in the motion-picture audience whose insecurities and chief preoccupations ran more toward members of the opposite sex, Charlie's cute but libidinally outrageous screen image permitted both psychological identification and imitation in the service of courtship or dalliance. Sallying forth cockily in their Charlie Chaplin getups to fraternity house costume parties and masked society balls, swains of all ages and shapes approached

maidens of their choice — sometimes with romantically bash-
ful but persistent fortitude, other times with aggressive mock-
licentiousness bordering on good-natured but incorrigible lechery.
If romance failed, they could shrug their shoulders with philosophical resignation, gracefully back-kick a cigarette butt, and shuffle
down life's highway without looking back — as Charlie had just
done in *The Tramp*, his first picture with an unhappy ending. If
love succeeded but the pair did not happen to win the plaster-
of-Paris statuette of Charlie being awarded as first prize at the
next week's local dance contest, no matter — the statues too
were for sale.

Advertisements in *Photoplay* magazine announced that pin-
ning a dollar bill to the coupon and mailing it off to Chicago
would command a figurine of the most famous clown in the
world. They were selling like hotcakes. As public opinion polls
throughout the world soon revealed, in some remote corners of
the globe the Little Tramp's graven image was becoming as well
known as Jesus Christ's, or better.[1]

The popularity of "The Moon Shines Bright on Charlie
Chaplin" spread swiftly from the Dardanelles to the Hindenburg
Line, where foot-slogging, battle-weary veterans of the European campaign, trudging through the mud and huddling in the
trenches, found themselves conjuring, to the tune of "Red
Wing," sweet memories of sitting as civilians in the peaceful Saturday afternoon darkness of their local nickelodeons and Bijoux
while images of Charlie Chaplin's familiar baggy-trousered, flat-
footed, scrappy Little Fellow flickered on the silver screen.

Behind the lines, in military hospitals, special vertical movie
projectors were being rigged to allow Chaplin's morale-boosting
Little Fellow to leap to life and waddle on the ceilings of surgical
and medical wards for those too weak or wounded to sit up in bed.
There were even physicians' case reports of the Little Tramp's
humorous screen image speeding the recuperation process of individual patients; sensation-hungry tabloid journalists took to re-

ferring to them as Chaplin's miracle cures. No less thoughtful a writer than Alexander Woollcott would conclude that "such a bearer of healing laughter . . . the world had never known."[2]

Almost from the start of his movie career, Chaplin appreciated that his screen character's instant popularity and universal appeal stemmed in large measure from his apparent ability to alleviate misery:

> In a world where so many people are troubled and unhappy, where women lead such dreary lives as my mother did when I was a boy, where men spend their days in hard unwilling toil and children starve as I starved in the London slums, laughter is precious. People want to laugh; they long to forget themselves for half an hour in the hearty joy of it. Every night on a hundred thousand motion-picture screens my floppy shoes and tricky cane and eloquent mustache were making people laugh, and they remembered them and came to laugh again. Suddenly, almost overnight, Charlie Chaplin became a fad, a craze.[3]

But after the initial thrill of overnight celebrity wore off, Chaplin would grow more circumspect and ambivalent as he came to realize that being the object of a fashionable craze posed the hazard of pursuit by admirers who behaved in a crazed fashion.

During the years that followed, there would be times when Chaplin's reaction to his screen character's enormous popularity and the resultant idolatry lavished on his actual person by vast crowds was tinged with distaste (and concern for his personal safety). On one such occasion, a return visit to London in 1921, after being mobbed by throngs of well-wishers including many thousands from his native slums, he confided to a friend, Thomas Burke:

> Oh, God, Tommy, isn't it pathetic — isn't it awful? That these poor people should hang round me and shout "God bless you, Charlie," and want to touch my overcoat, and laugh, and even

shed tears — I've seen 'em do it — if they can touch my hand. And why? Why? Because I made 'em laugh. Because I cheered 'em up. Cheered 'em up! Ugh! Say, Tommy, what kind of filthy world is this — that makes people lead such wretched lives that if anybody makes 'em laugh they want to kiss his overcoat, as though he were Jesus Christ raising 'em from the dead? Eh? *There's* a comment on life.[4]

Having managed to escape poverty and misery by creating the Little Tramp, Chaplin could find such encounters with members of his former social class disquieting. But it was not the pathos he perceived behind the crowd's collective identification with both his fictional character and the meteoric success story of his actual life that he found most upsetting.

If an archetype is, in a Jungian sense, an image or icon powerful enough to stir dormant communal emotions and, by doing so, unleash primordial group behavior, there were moments when the public's reaction to Charlie Chaplin the screen character and Charlie Chaplin the film star could be said to resemble that primitive behavior. Those mobs of fans with outstretched arms could be transformed, through their collective admiration — and equally passionate, unconscious envy — into hordes of souvenir-hunting scavengers swept up in a feeding frenzy.

On one occasion (the New York premier of a friend's movie) clothes were literally torn from Chaplin's back by admirers who, in their hunger for some memento of the rags-to-riches story of their movie star hero, seemed determined to return elegantly dressed Charlie to the abject and tattered aboriginal state of his Little Tramp:

The tide changed. I was swept back towards the entrance of the theatre. . . . My hat flew towards the heavens. It has never returned to me. I felt a draught. I heard machinery. A woman with a pair of scissors was snipping a piece from the seat of my trousers.

Another grabbed my tie and almost put an end to my suffering through strangulation. My collar was next. But they only got half of that. My shirt was pulled out. The buttons torn from my vest. My feet trampled on. My face scratched. . . . I kept insisting that I was Charlie Chaplin and that I belonged inside. . . . Insistence won. As though on a prearranged signal I felt myself lifted from my feet, my body inverted until my head pointed towards the center of the lobby and my feet pointed towards an electric sign advertising the Ziegfeld Roof. Then there was a surge and I moved over the heads of the crowd through the lobby.[5]

And inside those dream emporiums, image-hungry movie audiences suspended their disbelief and gorged themselves weekly, or even more frequently, on their favorite comedian, until the Little Tramp's essence was digested and assimilated into their own lives and daily routines and he felt as much a part of them as friends or family. So why not reach out and touch the actor who played Charlie Chaplin? What if he was pummeled and his clothes torn in the process? After all, their celluloid hero was an immortal slapstick god, invulnerable to the cuffs and blows and kicks of fate, fortune, and neighborhood policemen.

As children the world over have always known, clowns can be crushed, mangled, or strangled but never killed. No matter how dire Charlie's predicament at the end of one Keystone farce after another — being knocked unconscious (*Tango Tangles*), dynamited (*Dough and Dynamite*), clubbed over the head repeatedly with a cop's nightstick (*His Prehistoric Past*), "liquidated" by mock drowning on a sinking ship (*The Rounders*), or collapsing into an apparently fatal drunken stupor (*Face on the Barroom Floor*) — he could always be relied upon to resurrect himself by the following Saturday afternoon. The life-size cardboard image of the Little Tramp would be hauled again out of the box office and placed on the sidewalk in front of the neighborhood movie theater, announcing — like some miraculous second coming — the arrival of his latest and greatest celluloid incarnation with the sign caption "I am here to-day!" Singing in praise of their film god's comedy, children of privilege and slum urchins alike would eventually warble (to the tune of "Gentle Jesus"):

> Charlie Chaplin, meek and mild,
> Took a sausage from a child.
> When the child began to cry,
> Charlie slapped him in the eye.

A screen character whose transcendent appeal would still be compelling a full century after the birth of his creator, the Little Tramp had barely completed the first leg of his journey toward fame and fortune by the time those soldiers marched off to meet their fate on the shores of Gallipoli. Unlike the forgotten men who once sang his song, the Tramp's odyssey would eventually bring him to the ranks of Falstaff, Don Quixote, and a handful of other comic immortals who, ironically, the world remembers largely for their mock valor.

But on the rainy February afternoon of the Little Fellow's birth back in 1914, all of those developments lay in the future. That day the scrawny newcomer to the Keystone Film Company rummaged through the wardrobe department in the bungalow that served as the male actors' dressing room, borrowed a pair of Fatty Arbuckle's billowing pantaloons, trimmed down mountainous Mack Swain's prop moustache, slipped his delicate feminine feet into Ford Sterling's size-fourteen gunboats, and soon waddled onto the streets of Venice, California, where a children's soap box derby was in progress.

As the signs posted on the big red Pacific Electric trolleys that rattled and bumped their way across the Los Angeles city limits into the remote backcountry wilderness of Southern California reminded the passengers, shooting jackrabbits from the rear platform of the cars was strictly forbidden. It took three consecutive days of anxiously commuting back and forth on the Tropico Line, which ran all the way from his hotel to far-off, exotically tropical Glendale, before Chaplin finally gathered the resolve to physically enter Keystone Studio headquarters. The studio occupied an old farm in the formerly sleepy but now bustling trolley stop of Edendale. Edendale's wooden storefronts, quaint shacks, and lumberyards looked sufficiently frontierlike that the studio's previous occupant, Thomas Ince, had encountered no difficulty in producing a convincing series of cowboy one-reelers there before moving his home on the range to Santa Monica.

Each of the two preceding days Charlie had ventured no farther than the ramshackle green fence that demarcated the boundaries of the Keystone lot. He had lingered for half an hour at the "safe distance" of a street corner located directly across from the studio's Alessandro Street entrance, and then, unable to muster "the courage to go in,"[6] retreated from that alien environment to his digs at the Great Northern Hotel in downtown L.A., just a short walk from the old Empress Theatre where he had played so often with Alf and the rest of the Karno bunch. Filled with such "qualms about leaving the troupe in Kansas City"[7] a week earlier that he had wept in private after the final curtain on closing night, Charlie was still beset by misgivings as he wavered at the gates of Keystone and on the threshold of a radical change in career direction.

Chaplin's reservations were not just about bidding farewell to the small band of friends and countrymen with whom he had worked and toured in a foreign land for three years. Nor was he merely insecure over lapsing from seasoned veteran and well-established headliner to untested new kid on the block, and foreigner to boot. The "little Englisher" or "limey" comedian was what the back-slapping he-man gang of Keystone regulars would soon call him.[8] (Further, they would welcome the newcomer with their traditional practical joke, which consisted of electrically wiring the john seat in the male actors' dressing room with the studio's Ford generator.)

Professionally speaking, Chaplin was moving from an established and respected mainstream branch of the theatrical profession to what was still looked down on as a disreputable, vulgar form of cheap mass entertainment. By the end of 1913, America's burgeoning film industry was in fact beginning to emerge from its artistic infancy — a development in which Chaplin himself would be instrumental — but this was not a consideration in which the twenty-four-year-old music hall star could take comfort as he vacillated at the gates that December. Despite the indisputable logic of doubling his salary overnight, Chaplin retained traces of a popular prejudice still held by middle-class theatergoers and many actors as well: that abandoning an established stage career for the movies was professional suicide. As one film historian put it:

> There was good reason why the movies were held in contempt by polite society. The nickelodeons weren't quaint prototypes of the present-day neighborhood theatre, as they are often remembered. They were smelly, urine-stinking, unsanitary firetraps, tucked away in tenement districts, patronized only by immigrants and the poor, sometimes by prostitutes and pickpockets and other denizens of the dark. Nice people didn't go to nickelodeons, or if they did, they wore big hats and looked over their shoulders before entering. The stage community looked down on the movies. . . . the average movie ran ten minutes or less, enough time to sketch in a brief dramatic anecdote, but not long enough for any detailed plot or character development. Film acting wasn't real acting — it was making faces and funny gestures in front of a blackbox that added ten pounds to your waist and ten years to your face.[9]

As ambivalent about catering to the coarse appetites of nickel customers as he had once felt about pandering to the unsophisticated two-penny tastes of working-class stiffs in the music halls where he had been forced to play after leaving the Duke of York's, Chaplin was "not terribly enthusiastic about the Keystone type of comedy," which in his professional opinion was little more than "a crude mélange of rough-and-tumble." Still, having seen examples of Keystone's already famous productions before signing his contract — they were, as he mentioned in his letter to Syd, considered the best comedy films being made in the industry at that time — Charlie reassured himself: "A year at that racket and I could return to vaudeville an international star."[10] Undoubtedly it was a comforting rationalization to ponder as the Tropico trolley rumbled past exotically tropical palm, eucalyptus, acacia, pepper, and night-blooming jasmine on its way again to the Edendale studio.

Chaplin's first glimpse of Keystone occurred at the studio entrance at noon, just as a steady stream of carpenters and cameramen, errand boys and extras, costumed actors and actresses, including the Keystone Kops themselves, poured noisily onto Alessandro Street in search of their midday meals at the general store across the way. Desserts could be purchased at Greenburg's Bakery down the street, which, apart from feeding the hungry actors, did a thriving business supplying the studio with a never-ending stream of inedible prop "custard" pies (actually made of a paste that registered better on film) for Keystone's most famous trademark gag — a pie in the kisser. The incredible ambidextrous ease with which he could simultaneously splatter two opponents with pies in the puss as they charged him from opposite directions would soon earn Fatty Arbuckle recognition as Keystone's most valuable pastry thrower.

It was through that same studio gate that Keystone's other hallmark gag — the comic chase — periodically erupted in the form of wild pursuits by the Keystone Kops. Spilling out onto local streets and highways that had been made slick with a mixture of soapsuds and motor oil, a dazzling procession of paddy wagons, motorcycles, bicycles, baby buggies, tin lizzies, and flivvers slipped, slithered, and careened into one another, mowing down pedestrian stuntmen, knocking over water-spewing prop fire hydrants, and strewing comic policemen in the wake of their expertly choreographed near misses with Pacific Electric trolleys and speeding locomotives. (The breathtaking accuracy was a camera trick accomplished by shooting near collisions in reverse action and projecting the film backward to create the illusion of forward motion.)

As one might expect, public opinion among the citizens of Edendale was divided over the good-natured chaos and mayhem emanating from the fun factory in their midst. Keystone was clearly good for business, but the town's founding fathers were a stern band of God-fearing, Bible-toting ex-farmers from the Midwest who had selected the name Edendale as a scriptural tribute for the garden paradise that had been their sleepy hamlet and many of them were less than sanguine over the prospect of having the town overrun by "movies" — a nickname applied to those blasphemous East Coast actors themselves.

While that raucous lunchtime gang of "movies" spilling out of the studio was already enough to stimulate Chaplin's worst fears of crude assembly-line practices within, his first glimpse of its inner sanctum intensified his anxiety. On his third try — "dragging myself by the collar"[11] — Charlie forced himself through the gates, and into a sleepy bungalow whose rustic facade belied the madness of the mass-production operation going on just beyond:

A glare of light and heat burst upon me. The stage, a yellow board floor covering at least two blocks, lay in a blaze of sunlight, intensified by dozens of white canvas reflectors stretched overhead. On it was a wilderness of "sets" — drawing-rooms, prison interiors, laundries, balconies, staircases, caves, fire-escapes, kitchens, cellars. Hundreds of actors were strolling about in costume; carpenters were hammering away at new sets; five companies were playing before five clicking cameras. There was a roar of confused sound — screams, laughs, an explosion, shouted commands, pounding, whistling, the bark of a dog. The air was thick with the smell of new lumber in the sun, flash-light powder, cigarette smoke.[12]

There, on that infinitely adaptable open-air stage, in the intense glare of a hot Southern California sun whose ovenlike radiance was magnified, reflected, and diffused in order to ensure that figures in dizzying motion would register crisply on the low-emulsion film of the day, at an average rate of two to three per week, some 140 movies of exceedingly variable artistic quality had already been ground out in the course of the year just ending, 1913.

But the demands of the moviegoing public for Keystone's product were so insatiable, and the box-office rewards so compelling, that the expenditure of time and effort required to produce motion pictures with higher technical values (finer photography, better shot matching, tighter editing) or more thoughtful construction (character development, plot continuity) was not something the director of the Edendale studio was likely to consider seriously. A shanty Irish former construction worker who had been employed at the American Iron Works in East Berlin, Connecticut, before making his show business debut in New York City's tenderloin district playing the hind end of a horse on the burlesque stage, Michael Sinnott, aka Mack Sennett, was supremely confident that his own working-class tastes faithfully reflected what America's working-class audiences wanted to see. According to Keystone's leading comedienne (and Mack's sometime girlfriend), a sassy Staten Island girl by the name of Mabel Normand, the big lug's crude sensibilities made her think of "a flatfoot store detective"[13] when they had first met back East five years earlier at the old Biograph Studio.

Anxious to impress that pretty, dark-eyed, sixteen-year-old artist's model with the sexy gams, twenty-eight-year-old Mack had boasted to Mabel of his plans to start a comedy studio of his own, hinting that there might be a place for her in those operations. And with characteristic Sennett braggadocio, Mack announced that he was preparing for his life's goal by learning all there was to know about moviemaking from his good friend D. W. Griffith. While any claim of a deep personal intimacy or shared artistic vision with that lanky, hawk-beaked, aristocratically aloof Southerner was pure blarney on Mack's part — Griffith would use adjectives like "burly," "good-natured," and "bear-like" in the characteristic detachment with which he later remembered Sennett as a character actor who had reminded him of someone's "idiot brother,"[14] a low comedy role in which D.W. typecast him on several occasions — it was also true that, appearances aside, Mack was no dummy. Quick to recognize Griffith's as yet undiscovered genius, that crude but highly intelligent Son of St. Anthony made up his mind to pump the reserved and humorless Son of the Confederacy for as much cinematic wisdom as he could get.

On discovering that Griffith loved to unwind at the end of his sixteen-hour workdays by walking from Biograph's East Fourteenth Street brownstone on Movie Exchange Row to his apartment on East Thirty-seventh Street, Mack developed a sudden yen for hiking:

> When Griffith walked, I walked. I fell in, matched strides, and asked questions.
> . . . We used to . . . wander the streets, and talk about the future of motion pictures.
> "I want to put together full-length stories," he would say. "Not merely little scenes such as we photograph now. . . .
> "Writers do it. It's done on the stage. Why not in movies?"
> . . . I learned all I ever learned by standing around, watching people who knew how, by pumping Griffith, and thinking it over.
> I would have pumped anybody. It was sheer good fortune that made it possible for me to pump a genius.[15]

Hannah Chaplin (stage name Lily Harley), circa 1885, at the height of her beauty. The loss of her mental faculties in 1903 devastated fourteen-year-old Charlie. (Courtesy Jeffrey Vance Collection)

Charlie Chaplin Sr., 1885. His father's premature death from severe alcoholism affected young Charlie profoundly. (Photograph by H. T. Reed, courtesy Jeffrey Vance Collection)

The Lion Comique, early 1890s. Chaplin Sr., a famous stage actor in his day, portrayed himself as an elegant man-about-town with a fondness for the bottle and the ladies. "I can't remember a time when I wasn't trying to follow in my father's footsteps," Chaplin said. (Courtesy Jeffrey Vance Collection)

Center, circled, Chaplin at age seven, at the Central London Poor Law School at Hanwell, 1897. "My childhood ended at the age of seven," Chaplin once told a reporter. (Courtesy Jeffrey Vance Collection)

Center, in bowler hat, Chaplin with Casey's Court Circus Company, 1906. He was the star of the company. (Courtesy Jeffrey Vance Collection)

Young Chaplin impersonating Dr. Walford Bodie, a famous music hall medical charlatan who "cured" patients with electricity and hypnosis, 1906. This was one of Chaplin's first solo comedy sketches in *Casey's Court Circus*. (Courtesy Jeffrey Vance Collection)

Chaplin arrived in Los Angeles in late 1913 when Hollywood was still a dusty farm town and Beverly Hills little more than an undeveloped sagebrush wilderness full of jackrabbits and coyotes, an image he captured here in *The Idle Class*, 1921. (Courtesy Roy Export)

Chaplin in his first film, *Making a Living*, 1914, in which he plays an impecunious charmer. Chaplin's character bears a striking resemblance to Ella Shields's famous Burlington Bertie, who also sported a monocle and cane, pleaded an empty belly, and projected the false facade of a man of the world. (Courtesy Jeffrey Vance Collection)

Chaplin, age twenty-six, circa 1915. *Charlie Chaplin's Own Story*, narrated that year, was a cavalier concoction quite unlike *My Autobiography* a half-century later. (Courtesy Jeffrey Vance Collection)

Mack Sennett and Keystone Studios in 1916. Chaplin made thirty-five shorts for Sennett during the first year of their working relationship, and the Little Tramp debuted in Chaplin's second Sennett film, *Kid Auto Races*. (Courtesy *Los Angeles Herald-Examiner* and Los Angeles Public Library)

Sennett advertising for one of Chaplin's shorts, *Dough and Dynamite*, 1914. (Courtesy Jeffrey Vance Collection)

Birth of the Tramp, circa 1915. Chaplin's evolving screen character parodied and memorialized his father, but he warned his fellow actors, "You're liable to kill your enthusiasm if you delve too deeply into the psychology of the characters you are creating." (Courtesy Jeffrey Vance Collection)

The Champion, 1915. Chaplin's screen character developed gradually into a comic Everyman underdog. (Courtesy Jeffrey Vance Collection)

The Immigrant, 1917, Chaplin's comic valentine to the America Dream.
(Courtesy Jeffrey Vance Collection)

Brothers in arms, 1918. Charlie and Sydney Chaplin on the set of *The Immigrant*. After their mother's hospitalization, Sydney became Charlie's legal guardian when Charlie was only fourteen. A music hall star in his own right, Sydney helped Charlie get his first big break in show business and later put his career on hold to act as Charlie's financial manager and advisor. "If Sydney had not returned to London, I might have become a thief. . . . I might have been buried in a pauper's grave," Chaplin confessed. (Courtesy Jeffrey Vance Collection)

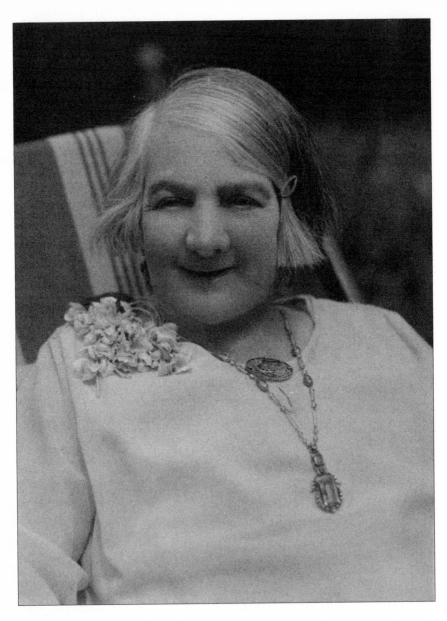

Hannah Chaplin, circa 1926. Though her beauty had been lost two decades before, she was now comfortable after a life marked by neurosyphilis, severe malnutrition, and chronic physical exhaustion. (Courtesy Roy Export)

Final scene from *City Lights*, 1931. The theme of rescuing and redeeming fallen women — stand-ins for his mother — runs throughout Chaplin's films. Eminent film critic James Agee said this scene, in which Chaplin rescues a blind flower girl from poverty, was "enough to shrivel the heart to see," and called it "the greatest piece of acting and the highest moment in movies." (Courtesy Roy Export)

A Chaplin family Christmas card, 1964. *Counterclockwise, from center:* Oona O'Neill Chaplin, Charlie Chaplin, and their children Josephine, Victoria, Eugene, Jane, Annette, and Christopher. Absent from the photo are their two oldest children, Geraldine and Michael. (Courtesy Yves Debraine)

Although there was no way then he could have appreciated it, it was likewise Charlie Chaplin's equally "sheer good fortune" not only to arrive at a critical point but to have the opportunity to "pump" the man who had just finishing pumping the man whose pioneering imagination, more than anyone else's, was directly responsible for the revolutionary artistic, economic, social, and cultural changes about to take place in the movie industry.

Mack would later sum up his five-year association with Griffith as "my day school, my adult education program, my university."[16] And with a smart click of the heels and courtly bow, Erich von Stroheim would deliver his own estimate of such a priceless educational opportunity: "For you, Mr. Griffith, I would work for a ham sandwich a day."[17] While at Keystone — paying Chaplin double his Karno salary — Mack Sennett would distill what he had just learned from the master and provide a completely untutored Charlie Chaplin with a highly condensed, state-of-the-art, one-year crash course in all aspects of filmmaking.

"There's another sausage," Griffith is reputed to have remarked after one of his 450 films rolled off the assembly line during his six-year stint at Biograph from 1908 to 1913.[18] Roughly 15 percent of that output was comedy, a fact generally overlooked in view of Griffith's subsequent lack of interest in the genre. By March of 1911, D.W.'s indifference was sufficiently strong that he gladly turned over the directorial responsibility for almost all of Biograph's slapsticks to a very eager Mack Sennett who, in addition to serving as Griffith's faithful walking companion, had already written and/or directed a handful of immemorable half-reelers and acted in about fifty Griffith films, including some twenty-five comedies. (A second-rate, one-note comedian, Mack typically played the rube, hayseed, yokel, bumpkin, and, of course, dumb department-store gumshoe — the part he happened to be playing when Mabel first saw him.)

Griffith's reluctant descent, from a creative inclination to zoom and soar gracefully in the ethers of the heroic, back to the requirements of earthbound, seat-of-the-pants low comedy, was an artistic compromise forced upon him by his new employer's need to remain competitive with other filmmakers by furnishing America's moviegoing public with programs containing a broad range of subjects, varying from serious drama, including old-fashioned melodrama, to cops-and-robbers adventure and cowboy-and-Indian westerns, as well as broad slapstick farces. Half-reelers ran some five hundred feet and lasted seven to ten minutes, with full-reelers and two-reelers of commensurate length. Theater programs were generally an hour long.

Arriving on the New York filmmaking scene near the end of 1907, at the height of the Nickelodeon Era, when many movies were little more than crudely assembled entertainments for the illiterate and the uneducated, projected on bedsheets tacked up on the rear walls of improvised storefront theaters in working-class neighborhoods and shown to the musical accompaniment of scratchy gramophones and tinkly secondhand pianos, D. W. Griffith had caught a train to the Bronx with his first film script in hand. Making an instinctive beeline for the one man, Edwin Porter, who had produced anything of notable artistic quality in American film up to that time (*The Great Train Robbery*, 1903), Griffith had been crestfallen to have his own first effort rejected by the Edison Studio.

Within a month, however, he had moved downtown to one of Edison's major competitors, Biograph, where, in addition to acting and writing, he began to direct. The full name of his new employer was the American Mutoscope and Biograph Company, a reference to those old hand-cranked movie viewers, and the studio was also in the business of keeping America's penny arcades well supplied with their product. Griffith's bosses had made it clear that they expected him to tell stories in pictures with a simplicity that anyone coming in off the street would be capable of understanding.

Griffith had grown up in a family in which Shakespeare's plays were read aloud; he had come to films from a failed career attempt as a dramatic actor on the legitimate stage. His literary tastes ran to Dickens (his favorite), Tolstoy, Poe, Browning, Twain, R. L. Stevenson, James Fenimore Cooper, and Jack London — to name but a few of the many writers whose lively tales he would adapt to the taste and the grasp of Biograph's nickel-and-dime customers. In an incredibly feverish five-year period of trial and error, translating into film the narrational techniques of other people's novels, short stories, plays, poems, and operas — in addition to the many tales he wrote himself — Griffith synthesized the basic storytelling grammar of cinema as we know it today.

The term "synthesized" is chosen advisedly, because as film historians are quick to point out, almost every narrative device Griffith employed had already been stumbled upon, if barely utilized, by filmmakers before him. Working without such modern aids as formal shooting scripts or storyboards, composing shots and sequences and entire tales from his head as he went along, Griffith refined the techniques of his colleagues and predecessors until at last his creativity could no longer be stimulated by the previously useful exercise of compressing entire epics into half-hour films. After seeking permission from Biograph to make his first feature film and being refused, Griffith went off on his own in 1913 — Sennett having left to start Keystone in August of the preceding year.

That "full-length" story Griffith most wanted to tell, and for which he is most remembered, was a legendary one that he later recollected having first overheard in bits and snatches during mealtime conversations when he was a small boy playing under the dinner table of his family's rural Kentucky home. Griffith's father, Colonel Jacob Griffith — also known as Thundering Jake and Roaring Jake for his powers of oratory — loved to spin "boozy yarns,"[19] especially of his very real adventures as a Confederate cavalry officer who had been wounded on multiple occasions.

Shiloh and Chickamauga were household words, and Sherman's march to the sea loomed as large in the ten-year-old boy's imagination as did the sudden death at that time of his father, "the one person I really loved the most in all my life."[20]

Informed by their family physician that his father had died of peritonitis caused by the dehiscence of an old, poorly cicatrized war wound — allegedly sutured with inferior thread as a result of the Union's punishing naval blockade on Southern shipping — the small boy coped as best he could with that "blow out of the past,"[21] whose bitter memory he tucked away alongside his daddy's treasured tales.

Some thirty years later, having finally earned the artistic freedom to give full rein to his passions and his cinematic imagination, Griffith would select a novel, Thomas Dixon's *The Clansman*, in which he would unconsciously embed those memories of his father to create a monumental historical evocation of the War Between the States. As the title of that book implied, Griffith's incredibly powerful film — in the outraged eyes of black leaders and liberal intellectuals alike — was rabidly pro-Southern and poisonously racist in its attitudes. Truly astonished and hurt by the vehemence with which that small but vocal minority denounced him for reopening a nation's wounds — to the point of demonstrating and picketing as well as raising the fear of race riots and circulating "crazy talk of dynamite"[22] — a by then unstoppable Griffith would respond by making his very next film a passionate indictment of other people's intolerance, of course including the moral hypocrisy of supposedly liberal do-gooders and social reformers.

But message aside, Griffith's groundbreaking *Birth of a Nation* would be hailed as an infant industry's first great work of art and honored with the first screening of a motion picture in the White House, in February 1915 — just as those Dardanelles-bound convoys set sail for the port of Alexandria. Not only would Griffith's opus serve as a magnet to draw respectable middle-class audiences into America's movie theaters, broadening forever the economic and social base of film by demonstrating conclusively that for as many as forty-eight consecutive weeks, in clean, handsomely appointed theaters located in good neighborhoods, respectable, well-educated people were willing to part with as much as two dollars of their hard-earned money for reserved prime-time seats to witness what they considered, for the first time, a cultural event on a par with the legitimate stage. As Woodrow Wilson put it, "It is like writing history with Lightning."[23]

But back in early 1914, while D. W. Griffith labored feverishly to create his brainchild out of the legacy of his childhood, an equally industrious Charlie Chaplin — who had just begun to learn the ropes by working as a comedian for the empire-building, crude ape of a man who had only recently finished picking up the tricks of the trade from D.W. himself — was about to dip into his own paternal legacy and invent that screen character whose image would, almost overnight, become legendary.

Birth of a Tramp

He could fall, trip, stumble, somersault, slap, and make faces.
These were stock-in-trade items which we could use.

— Mack Sennett[1]

H E HAD ONLY GLIMPSED CHAPLIN ONCE — onstage in his "Limey make-up and costume"[2] — before luring him to the West Coast by doubling his salary, and when they finally met in person that December 1913, crass and brassy Mack Sennett made no attempt to hide his doubts over his new star's apparent youthful inexperience. "What I had seen in New York was a deft, experienced, knockabout, roughneck, middle-aged comedian of the English music-hall type. In Los Angeles I met a boy."[3] Although Chaplin was now twenty-four, he still looked like that unimpressive and underfed teenage actor whom the Guv'nor had intimidated five years earlier. By Charlie's own estimate, he "looked about eighteen. A callow youth."[4]

"I thought you were a much older man," Mack griped.

"I can make up as old as you like," Charlie replied.[5]

Since Mack (on Mabel's advice) had spent a hefty bundle to hire the "little Englisher" to replace Keystone's departing principal comedian, a veteran ex–circus clown by the name of Ford Sterling, his tactlessly expressed concerns over Charlie's youthfulness were understandable enough. Each man had trepidations of his own.

Mack was afraid he had trapped himself in an expensive one-year contract with a wet-behind-the-ears adolescent comedian. Those fears were aggravated when the "scared little Englishman"[6] failed to report for work for several days. It took a phone call from Sennett himself, demanding to know why he had not shown up, before Charlie timidly inched his way through the Keystone gates at 1712 Alessandro Street and presented himself to "Mr. Sennett," the formal title by which he continued to address his new employer for the next several months. Unaccustomed to such deference, Sennett was used to being called Boss or Mack by his roughneck gang of Keystone regulars, who referred to him behind his back as the Old Man.

They were a motley collection of circus clowns, steeplejacks, sign painters, trolley conductors, ex-prizefighters, vaudeville vets, and acrobats. Their snappy vernacular language, wisecracking informality, and back-slapping camaraderie stood in stark contrast to the comparatively polite expressions of good fellowship expressed in Charlie's former Karno troupe.

Sennett took Chaplin on a brief tour of his bustling fun factory, which was producing several one- and two-reelers at the time. As they walked through the confusion and mayhem, Mack outlined his commercially successful formula for grinding out slapstick films: "We have no scenario — we get an idea, then follow the natural sequence of events until it leads up to a chase, which is the essence of our comedy."[7]

Escalating the pace of a comedy sketch until it exploded in nonsensical mayhem and a wow ending was not new to Charlie. Although the cramped confines of theatrical stages did not permit full-scale chases, Keystone style, he had led the *Mumming Birds* cast in unruly food-throwing, clothes-ripping riots at final curtain, night after night. But the world-without-walls of an open-air silent film studio in exotically tropical Southern California bore such a remote resemblance to the tight, boxlike, proscenium arch intimacy of darkened London music halls that — as he listened to Sennett's pet chase formula — the Cockney comedian was at a temporary loss to translate Karno into Keystone or vice versa.

Mack's larger-than-life, wide-open-spaces, shot-on-location, high-speed vehicular version of a standard crash comedy ending felt unfamiliar to Charlie and filled him with misgivings over his new guv'nor's lack of subtlety. Or maybe his qualms had more to do with America and Americans in general. From his first day in New York, there had been something disquieting about the hurried rhythms and throbbing urgency of life in the United States, which those highly popular Keystone comedies embodied and typified.

He had felt instantly "alien to this slick tempo" of a nation on the move and a people in a hurry. Americans' fast-paced lives, clipped speech, and brusque manners made him "uncomfortable for fear I might stutter and waste their time." A sensitive observer of other people's idiosyncrasies and an astute student of tempo and movement, Charlie had been quick to notice how the lowliest shoeshine boy, soda jerk, or bartender self-importantly performed the tasks and routines of his job like a "hopped-up juggler" with "a fury of speed."[8]

Coming from a tight little island whose lack of an expanding frontier and rigid class boundaries imposed more restrictive rhythms on its inhabitants, Chaplin was fascinated by the stylized manner and snappy pace with which Americans moved in their land of infinite social and geographic mobility. The manic energy of their entrepreneurial tempo reflected the national obsession with getting ahead and a Horatio Alger optimism. Or as Charlie put it, "The American is an optimist preoccupied with hustling dreams, an indefatigable tryer. He hopes to make a quick killing. Hit the jackpot! Get out from under! Sell out! Make the dough and run! Get into another racket!"[9]

Celebrating the modern industrial age and bidding farewell to the passing of pastoral agrarianism, twentieth-century urban America was abandoning the stately waltz of the 1890s in favor of the jerky two-step. And if the go-getter tempo of modern life in the United States ran like a Krazy Keystone Komedy, the resemblance was not accidental. The hopped-up pace at which Sennett's fun factory churned out 140 crude slapstick films in its first year occurred even as Henry Ford's Model T's were beginning to roll off his Dearborn plant's first assembly lines. The two events reflected that same Yankee ingenuity for mass production. The Rube Goldberg miracle of miles of tin lizzies or miles of near-identical celluloid one- and two-reelers was virtually the same. As Mack put it, Keystone movies sold "like gingham for girls' dresses — at so much per yard."[10]

The tightly formularized make-believe world of slapstick that Sennett slickly packaged in can after can of chase films as they rolled off his Edendale assembly line bore the unmistakable stamp of the studio-factory in which they were so rapidly shot and assembled. Burlesque-trained Sennett specialized in creating a wacky mechanical universe in which his clowns were reduced to the antlike scale and robot status of windup toys. He relied on long shots and far shots to establish this perspective cinematographically and also resorted to trick photography devices like animation, stop-motion, double exposures, and reversed film to enhance the effect. He had no time for subtle but slow-moving character comedy.

What gave Mack's comedy chases their distinctive flavor was his unique technique for creating the illusion that his film actors walked or ran at a high speed, by artificially causing their bodies to hop in a jerky fashion onscreen, more like krazy self-propulsion machines than real people. This special effect was accomplished by undercranking the camera intentionally. When those sequences were later projected at a normal rate, Sennett's marionettes spilled and somersaulted higgledy-piggledy across America's movie screens in apparent defiance of the laws of logic and gravity. Never giving spectators time to relax or to notice holes in a story, Mack believed that "once we stop to let anybody analyze us, we're sunk."[11]

The signature cutting-room rhythms that he achieved by rapidly alternating shots of pursued and pursuing comic chase figures at an ever-increasing tempo, coupled with his special trick of removing every fourth frame, came to be known as Keystone editing. Not surprisingly, almost all of this technical emphasis on speed derived its original inspiration from the breakneck pace of D. W. Griffith's famous Biograph editing with its much more skillful portrayal of smooth-flowing, natural actions as they gracefully unfolded through the combined use of crosscutting and parallel editing in his suspenseful last-minute rescues.

Just as Marcel Duchamp's fragmented, stop-action, co-simultaneous depiction of superimposed layers of motion in his *Nude Descending a Staircase* in the New York Armory Show that year reflected the increasing speed-consciousness of modern industrial European society, so D. W. Griffith had captured the hectic beat of his world and successfully translated its frenzied tempo into the cinematic time equivalent of ragtime.

Having taken the pulse of the nation, it was Griffith, not Sennett, who originally discovered the hypnotic fascination created by steadily quickening a film's tempo until it crescendoed in a spellbinding climax. Mack's commercial genius lay in his homespun comic transposition of his former walking companion's dazzling artistic genius by artificially souping up film speed in a slapstick world and choreographing his clowns in those slam-bang pileup finishes for which he became famous.

A comedian's ability to capsize convincingly was of far greater importance to Sennett than his talent as a comic actor.

Walking in off the street and asking for a tryout, decked out in "white pumps, white trousers, white shirt, blue bow tie, blue coat" and straw boater, natty Fatty Arbuckle — a sylph who tipped the scales at 265 pounds — had been hired on the spot to apprentice as a Keystone Kop because he could do "a backward somersault as gracefully as a girl tumbler."[12]

Nine months later, it was Chaplin's acrobatic agility that Sennett remembered when, facing that vacancy in his troupe of loonies, he decided to lure the little limey to California. But what was so uncharacteristic about Mack's offer of a hundred and fifty bucks a week, guaranteed, was that he was recruiting a completely unproven film talent into his organization at the starting salary of an established principal without so much as a screen test. All the other comedians on the roster — Mabel, Roscoe, Mack Swain, Chester Conklin, and Ford Sterling included — had worked their way up from the ranks in pay and status at Biograph or Keystone. To outsiders, it might have appeared to be a case of Mack's well-known gambler's instinct triumphing over his equally notorious penny-pinching ways. But as Sennett put it, he offered Chaplin such a princely sum because he had all the right moves.

Sennett understood that the financial soundness of that investment could not be tested without additional training. It took six weeks before Charlie attempted his first film. During those early days, Mack remembered him as "a shy little Britisher who was abashed and confused by everything that had anything to do with motion pictures,"[13] while Chaplin recalled:

> For days I wandered around the studio, wondering when I would start work. Occasionally I would meet Sennett crossing the stage, but he would look through me, preoccupied. I had an uncomfortable feeling that he thought he had made a mistake in engaging me which did little to ameliorate my nervous tension.[14]

Chester Conklin's description of Chaplin during this orientation period was "a serious little fellow, very curious, always listening and observing and saying practically nothing except to ask a few pointed and professional questions. He watched everybody all the time."[15]

Chaplin discovered that virtually every aspect of filmmaking required a major adjustment to his theatrical technique. Even the greasepaint was different. Dismayed to learn that the flesh tones and broad character lines of traditional stage makeup registered a garish gray on film shot in the bright glare of a California sun, Charlie was "bowled over" by his first glimpse of his image on the silver screen, exclaiming, "It caw'nt be. Is that possible? How extr'ordin'ry. Is it really me?"[16]

As accustomed as he was to commandeering stage space in his graceful impersonations of klutziness, it took every ounce of concentration and effort he could muster to convey with his movements an appearance of naturalness and relaxed spontaneity, while constantly reminding himself to stay at all times within the rigidly defined limits of the camera's range in order to remain in focus.

He found Keystone's production methods equally disorienting. Scenes were shot out of chronological sequence, piecemeal. Rushes were viewed, confusingly, in negative (black face, white moustache) rather than the more visually recognizable positive print form of ordinary photographs. And in certain scenes, Charlie was dismayed to discover, actors were expected to react convincingly to imaginary off-camera characters instead of to live fellow performers, whose partnering might enhance their performances.

Attempting to do his funniest business in front of an impassive recording device was unnerving for an actor whose years of live performance experience had trained him to instinctively play to a house. Instead of the familiar feedback of the audience's laughter to help time gags, and an intuitive sense of the mood of the crowd to gauge the pace and build of his material, Chaplin found himself confronted with the impersonal click and whir of the camera gearbox and the cyclopean fish-eye stare of its distracting "round black lens," which "seemed like a great eye watching me."[17] (After he got the hang of it, he would, of course, be enormously relieved never to have to face a live audience again.)

Instead of providing Chaplin with the benefit of his own personal tutelage, or at least giving him a sympathetic director who could teach him the ropes and encourage him to improvise, Sennett threw Charlie to the wolves. Going off on location to supervise Keystone's first unit, which was shooting a Mabel Normand comedy at the time, Mack assigned Chaplin to Henry Lehrman, the departing director of his second unit.

Lehrman's inherent tendency to browbeat actors was aggravated by the fact that he was then in a hurry to wind up his commitment to Keystone. He had an offer from Universal to become a producer like Sennett, with the prospect of eventually establishing his own film company, and his vanity was at a peak. Filled with self-important dreams of becoming a movie mogul, the arrogant, ambitious director was in no mood to answer questions or take suggestions from a newcomer.

Around the Keystone lot, and throughout the industry, the former trolley conductor and self-styled impresario was better known as Pathé Lehrman. It was a nickname that D. W. Griffith had personally bestowed in recognition of the brashness with which he had attempted to bluff his way onto a Biograph set with a phony French accent and equally false claim that he'd worked in Europe for prestigious Pathé Frères. But with less irony and much more resentment, the actors and stuntmen at Lehrman-KO (Knock Out) Studio would later redub him Suicide Lehrman, a nickname that testified to the reckless indifference he consistently displayed for their physical safety. A technically competent but second-rate disciple of the Mack Sennett school of high-speed slapstick, Pathé considered film actors dispensable commodities and liked to brag about the fact that "he got all his laughs from mechanical effects and film cutting."[18]

Apart from enjoying the historical distinction of directing Charlie Chaplin in his first movie, *Making a Living*, a film that he later admitted to spitefully butchering in order to teach Chaplin a lesson because he "knew too much,"[19] Henry Lehrman is best remembered for the equally malicious delight he took in helping to wreck Roscoe Arbuckle's career. Roscoe had suddenly fallen from grace and was being accused unjustly of drunkenly raping and accidentally killing an aspiring starlet by rupturing her bladder during a wild Labor Day gin blast and sex spree in a suite at the St. Francis Hotel in San Francisco. Publicity-seeking Lehrman was more than happy to oblige sensation-hungry Hearst journalists in their scathing pretrial indictment of Arbuckle in the tabloids of the day.

He furnished them with false denunciations of his old pal's moral character. For flabbergasted Fatty fans, who found it hard to imagine their boyishly innocent, chubby comic hero as physically or temperamentally capable of behaving in such an obscene manner, Lehrman would lend considerable credibility to that image by depicting Roscoe as a lecherous swine whose infamous Sabine forays into the actresses' dressing room had been a regular occurrence at Keystone.

Before starting to shoot *Making a Living*, Chaplin had been instructed to select his own character costume. He chose a standard man-about-town getup which he fashioned out of an old Karno outfit. It consisted of a tall silk hat, a frock coat with matching trousers, starched cuffs with an equally stiff bib dickey and formal batwing collar, around which was fastidiously knotted a fashionably billowing cravat. To heighten the effect, Charlie selected a flowing moustache and those twin insignias of every strutting and peering gentleman on the Strand who is — or aspires to be — a member of the upper class: a walking stick and a monocle on a chain.

When the shooting began, Chaplin even managed to squeeze in a highly condensed but thoroughly polished pantomime vignette of the particular type of elegant swell he had in mind. Since his portrayal occurred in the film's opening sequence, at a point when his screen character is first being introduced to the audience, it would have been next to impossible, even for scissor-happy Henry Lehrman, to completely extirpate our first glimpse of the considerable skills as a comic character actor that Charlie Chaplin had already developed at this earliest point in his film career.

But after those revealing opening moments, the production plunged headlong into a typically fast-paced chain of slapstick events, Keystone-style. With the exception of one other brief bit of retained but badly mangled funny business that Charlie managed to squeeze in (see below), a very impatient Lehrman allotted Chaplin no time for character comedy. The entire film was shot in three days. And in what amounted to a curious case of art mirroring life, or vice versa, the film's contrived plot, such as it was, bore an uncanny resemblance to the real-life drama unfolding on the Keystone set.

Taking the other principal role in *Making a Living* — in addition to directing it — Henry Lehrman played the part of Chaplin's rival in a competition that was as hard fought offscreen as on. Cast as the villain in the piece, Charlie played an impoverished English swell who succeeds in stealing Henry's girl by impressing her with his phony urbane manners and elegant dress. Aware that Chaplin is actually broke and therefore no gentleman at all, at least in his eyes, Henry attempts to win back his girl by denouncing Charlie. But the young lady, already smitten, refuses to listen and sends Henry packing.

Coincidences multiply. Henry and Charlie next end up competing for the same job as a newspaper reporter. Once again

Henry attempts to denounce his rival: "He is a bum!" a subtitle informs their prospective employer. Affecting gentlemanly outrage at such heinous slander, Charlie strikes an elegant pose of righteous indignation by dashing his walking stick to the ground — only to discover that he is holding it wrong side up (shades of his Bodie impersonation).

Choosing this inopportune moment, a loose cuff from Charlie's shirt lazily tumbles down the full length of his cane. Undaunted, Charlie prepares to defend his sullied honor by challenging Henry to a fisticuff duel.

Stripping for action, Charlie begins to remove his frock coat only to reveal the true extent of his poverty: he doesn't even own a shirt. The cuff tumbled because it was unattached. Disgracefully exposed as a false swell whose surface pretensions to gentility rest on a sartorial understructure as weak and artificial as the moral foundations of his character, Charlie makes a hasty exit from the newspaper office.

After that deflating departure, Charlie manages to steal Henry's reporter's camera and run off with his rival's exclusive photos of a news scoop, which he peddles as his own. The rest of the story — at least half the film's footage — is spent running. Henry chases Charlie. An irate husband of an innocent woman bystander chases Henry. A comic policeman chases Charlie. A highspeed Pacific Electric Line trolley chases Charlie and Henry as they chase and fight one another. As far as Henry Lehrman was concerned, the film's plot was only ever intended as a vehicle for comic chase scenes.

While repeated, slower viewings (on a hand-turned Steenbeck flatbed editing machine at the Library of Congress) permit more considered analysis of the specific type of British music hall pantomime and social class comedy that Chaplin was attempting to insert, a single normal-speed viewing reveals the film Henry Lehrman succeeded in making: a fast-paced, typically American slapstick tale of two rival go-getters struggling for a fast buck and fighting over a pretty girl. As to their equally hard-fought offscreen competition, what provoked Pathé's ire and his resolve to take vengeance in the cutting room was the way the earnest little Englishman innocently kept offering Lehrman help, by suggesting bits of funny business for other members of the cast.

"When I saw the finished film it broke my heart," Charlie ruefully recalled, "for the cutter had butchered it beyond recognition, cutting into the middle of all my funny business."[20] And after Mack saw the film, Mabel recalled, he "screamed that he had hooked himself a dead one."[21] But attempting to calm down his even more nervous business partners back in New York after they previewed Chaplin's first outing, Sennett reassured them that it was the same old problem they encountered with each new Keystone comedian: "We haven't got his character right yet. . . . Or his make-up and costume."[22]

Equally filled with misgivings over his disappointing first effort, Charlie confided to Chester Conklin: "I'm going to get out of this business. It's too much for me. I'll never catch on. It's too fast. I can't tell what I'm doing." Then, shifting part of the blame onto the crudeness of the medium itself, Charlie rationalized, "I'm not sure any real actor should get caught posing for the flickahs." Taking pity, Chester recalled,

> I told him to stick it out. I told him he was going to be something very big in motion pictures. I lied like hell. I didn't think any such thing. I can't claim I had the foresight to see Chaplin's future. But I have as tender a heart as the next roughneck and I couldn't help trying to cheer up that doleful Englishman. His criticisms of movies were nothing but whistling in the dark. Charlie was humiliated and needed encouragement. I talked him out of quitting.[23]

As Sennett reminded the management at Keystone financial headquarters, it was standard procedure at the California studio for each new comedian to experiment until he developed an identity, which then became a stock character he would play in film after film. Ford Sterling specialized in a comic Dutchman, Mack Swain was Ambrose, Chester Conklin was best known as Walrus, and of course Roscoe Arbuckle, with his glowing face and winning grin, played boyishly lovable Fatty. In a sense, Sennett's operation was not unlike a commedia dell'arte company with its Harlequin, Pantaloon, Pierrot, Columbine, and other familiar figures. But the crucial difference was that instead of narrowly prescribed stock characters based entirely upon strictly defined, time-honored theatrical traditions, each Keystone performer was free to invent himself.

On a rainy February afternoon about a week after his debut debacle in *Making a Living*, Charlie Chaplin did just that. Unable to work because of the downpour, some of the boys (Chester, Roscoe, Mack, Ford) were holed up in the male actors' dressing room, playing a friendly game of penny pinochle for beers, while Charlie "ambled about the room looking pale and worried."[24] Borrowing something from almost all of the assemblage — a pair of Fatty's baggy trousers, Ford's equally capacious clodhoppers, Charlie Avery's skimpy formal cutaway jacket, Roscoe's father-in-law's tight-fitting derby, and a trimmed-down version of Mack Swain's moustache — Charlie fashioned himself a set of comic "moes" and instantly began to improvise the character for which he would become famous.

Selecting a flexible bamboo cane in place of the stiff one he had used in *Making a Living*, Chaplin brought his Little Tramp to life. His character actions felt more spontaneous and would register with less rigidity than they had in his stereotypical English dude get up. A supple series of trademark movements, gestural inflections, and facial expressions soon began to appear as well. Some could be traced back to their origins: the Rummy Binks shuffle from his Methley Street days with Lily and Syd; that old standby one-legged corner turn from the Dick Turpin sketch in *Casey's Court Circus*; Fred Kitchen's ashtray kick. But for the most part, as if by some miracle, mannerisms materialized from sources Chaplin could not explain. He realized it immediately, and the boys in the backroom also sensed a breakthrough. He had no conscious preconception of his tramp character,

> But the moment I was dressed, the clothes and the make-up made me feel the person he was. I began to know him, and by the time I walked onto the stage he was fully born. When I confronted Sennett I assumed the character and strutted about, swinging my cane and parading before him. Gags and comedy ideas went racing through my mind.[25]

Deciding that Chaplin's new character looked promising, Sennett assigned him to Lehrman again and dispatched the ill-matched pair with a camera crew to the nearby beach town of Venice where a children's soapbox derby would be taking place a few days later. It was Mack's custom to film all photographically interesting public events — parades, dance contests, international expositions, fires, accidents, building demolitions, reservoir drainings, ship launchings — and use them as backdrops for his low-budget comedies, in order to economize on production costs.

Shot in forty-five minutes, the split-reeler was conceived as an improvisationally plotless film, whose primary purpose was to serve as an informal screen test. For Chaplin and Sennett, it was a chance to see how Charlie's new character registered and played. But ever loath to waste a penny or a foot of film, Mack undoubtedly told Pathé to take his shots in such a way that they could also be assembled and vended as a ten-minute "quickie," which they were. An educational documentary titled *Olives and Their Oil* occupied the other half of the reel.

Like the olive-oil opus, Lehrman's *Kid Auto Races at Venice* begins documentary style in a newsreel format. The only catch is that film coverage of the real-life event is constantly disrupted by an eccentrically dressed, unidentified wise guy and show-off in the racetrack audience who inserts himself in front of the filmed action. Only after the opening few minutes is that original narrative premise broken and the picture-show audience presented with shots taken from the fresh perspective of a second camera. It now becomes clear that all along we have been watching a professional actor playing the role of camera hog and disruptive nuisance, and that this is a comedy film about making a documentary movie.

Directing the film as well as acting the part of the newsreel director in the film-within-a-film, Henry Lehrman delights in giving Charlie the bum's rush. Heaving, shoving, pushing, collaring, and booting an ever-persistent Charlie out of the frame time and again, Pathé puts passion into his performance. Behind-the-scenes undertones from the real-life drama of Charlie's earnest attempt to break into the movies and ill-natured Henry's equally energetic determination to keep him from succeeding add life and vitality to this otherwise limited slapstick situation.

Theater critic and silent film historian Walter Kerr's verdict on the Little Tramp's maiden voyage is:

> He is elbowing his way into immortality, both as a "character" in the film and as a professional comedian to be remembered. And he is doing it by calling attention to the camera as camera.
>
> He would do this throughout his career, using the instrument as a means of establishing a direct and openly acknowledged relationship between himself and his audience. . . . The seeds of his subsequent hold on the public, the mysterious and almost inexplicable bond between this performer and everyman, were there.[26]

Kid Auto Races at Venice did not make Chaplin an overnight star. Nor would his next several pictures, for that matter. But he had made a major breakthrough. After attempting, in *Making a*

Living, to project a standard music hall comedy swell whose impeccable exterior hides his impecunious interior, Charlie had gone on to create his own much more original and deeply personal version of a down-and-out dandy. Through a complex molting process, whose most easily observable external manifestation was an improvisational shedding of one set of togs for another, the Little Tramp was born. Chaplin later recalled that a psychological transformation of his character occurred as a direct result of his costume change:

> I hadn't the slightest idea what to do. I went to the dress department and on the way I thought, well, I'll have them make everything in contradiction — baggy trousers, tight coat, large head, small hat — raggedy but at the same time a gentleman. . . . Making an entrance, I felt dressed; I had an attitude. It felt good, and the character came to me.[27]

A definitive verdict on this new screen character's mass appeal would have to await the film's release. But Chaplin was able to sense from the atmosphere in the male actors' dressing room that he had made a promising start with his new character moes. On a streetcar ride home from the studio a few days later, one of the bit players confirmed that impression with an enthusiastic "Boy, you've started something; nobody ever got those kind of laughs on the set before, not even Ford Sterling."[28]

Charlie's pinochle-playing colleagues had never seen anything like his Little Tramp. As a matter of fact, neither had Charlie. "My character was different and unfamiliar to the American, and even unfamiliar to myself."[29] Although this disclaimer was not strictly true, Chaplin's remark was not meant to be coy or shroud the character in mystery. He knew the Little Tramp's cultural heritage and psychology could be traced back to his own Cockney roots. He never hid that fact:

The idea of being fastidious, very delicate about everything was something I enjoyed. Made me feel funny. There is that gentle poverty, quiet poverty about all the Cockneys who ape their betters. Every little draper, soda clerk wants to be a swell, dress up. So when I stumbled over some dog's leash, got my hand stuck in a cuspidor, I knew instinctively what to do. I tried to hide it. They yelled — the mere fact that I didn't want anybody to see it.

I never thought of the tramp in terms of appeal. He was myself, a comic spirit, something within me that said I must express this. I felt so free. . . . That was the thrill.[30]

If Chaplin ever was fully aware that his comic screen character had emerged from his tragic childhood, he never recorded the insights in print or dictated typescript (as opposed, possibly, to handwritten private notes or off-the-record conversations). Skeptical about the value of so-called method acting technique, he also believed that introspection had the power to destroy an actor's performance by robbing it of all spontaneity:

> I think you're liable to kill your enthusiasm if you delve too deeply into the psychology of the characters you are creating. I don't want to know about the depths; I don't think they're interesting.[31]

But for students of the creative process, the cultural and personal forerunners of Chaplin's Little Tramp are of more than passing interest. His second screen character, the tramp in *Kid Auto Races at Venice*, was unfamiliar to American audiences. But his previous one, the impecunious swell in *Making a Living*, was well known to his countrymen.

Had they given it much thought, thousands of English music hall patrons could have identified Chaplin's first screen character in *Making a Living* as a near ringer for Burlington Bertie from Bow, a famous stage character from the song of the same name. The song had just become popular in British music hall around the time Charlie was departing on his second American tour. It is impossible to establish with certainty where and when "Burlington Bertie from Bow" was first performed. After it became a great hit, it was copyrighted in 1915, but that followed its reception by at least a year. In those days, songs were protected by copyright after their popularity was established, if at all. To identify a few of the song's references: Tom Lipton was the tea importer, Lord Rosebery the former prime minister, and Lady Diana Manners the reigning beauty of the day. The earliest identified date of performance is 1914, but that date does not mean it wasn't performed before that. The lyrics ran:

I'm Bert
P'raps you've heard of me
Bert
You've had word of me,
Jogging along
Hearty and strong
Living on plates of fresh air

I dress up in fashion
And when I am feeling depressed
I shave from my cuff all the whiskers and fluff
Stick my hat on and toddle up West

I'm Burlington Bertie I rise at ten thirty
And saunter along like a toff
I walk down the Strand with my gloves on my hand
Then I walk down again with them off
I'm all airs and graces, correct easy paces
Without food so long I've forgot where my face is
I'm Bert, Bert, I haven't a shirt
But my people are well off you know.

Nearly everyone knows me from Smith to Lord Rosebr'y,
I'm Burlington Bertie from Bow.

I stroll
With Lord Hurlington,
Roll
In The Burlington
Call for Champagne
Walk out again
Come back and borrow the ink
I live most expensive
Like Tom Lipton I'm in the swim
He's got so much "oof" he sleeps on the roof
And I live in the room over him.

I'm Burlington Bertie I rise at ten thirty
And saunter along Temple Bar
As round there I skip
I keep shouting "Pip Pip!"
And the darn'd fools think I'm in my car
At Rothschilds I swank it
My body I plank it
On his front door step with "The Mail" for a blanket
I'm Bert, Bert, and Rothschild was hurt
He said "You can't sleep there" I said "Oh"
He said "I'm Rothschild sonny!" I said "That's damn'd funny
I'm Burlington Bertie from Bow."

. . .

My pose,
Tho' ironical
Shows
That my monocle
Holds up my face, keeps it in place,

Stops it from slipping away.
Cigars,
I smoke thousands,
I usually deal in The Strand
But you've got to take care when you're getting them there
Or some idiot might stand on your hand.

I'm Burlington Bertie I rise at ten thirty
And Buckingham Palace I view.
I stand in the yard while they're changing the guard
And the queen shouts across "Toodle oo"!
The Prince of Wales' brother along with some other
Slaps me on the back and says "Come and see Mother"
But I'm Bert, Bert, and royalty's hurt,
When they ask me to dine I say no.
I've just had a banana with Lady Diana
I'm Burlington Bertie from Bow.

Chaplin's impecunious swell in *Making a Living* was the very embodiment of Bert: monocle, walking stick, empty belly, flashy sartorial exterior, swollen false pride, ironic pretensions toward gentility. It is in the opening sequence of that film that Chaplin the actor mimes his man. He accosts Lehrman with one of those bluff, hail-fellow-well-met greetings that men-about-town customarily exchange upon casually encountering one another. Then, after flattering Henry and establishing their mutual good taste by admiring Lehrman's pinky ring, Charlie shifts gears. Swallowing his pride with a visible gulp and leaning forward to whisper into a cupped hand, Chaplin skillfully pantomimes, with lowered eyes, the portrait of a gentleman of leisure who, having forgotten his wallet, has just made the deucedly embarrassing discovery that he is short of cash. Charlie attempts to negotiate a loan from Henry, one gentleman to another.

Upon being refused, Chaplin again shifts gears and confesses the true nature and urgency of his immediate needs. Pleading his belly, which he pathetically demonstrates to be as empty as his pocket, he readjusts the scope of his request for assistance. Offered a small coin whose meanness (on closer inspection) precludes accepting, Chaplin proudly turns away the proffered sum. Then, thinking better of it, he gratefully snatches the pittance. Parting with Henry, he immediately resumes his pose.

Sauntering along "like a toff," he flourishes his cane as if it were a field marshal's swagger stick or country squire's riding crop, and resubmerges his secret hunger and pennilessness beneath the glitzy exterior of a false swell who is "all airs and graces, correct easy paces."

Only later, in the screen character's final mortifying comic denouement, does he accidentally reveal the full extent of his shabby gentility by losing his temper (and his cuff) while starting to strip for battle. At this point we discover: he's Bert, Bert — and he hasn't a shirt (though his people are well off, you know!).

That Chaplin knew this famous song, which was first introduced in the halls with immense success by an American-born vocalist and male impersonator by the name of Ella Shields, there is little doubt. Apart from the internal evidence of the striking resemblance between Charlie's elegant swell in *Making a Living* and Shields's equally illustrious member of the shabby genteel, residual traces of Bert are to be found in Chaplin's principal character, the Little Tramp, throughout his screen life. On three separate filmmaking occasions, the Little Tramp resorted to his first cousin Bertie's practice of hand-selecting his Havanas on the Strand (see Chaplin's smoking-case gag in *The Kid* and his cigar-butt routines in *The Gold Rush* and *City Lights*). And like Bertie — who can be played either as a well-born gentleman who has fallen from society's upper ranks or a daydreaming Cockney who is attempting to escape its lower depths — his cousin Charlie also embodies the ambiguous amalgam of the has-been gent and would-be dandy.

But if Bertie the seedy stage character and Charlie the shabby screen character are relatives, it was their common cultural heritage with its complex comic traditions that Chaplin the actor drew upon for the depth, power, and universality of his personal creation. Down-at-the-heels gentlemen shambled across the stage throughout the history of stage comedy. But the most immediate limb of the long English branch of Charlie and Bertie's family tree grew from the music halls of the 1860s.

It was a tall, handsome day laborer by the name of Joe Saunders, who earned his bread as a construction worker in the Westminster Bridge Road just a stone's throw from the Canterbury Music Hall, who had been their progenitor. Setting his sights on the finer things in life, Joe adopted the more dignified stage name George Leybourne and exchanged his workman garments for an elegant swell's clobber, which he wore with the ease of someone to the manner born.

Shedding his working-class dialect — except when he occasionally sang Cockney character songs like "The Mousetrap Man" — Leybourne played the part, onstage and off, of an impeccably groomed and stylishly mannered man-about-town. Singing of his fondness for champagne, which he drank by the tankard, and his fondness for the ladies, who flocked to him by the score, George became an overnight superstar and folk hero to members of the working class. It was the chairman (emcee) at the Canterbury who first declared Leybourne a regular lion of a comic, and it was the elegant gallicized version of that term, *lion comique*, that stuck and finally came to describe both George and his rivals.

While the issue of originality was hotly contested in its day, particularly between Leybourne and that equally popular *lion comique* the Great Vance (a middle-class actor by the name of Alfred Peck Stevens), the issue of priority is moot from a contemporary perspective, since there is good reason to suspect that Saunders and Stevens originally invented themselves in recognition of a far more prominent gentleman of the time.

Born one year apart from their illustrious and better-bred contemporary Albert Edward of Saxe-Coburg-Gotha, the Prince of Wales, known to his intimates as Bertie, both Leybourne and Vance adopted their prospective ruler as their role model. An urbane and relaxed, sartorially elegant, trendsetting man-of-the-world, England's crown prince was renowned for the connoisseur's delight he took in fine champagne, thoroughbred horseflesh, good cigars, and pretty women. His loyal subjects — including the low-born Cockneys — took pride in the fact that the heir apparent and royal lion was a sporting man. When Coronation Day rolled around many years later in 1902, they would look forward in music hall song to the good times to come "On the Day King Edward Gets His Crown On."

Even as early as the mid-1860s, when Bertie, Alf Stevens, and Joe Saunders were coming of age and beginning to polish their performance skills, admiration between commoner and prince already ran high in both directions. Not only would the fun-loving and democratic heir apparent frequent the halls, he would invite Leybourne to perform for him in private. Leybourne's rival lion, the Great Vance, could and did boast that he was nicknamed the Beau Brummel of the Halls, a reference to the equally well-groomed boon companion of that other playboy prince, the regent of days gone by, George Augustus Frederick. While it isn't likely that Vance ever dared to address his monarch as Bertie — unlike Brummel, who tweaked his "fat friend" by dubbing him Prinny — the Prince of Wales's personal but casual friendship with Alfred Peck Stevens is a matter of historical record. Their mutual interest in fashion was sufficient to cement ties between the two dandies. Offstage, Bertie set the style for the gentlemen of his class while Vance, who was considered the best-groomed singer among the *lions comiques*, served up an on-stage version for the lower orders to imitate vicariously during such snappy music hall numbers as "Strolling in the Burlington," invoking the West End shopping arcade still renowned today for its elegant men's shops.

Courtesy of the competing managements of their respective halls — the Canterbury and the Oxford — Leybourne and Vance were both able to adopt lifestyles fit for a king. Not only were they lavishly paid, but their employers also furnished each man with a handsomely appointed horse-drawn carriage complete with liveried footmen and coachmen as part of a highly visible rivalry encouraged for publicity purposes. Both men also received much of their *lion comique* wardrobes gratis from rival tailor shops, in an equally intense publicity campaign waged by enterprising merchants.

Unfortunately, the darker side of this felicitous mixture of commerce and class culture lay in the music hall owners' intent to turn a handsome profit by vending wines and spirits to their patrons. As well known by his theme song "Champagne Charlie" as his stage name, it was George Leybourne's responsibility at the Canterbury to stimulate his audience's thirst by song and example. The Great Vance was expected by his management to keep the fizz flowing at the Oxford. Onstage, this rivalry took the quaint but thirst-provoking form of a duel between the two lions as they gaily sang, quaffed, and tippled their way down the beverage lists of their respective establishments with a series of convivial drinking songs like "Cool Burgundy Ben," "Moet & Chandon," "Sparkling Moselle," and "Cliquot." Quick to capitalize on the prospect of promoting those costly luxury items, which they were hoping to introduce as staples into the daily diets of the status-seeking but beer-drinking Cockneys from Bow, importers for the wine and spirits industry lost no time in following the example of their colleagues in the haberdashery trade, by furnishing the *lions comiques* with cases of their favorite beverages of the moment in exchange for their endorsements.

But those complimentary wine samples were a trickle compared to the torrent of alcohol that poured nightly down the throats of men like Joe Saunders and Alfred Stevens, who managed to drink themselves to death while still in their forties. *Lions comiques* died young and penniless, and alcoholism was endemic to their peculiar profession.

The chronic alcohol abuse that also destroyed the lives of hard-drinking working-class worshippers of the *lions comiques* eventually became the subject of clever satires by a group of music hall seriocomediennes who ironically served as unintentional social critics. With good-natured charm, their droll stage characters cautioned of the folly and tragedy of following in the footsteps of *lions comiques* by holding an uncompromisingly frank but funny mirror up to them. These female entertainers donned the garb and regalia of the dandies of the day to drive their point home. Working in realistic drag, skillful male impersonators like Nellie Power in the 1880s and Vesta Tilley in the 1890s created telling psychological portraits that poked fun in song at the self-deluding pretentiousness of the swells in the music hall audience. On one occasion, a young and presumably drunken swell in the audience heaved a heavy soda syphon at Nellie as a token of his esteem. Her best-known *lion comique* satire — "The City Toff" doing the la-di-da — was directed at the blokes in the balcony, while Vesta Tilley aimed her salvos at the sports in the stalls with her equally famous "Burlington Bertie."

Not to be confused with Ella Shields's "Burlington Bertie from Bow" who orders champagne but sleeps under a newspaper on Rothschild's doorstep, Vesta Tilley's "Bertie" is a flighty creature of real financial but no personal substance. In addition to "renting a flat somewhere Kensington way," he "spends the good 'oof' his Pater has made, along with the Brandy and Soda Brigade." Both characters have drinking problems, but they belong to different social classes.

As is the case when a few fragmentary anecdotes survive describing the quirks and eccentricities of a real-life individual's distant relations, it is possible to cobble together a miscellaneous genealogy tracing the Little Tramp's habits and mannerisms back to these theatrical ancestors. Ella Shields's secretly shirtless Bertie begat the false swell in *Making a Living* who then begat the Little Tramp.

"Cradled in the profession," Chaplin was steeped in the lore and traditions of the music hall comedy swell. He was as familiar with character gags tracing all the way back to the original *lions comiques* of the 1860s (such as the cuff routine of George Leybourne) as he was conversant with the comedy material of contemporary male impersonators like Vesta Tilley and Ella Shields. But far more persuasive than these spotty conjectural identifications of the elegant swell ancestry and the rich theatrical pedigree of the screen character Charlie, as reflected in Chaplin the actor's costume and gag selection as he experimented with props and moes in the actors' dressing room at Keystone in 1914, is the genealogical evidence — written and cinematographic — we have from the Little Tramp himself when he looked back over his entire life and thoughtfully summed up the comic influences on his career half a century later.

Nothing revealed Chaplin's conscious identification with the *lions comiques* more conspicuously than the death scene he chose for his alter ego Calvero in *Limelight*. Like the Great Vance, who collapsed onstage at the Sun Music Hall in Knightsbridge after his final number — to immense applause from the audience, who mistook his prostration as part of his act — and then died in the wings of a heart attack, so Calvero would make his exit by falling into a drum onstage and then dying offstage, going out in a similar burst of glory to equally deafening applause.

Chaplin was undoubtedly aware of that connection between Vance, Calvero, Charlie Sr., and himself when he made *Limelight* in 1952. Twelve years later he elaborated some of the factual details of his father's professional career as a *lion comique* in *My Autobiography* without connecting it directly to his screen character's identity. Where Chaplin's Little Tramp had condensed the double identities of a down-and-out dandy and a would-be swell into one persona, Chaplin's father had traversed a similiar but more protracted course from elegance and celebrity to decadence and obscurity over a ten-year period from 1890 to 1900. Charlie had witnessed his father's descent. His screen character commemorated it symbolically.

Like ten-year-old David Wark Griffith, who never forgot his formerly glorious military father's sad alcoholic descent into marginal poverty and untimely departure from a world that had long since passed him by, so amid the pomp and ceremony of an elaborately fancy, rented funeral procession for his once immaculately glamorous but now seedy fallen *lion comique* father, twelve-year-old Charlie Chaplin had tossed a handful of earth on a polished oak coffin as it was lowered into a pauper's grave, and perhaps silently vowed to remember.

Both of these loving sons commemorated and evoked the legacies of their fallible fathers with nostalgic brilliance as they labored passionately, so many years later, in the make-believe, Arabian Nights film world of props, costumes, and sets, where time could be magically reversed by the creative imagination in order to bring fallen idols back from the dead. And so, in that momentous turning-point year in the life of a film industry that was just starting to emerge from its own infancy, D. W. Griffith absorbed himself mightily in recreating and redirecting his warrior father's glorious battles, while Charlie Chaplin began with equal power and poignancy to restage and relive long-buried memories and images of his own fallen father by begetting a screen character who memorialized his image. To an English visitor who had known Charlie Sr. and met Chaplin in Los Angeles in the winter of 1919, Charlie confided: "I can't remember a time when I wasn't trying to follow in my father's footsteps."[32]

The Moon Shines Bright
on Charlie Chaplin

He does things and you're lucky if you see them.

— John Singer Sargent[1]

I used to do the most terrifically vulgar things in those days.

— Chaplin[2]

WITH A GROSS OF HALF A MILLION DOLLARS, 1913 was a banner year for Keystone, and 1914 promised to be even more profitable if Sennett could hold down costs and maintain his production schedule. Satisfied with Keystone's formula for comedy, Mack was more preoccupied with commercial expansion than artistic development. By the end of 1915, Keystone would boast "ten producing companies . . . and a herd of comedians."[3]

Keeping his herd corralled was crucial to his expansion plans. Inflated egos meant inflated salaries. His clowns were not permitted to think of themselves as prima donnas. He was the chief, they worked for him. Now that the new English clown was settling down and getting the hang of it, Sennett began to relax and congratulate himself on his astute decision to replace Ford Sterling with Charlie Chaplin at one-third the cost instead of agreeing to pay Ford five hundred dollars per week.

But by late March, when shooting on Keystone's forty-second film of the year abruptly ground to a halt, he began to reconsider the wisdom of that decision. Meeting the salary demands of a former circus clown was a minor annoyance compared to dealing with the endless personality conflicts being generated by the high-strung English comic who fancied himself an artist. Chaplin's latest and most outrageous act of defiance was a one-man sit-down strike on the curb of a suburban Los Angeles street. Miffed when his suggestion for a gag was ignored by the film's director because of time constraints and fading light, Charlie refused to continue.

When the crew returned to the studio with unexposed film in the can and Sennett heard the story, he stormed into the dressing room and bellowed: "What the hell's the idea?" Continuing to remove his makeup, Charlie calmly explained that his only interest had been in "gagging up" a weak story. As Charlie tells it, Mack fumed:

"You'll do what you're told or get out, contract or no contract."

I was very calm. "Mr. Sennett," I answered, "I earned my bread and cheese before I came here, and if I'm fired — well, I'm fired. But I'm conscientious and just as keen to make a good picture as you are."

Without saying anything further he slammed the door.

That night, going home on the streetcar with my friend, I told him what had happened.

"Too bad. You were going great there for a while," he said.

"Do you think they'll fire me?" I said cheerfully, in order to hide my anxiety.

"I wouldn't be at all surprised. When I saw him leaving your dressing room he looked pretty mad."

"Well, it's O.K. with me. I've got fifteen hundred dollars in my belt and that will more than pay my fare back to England. However, I'll show up tomorrow and if they don't want me — *c'est la vie.*"[4]

Reviewing the little Englishman's rapid transformation from a shy, polite greenhorn into a cocky veteran in three short months, Mack felt justified in firing Charlie if he refused to knuckle under. Without exception, every director Chaplin had worked for so far had found him equally impossible. First there was his running feud with Pathé Lehrman. But aware that Pathé was abrasive, Mack made allowances for Charlie. Sidelining him for a week as a slap on the wrist, he reassigned him to mild-mannered "Pop" Nichols's unit.

An easygoing man in his sixties, with ten years' experience as a director, "Pop" suffered from none of the vanities that caused Lehrman to seek vengeance in the cutting room. Nonetheless, three films later, Nichols threw up his hands and informed Sennett that Chaplin was "a son of a bitch to work with."[5]

Nichols's verdict was no surprise. After trying to direct Chaplin himself, Sennett knew how difficult he could be. Unwilling to bend his will to another's, particularly if he considered that person's concept of comedy inferior to his own, the scrappy bantam comedian had resorted to indirection in order to avoid a point-blank confrontation with Sennett until now. "He would agree to a scene as I outlined it, then discombobulate me by doing everything some other way," Mack recalled.[6]

Through mutual forbearance and tact, the two men had managed to postpone a showdown. But the way Charlie refused to continue working with his fourth director was the final straw. Informing his latest mentor, "I'm sorry. . . . I will not do what I'm told. I don't think you are competent to tell me what to do," Chaplin threw down the gauntlet.[7] In front of the entire shooting crew, he flouted Sennett's authority.

The fact that Chaplin's latest director was also Mack Sennett's longtime sweetheart and sometime fiancée, Mabel Normand, didn't help. But personal considerations aside, there was something unbearably arrogant about a newcomer with three months' studio time turning a deaf ear to a seasoned veteran with four years of filmmaking experience at Biograph and Keystone. It was true that the film Chaplin boycotted (on the first day of shooting) was Mabel Normand's maiden voyage as a director. But it was also true that she was a competent and experienced comedienne, who already had appeared in forty films as against Chaplin's nine.

The title of her debut as a director was *Mabel at the Wheel*, a comedy "vehicle" with feminist undertones in which Normand played a capable lady racetrack driver who succeeds in foiling the bungling slapstick attempts of an oily male villain to fix the outcome of her race. Instructed to put on his old music hall getup from *Making a Living* plus a Fu Manchu goatee, a very reluctant and out-of-character Charlie was cast by Mabel to play the heavy to her juicier role as the film's comic heroine.

If Chaplin's latest director was four years his senior in experience, he seemed to notice only the galling fact that "pretty and charming" Mabel was four years younger as well. As payback for Charlie's treatment of Nichols, Lehrman, and Sennett himself, Mack had turned a deaf ear to his persistent pleas "to write and direct my own comedies" and consigned him to a supporting role in Normand's film.[8] But instead of serving as an object lesson in etiquette, the strategy backfired and triggered an open clash between Charlie and Mack.

If the hot-tempered Irishman and feisty Englishman had been left to their own devices to resolve the dispute, undoubtedly Fred Karno would have been the principal beneficiary. But on the eve of their showdown, it was averted by a pair of cigar-chewing ex-bookmakers from Sheepshead Bay. Back at the Longacre

Building on Broadway, where they ran the distribution end of Keystone's bustling East Coast operations, Sennett's business partners, Adam Kessel and Charlie Bauman, sent Mack an urgent wire instructing him to "hurry up with more Chaplin pictures" as the demand was "terrific."[9]

By the time he poked his head into the dressing room the next morning to issue Charlie a warm invitation to a friendly chat in private, burly Mack Sennett was of a very different mindset than the door-slamming guv'nor of the night before. Soothing Chaplin's ruffled feathers by acknowledging he was "a fine artist," Mack coaxed him into agreeing to cooperate with Mabel for "the good of the picture," in exchange for a semipromise that, in the near future, he could write and direct a movie of his own. To assuage Sennett's financial anxieties and equally strong conviction that no novice with a mere nine films under his belt was capable of producing a Keystone comedy, Chaplin offered to plunk down fifteen hundred dollars — his hard-earned life savings — to guarantee that the picture he shot could be released and shown.[10]

Delighted at the possibility of gaining artistic independence to explore and develop his own brand of comedy, Charlie became all sweetness and tractability — as were his two new pals, Mabel and Mack. Stepping in gallantly to help his girlfriend to write, direct, and act in her directorial debut, Mack was able to restore an atmosphere of mutual respect and creative generosity in the crew — where a couple of extras had actually threatened to belt Charlie in the kisser for his rude behavior toward the popular young actress.

Offscreen and after hours, in a congenial arrangement that lasted long after the picture was completed, Sennett, Normand, and Chaplin dined companionably in the restaurants of downtown Los Angeles. One of their favorite after-work hangouts was Harlow's at Third and Spring where, apart from mixing with other members of the burgeoning film colony, film stars could rub elbows with celebrities like Clarence Darrow, Samuel Gompers, Barney Oldfield, Jim Jeffries, and Frank Chance (of Tinker-to-Evers-to Chance fame). Mack even got Charlie a temporary residential membership at the exclusive L.A. Athletic Club, whose posh but affordable facilities were palatial compared to his cheap digs at the Great Northern Hotel. Chaplin had such a tendency to hoard his money that during this early period he saved almost all his paychecks in a strongbox, erroneously assuming that a Keystone check was as good as cash, until someone finally pointed him to a bank.[11] Depositing the checks was another problem, since Charlie routinely arrived at the studio one hour earlier (7 A.M.) and left one hour later (7 P.M.) than everyone else, in his determination to learn all he could about filmmaking.

While Sennett may have sensed from the start that Chaplin was onto something with the *Kid Auto Races* costume he devised, neither he nor Charlie anticipated the instant mass appeal Chaplin's quaint character would hold for America's moviegoing public. But the soaring sawtooth graphic peaks representing Chaplin film revenues on Keystone's first-quarter sales chart told the story. By the time Charlie's fifth movie, *A Film Johnnie*, was released, orders for prints of films featuring the new comedian in that picturesque tramp outfit were arriving at New York headquarters from nickelodeons across the country at more than twice the usual rate for Keystone comedies.

The critics agreed. They had never seen an oddball screen character as amusing as that new English clown whose name most film reviewers had not yet matched with the quirky mannerisms, unforgettable facial expressions, and intriguing costume. As one of the few reviewers of those first nine Keystones who got the name straight put it, "Chaplin is a born screen comedian; he does things we have never seen done on the screen before"; Another talked of a "Chaplin touch," while a third concluded, "in the three months' experience that he has had in motion pictures . . . [Charlie Chaplin is] second to none."[12]

Stepping back to determine what made Chaplin's acting stand out from the rest of Sennett's thundering herd of slapstick comedians in those "galloping tintypes" of early 1914 is not as easy as one might imagine. Spotting him in a crowd is not the problem. The distinctive "moes" he wore in six of his first nine films solved that problem as handily as they would throughout his entire twenty-five-year career playing the Little Tramp. But determining exactly what the Little Fellow was up to in those grainy, blurry, flickering one- and two-reelers is another matter. The greatest impediment is that most commercially available print copies of Chaplin's first two years' output in the movies — thirty-five films at Keystone and fourteen at Essanay in 1915 — are currently being sold in chemically deteriorated and editorially mutilated states, which fail to do justice to the originals. (They are being restored.)

In almost all cases, the surviving prints have been so chopped up that, while various copies of the same Chaplin Keystone film may present identical scenes, they are often arranged in different order. In some print versions of a film, entire sequences are omitted. Concentrating on worn-out prints exhausts a viewer. It is tempting to dismiss Chaplin's entire year's output at Keystone as more artistically primitive than it was in reality, on the assumption that those original recorded performances were as crude and inferior as the poorly preserved celluloid strips on which they are viewed ninety years later.

Nor is the task of recapturing what contemporary audiences experienced in 1914 made easier by the modern setting and mindset through which our viewing takes place. The neighborhood nickelodeon has disappeared. The ragtime beat of the piano player synchronizing his tunes to rhythms supplied by his partner, the projectionist (who would fiddle with the rheostat to adjust the film's pace according to his own artistic interpretations), is long gone. There is no hushed whisper of excitement, no gentle rustle of shifting outer garments as a picture-show audience settles expectantly to witness a state-of-the-art entertainment event that is as much live as it is recorded. No hand-painted color slide of a bluebird of happiness flashes on the screen with a note in its mouth extolling the virtues of neighborliness by politely requesting the ladies to remove tall ostrich-plumed hats and discreetly reminding gents to remember the Johnstown Flood and refrain from expectorating on the floor (gleaming brass cuspidors have been provided). Viewing old Keystones on modern videocassettes and DVDs at home or in the ghost-town silence of a projection booth in an academic film archive misses the original social context in which they were received.

We cannot recapture the springtime enthusiasms of our grandparents' world of straw boaters and ankle-length skirts, when both they and those astonishing pictures in motion were at once adolescent and thoroughly modern. Their level of visual sophistication was a far cry from our own — a world in which D. W. Griffith, unable to resist the temptation to dramatize what he would soon hype in paid advertisements as one of his crowning cinematic achievements, the "switch-back," confided to readers of the *New York Dramatic Mirror* that January of 1914: "The switch-back I use with fear. . . . I must give a very good sound reason for its existence before I will attempt to use it." Later, rechristened the flashback, it would of course gain universal acceptance as a routine narrative convention. It took time for audiences to accustom themselves to emerging storytelling techniques and for Hollywood professionals to accept them as conventions.

For example, a few years earlier, a major studio chief had chastised a director for cheating the moviegoing public out of their full nickel's worth of entertainment by denying them full-length views of their favorite actors and actresses. And while "foreshortening" — that avant-garde technique that arbitrarily cut off photoplayers at the knees, waist, or shoulders — was now in fashion under the name "close-up," as late as May 1915 a cautious reporter for *Photoplay* still found it necessary to enclose the term in quotation marks while bravely declaring himself a firm believer in it.

But it was imagination's suspension of disbelief that made those choppily edited Keystones as visually engrossing and narratively seamless for our grandparents as films made with contemporary Hollywood's most modern editing techniques and high-tech special effects are for us. Back in 1914, an audience's desire to fuse with the dream screen and become one with the actors, action, and text of a movie like Chaplin's fifth Keystone, *A Film Johnnie*, was no less intense than a later filmgoer's hunger to merge and mingle with the players and plot in films like Buster Keaton's *Sherlock Jr.* and Woody Allen's *Purple Rose of Cairo.*

In all three of these movies-about-the-movies, the protagonist is a deeply engrossed, romantically inclined member of the audience who joins or is joined by a performer/screen character from the film within the film. In what must be the ultimate cineclimax, the viewer-voyeur manages to escape the drab everyday realities that have driven him or her to seek sanctuary in a dream palace in the first place by entering filmland magically and attempting to merge with a fantasy love object — with varying degrees of comic success.[13]

In 1914, lacking the sophisticated technology to depict photographically the physical act of walking through a movie screen into another story, and playing to audiences not yet accustomed to the fantasy-dissolve, Charlie, a movie-struck dreamer, is forced to take the long way around to pursue his desires. Physically ejected from the nickelodeon by the management because of unruly behavior — wildly enthusiastic applause, an extravagant outpouring of tears, kiss-blowing transports of rapture, an impassioned attempt to rescue the endangered heroine of the film within the film by shadowboxing the screen villain and, ultimately, getting into a real fistfight with his irate neighbor in the next seat — Charlie makes his way to the film studio where the movie was made.

Stepping through the looking glass, he arrives in wonderland: the Alessandro Street entrance to Keystone headquarters. Still dressed in his tramp outfit, in what now becomes an authentic behind-the-scenes documentary on a day in a modern movie studio, Charlie encounters a famous film star, dapper Roscoe "Fatty" Arbuckle, who, we discover, when he's not in his tight-fitting Fatty costume, is a sleekly handsome gentleman of substance, accustomed to arriving at work in elegantly tailored, obviously expensive double-breasted suits.

Attempting once more to break into the movies, this time the Little Tramp tries a new approach. Sneaking through the studio gates past the Keystone guard, he installs himself in a prop armchair in the midst of a set on an open-air stage where a new movie is being shot. Completely carried away as he watches the filmed action from this close-up spectator's perch, Charlie is no more capable of remaining a passive member of the audience in *A Film Johnnie* than he was as the music-hall swell in *Mumming Birds*. Impelled to rescue the costumed actress/heroine, Charlie assaults the actor/villain and is in turn physically attacked by the film's furious director for spoiling the picture.

What made moviegoers sit up and take notice of Chaplin in this early film? Viewing and re-viewing a medium-quality print of the far-from-seamlessly edited Keystone celluloid supports Chaplin's contention that, from the start, audiences were struck by his Little Fellow's personality as conveyed through his unique character gags and idiosyncratic style of pantomime. Clothes, too, made the man. In keeping with his tramp outfit, Charlie panhandles prosperous Roscoe Arbuckle, the famous movie actor, with an earthy, streetwise aplomb entirely in keeping with their obvious social differences. Instead of engaging in the fastidious fandangos of the elegant swell in *Making a Living*, a much more elemental Charlie sizes up Roscoe in *A Film Johnnie* and puts the touch on him.

The sight gag is simple. Taking the measure of his man, Chaplin expertly slips both hands around Arbuckle's waist as if to appreciate and demonstrate the full majesty of his girth and the full girth of His Majesty. Then, after comparing his prospective benefactor's magnificent paunch to his own scrawny-bellied, baggy-trousered lineaments — both for our edification and his patron's — Charlie gently prods Roscoe's gut in confident expectation of a forthcoming coin, which plops automatically into his outstretched palm.

Chaplin's pantomime is crystal clear. Arbuckle is a soft touch. Relying exclusively on nonverbal gestures and subtle facial expressions, the Little Tramp communicates his predicaments, motives, innermost feelings, and thoughts with idiomatic precision. He translates them effortlessly from figures of everyday verbal speech into a universal sign language. In *A Film Johnnie*, Chaplin's performance is inspired by touches of verbal-visual poetry with which he metaphorically identifies or underscores his emotions using sign language — while dramatizing them simultaneously with his extraordinarily mobile facial expressions. "Flipping his lid" over the heroine in the nickelodeon movie, Chaplin the actor reinforces his impersonation of moonstruck infatuation by making the Little Tramp's derby pop from his head, as if by magic.

But also in keeping with the Little Tramp's elemental psychology, some of Chaplin's expressions of rapture remain far more earthbound. In that same screen-gazing sequence in the nickelodeon, Chaplin portrays less ethereal aspects of passion by wetting his pants. "I have seen Mr. Chaplin blithely performing functions in the moving pictures that even I would decline to report," wrote one reviewer.[14]

Well schooled in the music hall tradition of the sly double entendre, Chaplin is careful to establish overtly a hysterical case of handkerchief-wringing, lap-drenching lacrimation as the official explanation for those dripping baggy trousers he discovers as he gets up from his seat. Nonetheless, there is a soupçon of mischievous bawdiness in that split-second, camera-conscious aside he tosses our way, as he pauses just long enough to jiggle a few dewy drops of emotional overflow down his pant leg while being given the bum's rush by an irate theater manager. It hints of a hidden wellspring other than his tear ducts. What was it Charlie Chaplin just did? Who can tell, it happened so fast.

His Little Tramp's manners and deportment certainly left something to be desired. Toying absentmindedly with a revolver he has filched from the film studio's prop room, he casually picks his teeth with it while musing on his next move. A few frames later he succumbs, for the first time on film, to what will become his screen character's lifelong penchant for rescuing cigar butts abandoned by their former owners. Stooping to scoop his prize, he lights up with a handy pull of the trigger and puffs away. When finished, he blasts the cigar into oblivion with another shot while casually discarding the firearm as if it were the cigar.

His vagabond character's hygiene is no more impeccable than his manners. Like some nomadic tribesman whose migratory lifestyle has taught him the virtue of making a single possession serve multiple functions, the Little Tramp employs his dirty old sock as a change purse and as a handkerchief to dab his eyes and blow his nose. Nor is there anything about this early Chaplin character that remotely resembles the soulfully poetic, self-sacrificing dreamer we came to know and love in the later Mutual and First National shorts and the full-length features.

We do get one tantalizing preview of the otherwise entirely absent soft and feminine side of the Little Tramp in Chaplin's twenty-fourth Keystone, *The Masquerader*, where he does a brilliant turn as "Señorita Chapelino." Dressed as a woman, he reveals his feminine side. No male actor can capture a female character's feminine essence if he is not entirely comfortable with his own. Chaplin's brief impersonation of a glamorous, flirtatious woman who seduces men and effortlessly twists them around her little finger is more than convincing; it is sexy. Not only is he more physically appealing than many of the silent film actresses of his own day, but he even makes the unforgettable star turns as women of such modern actors as Jack Lemmon, Tony Curtis, and Dustin Hoffman pale by comparison (except for the important fact that they do their distaff impressions for long stretches while Chaplin does his in one brief scene). Watching Chaplin impersonate a seductive woman is enough to make a psychiatrist wonder what it might have been like for the five-year-old boy to observe his twenty-nine-year-old showgirl mother's mesmerizing star turns. If the eagle-eyed child learned how to "do" drunks by studying his father, it is equally plausible that he first learned to "do" sexy women by watching his songstress mother, whose act he later copied to perfection, even to her laryngitically cracking voice at Aldershot.

Sennett recalled that it was only after Chaplin left Keystone that "he abandoned cruelty, venality, treachery, larceny, and lechery as the main characteristics of his tramp . . . and made him pathetic — and lovable."[15] To this list of questionable comic virtues should be added: slobbishness, selfishness, lewdness, crudeness, and bad manners. Entirely in keeping with the prevailing morality of the rest of Keystone's hard-hearted clowns, a not very altruistic Charlie bites, kicks, trips, burns, spritzes, shoves, and manhandles his fellow citizens out of his way in mad comic pursuit of life, liberty, and happiness.

In these early films, Chaplin scales every performance for the belly laugh. The sympathetic communion he seeks with audiences at this stage of his screen character's development is in the depiction of a picaresque misfit and incorrigible trouble-maker whose idiosyncratic mannerisms and clever imperson-ations are considerably more witty but not a shred more honorable or refined than his fellow performers' depictions of their desper-ate characters.

By the time of his showdown with Sennett in March 1914, what Chaplin the actor had already begun to realize was that to develop and project this new tramp character to its best cine-matic advantage, he had to break away from the Keystone chase formula, arbitrary casting, and unsubtle conventions (including dumb facial mugging that passed for acting) that seemed to sat-isfy Mack Sennett's standards as a film director. Being forced by Mack to play a wildly gesticulating, broadly grimacing, crude car-icature of a comic heavy, as he was in *Mabel at the Wheel*, did noth-ing to advance Chaplin's growing reputation or showcase his remarkable skills as an actor-pantomimist.

Choosing his own roles, slowing the pace of the stories, training and sustaining the camera on the Tramp to catch his gags and facial expressions, and making sure that the captured funny business didn't end up on the cutting room floor were his goals. Otherwise he ran the risk of becoming one of the crowd in the formula chases and fast-paced action sequences. Looking back years later, Chaplin would conclude that his phenomenal early success had been largely the result of his decision to set his character apart visually from the Keystone herd.

While Charlie's disagreement with Mack may have looked like a spontaneous temper tantrum, it was not unplanned. His determination to fight for artistic independence inspired his sit-down:

> I had an awfully difficult time. Again and again and again I argued that I could do the directing myself, to let me direct, but the answer was always the same: "Leave that to us; we've been in the game for ten years." The superior attitude . . . used to drive me wild.[16]

The full-page advertisement in the April 4, 1914, issue of *Moving Picture World* offering fans a complete set of eight-by-ten individual photos of Mack Sennett, Mabel Normand, Charlie Chaplin, and Roscoe Arbuckle for fifty cents attested to the resolution of his conflict with Mack, and to Chaplin's rapid rise in the Keystone organization. On practically the same day, Chaplin began shooting *Caught in the Rain*, his thirteenth Keystone and the first one in which he was granted total artistic control as writer and director.

Writing credits in those days did not imply that a film's author was capable of completing a shooting script comparable to today's screenplay. Nor is it likely that marginally literate Chaplin would then have been sufficiently adept as a writer to produce such a document with its orderly progression of shots, scenes, and sequences. But in 1914, lack of sophisticated writing skills was not a hindrance for "authoring" successful photoplays. Chaplin's lack of formal education actually may have helped him, as a pantomime storyteller, to reach many of the non-Western members of his worldwide audience.

Even twelve-reel epics like *Birth of a Nation* were being "written" largely on loose scraps of notepaper crammed in Griffith's bulging pockets, recording or complementing the outpouring of ideas from his boiling brain. Following his Biograph mentor's example, Mack Sennett had also learned to improvise films from the sketchiest of scenario outlines. It was this seat-of-the-pants approach to comedy and confidence in his own creative ability that Chaplin would credit fifty years later as the single most important lesson he took away from his year at Keystone (apart from his self-taught technical education in filmmaking).

> There was a lot Keystone taught me and a lot I taught Keystone. . . . they knew little about technique, stagecraft or movement, which I brought to them from the theatre. They also knew little about natural pantomime. . . . Their miming dealt little with

subtlety or effectiveness, so I stood out in the contrast. . . . I had many advantages, and . . . like a geologist, I was entering a rich, unexplored field. . . . that was the most exciting period of my career, for I was on the threshold of something wonderful.

. . . I had confidence in my ideas, and I can thank Sennett for that, for although unlettered like myself, he had belief in his own taste, and such belief he instilled in me. His manner of working had given me confidence; it seemed right. His remark that first day at the studio: "We have no scenario — we get an idea then follow the natural sequence of events . . ." had stimulated my imagination.[17]

In early April of 1914, having squawked and griped that he was as qualified as the next guy to write and direct his own pictures, Charlie suffered a slight panic attack when Mack finally gave him the green light. He decided to play it safe and return to his music hall roots by reprising two stage characters he had already played on film: the inebriate and the comic flirt. These roles that he combined in *Caught in the Rain* were actually take-offs on two standard *lion comique* roles, the cosmopolitan tippler and the suave ladies' man. Yet if Chaplin's bawdy depiction of a sloppily dressed, drunk flaneur, or urban loiterer, who ogles and flirts with women in parks and hotel lobbies can be seen as a tribute to the *lion comique* tradition, it was a backhanded one. Unlike the impeccably dressed, lady-killing comic flaneur gracefully strutting the Strand that his once-famous father had portrayed, Charlie's ill-clad man-about-town was a drunken klutz.

When he made this film, Chaplin was not openly satirizing his father. There is no evidence that he even connected his screen character's double identity in *Caught in the Rain* with his father's two signature stage roles. If a paternal influence inspired him, it was unconscious, not self-conscious. Chaplin's childhood was undoubtedly the last thing on his mind when he set out to write and shoot *Caught in the Rain*. More likely, he had been taking a mental inventory of his previous Keystone depictions of drunks and urban flirts.

Weaving his woozy way through barrooms and bedrooms, Chaplin had managed on those earlier filmmaking occasions to tangle hilariously with saloon doors and cuspidors. As graceful as he was clumsy, he had wowed moviegoers with his acrobatic skills. Vaulting a banister dead drunk in *His Favorite Pastime*, he could execute a miraculously perfect comic landing — upright and unharmed, blithely lighting and puffing a cigarette, gloriously oblivious to his near-fatal encounter with the force of gravity. And in his screen character's other major incarnation as a great lover, film fans across the nation cheered, howled, and egged on the Little Fellow as he strove, shyly and slyly, to accost, pick up, and seduce all manner of women — single or married, homely or sexy — encountered in his shuffling satyric rambles through the parks, hotel lobbies, dance halls, boardinghouses, and street corners of downtown Middle America. During his year at Keystone, Chaplin had frequently burlesqued his portrayal of romantic feelings when the need for a seduction arose in his screen character's life.

In *Caught in the Rain*, the Charlie we meet is more lust-driven than affection-starved. Satisfaction of desire is foremost. Every woman is a potential conquest. Filled with adolescent bravado and propelled by a testosterone surge that permits scant time for the niceties of courtship and preliminaries of dalliance, a very horny Charlie spies a respectable matron on a park bench, sidles up, and sits down. After crossing his legs modestly and averting his eyes bashfully, he launches a full-scale frontal assault by slinging his legs across her lap. Scolded for his audacity by this incongruously formidable-looking love object, he naughtily snatches her waggling finger and smothers her hand in kisses just as her irate husband, played by gigantic Mack Swain, shows up to give him the boot.

Discouraged, Charlie gets drunk. After striking a match on a passing cop and stunting a comedy spill in the wake of a tipsy brush with a speeding automobile, he toddles into a hotel lobby seeking shelter for the night. Stepping repeatedly on a gouty old gentleman's painful bandaged foot while ogling an attractive pair of young ladies and drunkenly scrawling his mark in the hotel register, Charlie then proceeds to flop, lurch, belly-slide, sprawl, crawl, totter, and stagger his way upstairs — somehow managing to inflict ever-increasing amounts of pain on the hapless hotel guest's gouty foot with almost every step.

Finally arriving at a room he mistakes for his own, Charlie tries unsuccessfully to unlock the door with a lighted cigarette. It swings open. Entering, he makes a beeline for a whiskey bottle. After taking a healthy swig, he pours the rest on his scalp and begins brushing his hair, only to discover he has forgotten to remove his derby. Suddenly, he makes the more sobering discovery that the room's occupants are none other than the married couple from the park. Beating a hasty retreat to his own room, directly across the hall, Charlie gets undressed and prepares to bed down for the night, polishing his by-now-iconic boots with his shirt before tucking them under his pillow.

Relying on the plot device of a sleepwalking tendency in the Margaret Dumont–like matron across the hall to transform her into a sexual aggressor who turns the tables on Charlie, the remainder of *Caught in the Rain* is a bedroom farce in which the Little Fellow struggles desperately to escape his somnambulant female pursuer's unwelcome attentions while dodging the mighty wrath of her husband. Although the humor is innocent by modern standards, Chaplin's film gags were considered sufficiently bawdy by 1914 norms for the movie to be banned by Sweden's Board of Censors.

*   *   *

"Well, are you ready to start another?" Sennett asked as they left the projection room after screening *Caught in the Rain*.[18] Not only was he willing to grant Chaplin carte blanche, but he also awarded him a twenty-five-dollar bonus for each new picture he wrote and directed. The offer was less generous than it sounds, considering the enormous profits that Keystone and its distributor, Mutual Films, had already begun to realize on Chaplin movies.

Charlie's biggest moneymaker was his twenty-ninth film, *Dough and Dynamite*. Completed by early fall of 1914, it grossed $130,000 in rentals in its first year alone — a tidy sum, considering the fact that a typical Keystone two-reeler brought in $40,000. But even in June of 1914, Chaplin's box-office drawing power had become so strong that a movie like *The Knockout* was advertised by Keystone's publicity department as a Charlie Chaplin film. In reality it was a Roscoe Arbuckle two-reeler in which Charlie makes a two-minute cameo appearance to referee Fatty's boxing match in a personally choreographed slapstick ballet sequence whose fancy footwork anticipates his great scene of comic pugilism in *City Lights*.

Film history was being made. Not only were consumers with established filmgoing habits asserting a preference for Chaplin films above all others, but "people who never went to the movies before were driven by the accounts of the new comedian," reported *Photoplay* magazine.[19] Chaplin *was* the movies. So much so that the Crystal Hall theater on Fourteenth Street would soon adopt the unprecedented policy of exhibiting Charlie Chaplin films exclusively. With the odd exception of four unaccounted days of alternative programming, it would successfully continue that booking practice until it burned down in 1923.

Though not yet aware of his burgeoning nationwide reputation and the astronomical earning power of his films — he was more than pleased to be earning two hundred dollars per week[20] — Chaplin was becoming aware of local manifestations of his skyrocketing popularity at the time of that showdown with Sennett in March of 1914. In search of crucial feedback to calibrate his timing and fine-tune his acting, Chaplin was just starting to supplement his Edendale studio viewing of the daily rushes with occasional expeditions to first-run theaters in downtown Los Angeles, to study audiences firsthand in live settings. Those visits were field trips, not ego trips. He needed to understand audience reception in order to polish his performances. As he watched, he incidentally noticed the anticipatory ripples of "ooh" and "ah" that routinely greeted his Little Tramp's first appearance in each new film, even before that character began doing his gags.

Chaplin had already mastered the art of funny business onscreen, but he was still studying how to connect intimately with his movie audiences without straining for effect. After Aldershot and Foresters, it was a relief never to face a live audience again. But he was determined to establish the same come-hither, absent-fourth-wall intimacy that Leno and Lloyd had achieved so effortlessly. In the years to come, his relentless pursuit of excellence would even extend to providing rent-free loft space in his film studio to a deaf painter, Granville Redmond, in exchange for the specialized feedback someone with a handicap like his was capable of providing. And he was constantly testing new material by regaling fellow partygoers in Hollywood and elsewhere with colorful bits, shticks, and improvisations.

In 1914, however, during this earliest phase of his filmmaking career, there was not much time for socializing. Laboring with the singleminded intensity he had always lavished on his work, from his days with the Lancashire Lads to his years with Karno, Charlie denied himself anything remotely resembling a well-rounded personal life. As Mack Sennett told Theodore Dreiser:

The average actor . . . is just an actor. When it's quitting time he's through. He's thinking of something else — maybe even when he's working! — and he wants to get away so he can attend to it. . . . personality people are different. . . . Chaplin used to fairly sweat if he thought he hadn't done a thing as well as he should have . . . and when the time came that he could see the film of the day's work, he was always there, whereas most of the others in the picture would never come around. And if anything in the run didn't please him, he'd click his tongue or snap his fingers and twist and squirm. "Now why did I do that, that way?" he'd say. "What was the matter with me anyhow?"[21]

There were even times when Chaplin's tendency to "fairly sweat" actually rendered him offensive (according to Minta Durfee, a Keystone comedienne who played in twelve films with him and remembered him as "plenty dirty"). What it probably amounted to was Charlie's habit of becoming so fanatically absorbed in filming that he absentmindedly neglected his personal hygiene from time to time. Stan Laurel recalled similar lapses in his ex-roomate's grooming habits at moments of intense absorption during their Karno days.

But it was none other than salty Marie Dressler who confronted the problem openly by stalking off the set of *Tillie's Punctured Romance* and taking Sennett aside to complain bitterly about the same rancid piece of banana that had remained on Chaplin's celluloid collar for sixteen consecutive days of shooting that July. "As a matter of fact, Mr. Mack Sennett, if the banana is not removed, I shall enact you the goddammedest vomiting scene in the annals of the drammer," Marie declared.[22] Dressler's remarks referred to Chaplin's character costume, not his personal wardrobe. But according to a former assistant, Jim Tully, Chaplin was less than fastidious in his personal dress as well during this time. Rather than launder shirts, Chaplin saved time and money by buying one shirt, wearing it until he could wear it no more, and throwing it away. Chaplin's cameraman Rollie Totheroh recalled his surprise over the fact that this extraordinarily well paid actor traveled so light that he had nothing but a toothbrush and torn pair of socks when he first unpacked his valise at Essanay's studio in Niles, California.

More interested in slipping on bananas than removing their traces from his character costume, the comedian simply lived and dreamed cinema. Of the remaining twenty-two Keystones in which he appeared after *Caught in the Rain*, Chaplin wrote and directed sixteen. Many contain fresh gems of comic invention, some successful, some less so. Each taught him valuable lessons: how long to let a scene run, where to place the camera, how best to edit sequences in order to showcase his own unique brand of humor.

Achieving a personal cinematic style as an actor and a director had meant breaking with Keystone's exaggerated emphasis on speed. "The plant must come as close as possible to the gag" was Roscoe Arbuckle's way of summing up Sennett's credo that both beats of a gag must be completed within twenty feet of film.[23] That narrow fifteen-to-twenty-second time frame denied comedians the opportunity to enrich their gags with suspenseful pauses or subtle twists of exposition. It also failed to permit sufficient time for a series of thematically related gags to grow naturally out of a situation and to be contained within a character's psychology. Fun flew furiously in a Mack Sennett comedy. Time passed at a snail's pace in a Chaplin film.

By the time of his nineteenth Keystone, *Mabel's Married Life*, Chaplin the director was beginning to experiment with the camera by recording Chaplin the actor for what seems like an eternity by Sennett standards. Playing a married souse who returns home after a night on the town to discover a fully clothed and very human-looking boxing dummy in his living room, which he mistakenly identifies as an archrival who has invaded his home, an incensed Charlie gets into a shoving match with this creature. In addition to turning a deaf ear to Charlie's demands that he leave at once, the flexibly rigged "rival" returns each blow measure for measure. Astounded by the intruder's audacity, and scenting foul play — which we immediately recognize as the residual aroma of the conciliatory bouquet of scallions he has brought home to placate his wife — a very tipsy Charlie wrinkles his nose and tilts forward precariously to sniff his opponent's breath to see if he has been drinking, before resuming their shoving contest.

The scene runs long enough for Chaplin the actor to showcase his inimitable talent for bringing inanimate objects to life by reacting to them with complex and intimate emotions usually reserved for interactions with human beings. But if capturing the funny business of character and situation meant training the camera on himself and letting it run, Chaplin also had to learn to restrain himself (and others) in the cutting room in order maintain the continuity of his comedy scenes. In his very next Keystone, *Laughing Gas*, Chaplin mutilates the Tramp's best take — a long "love" scene in which our horny hero attempts to seduce a maiden in distress.

Playing a lowly dental assistant who takes advantage of his boss's temporary absence to impersonate him, Chaplin treats us to a clever parody of the diabolical profession of dentistry as licensed sadism and seduction which, in a properly edited version, would have easily rivaled or surpassed W. C. Fields's hilarious treatment of that subject eighteen years later in *The Dentist*. Mustering his most masterful manner, Charlie enters the waiting room and selects a pretty young woman as his victim. While diplomatically devoting his full attention to the complaints of a homely dowager with a painfully swollen, heavily bandaged jaw as she angrily protests her need to be seen first, Charlie suavely ushers the maid of his choice into the operating room suite with the latest and gentlest of his seemingly endless repertoire of idiosyncratic back-kicks.

Having dispatched the old biddy, he turns to the young

woman. Seating her in the dental chair and tilting it back with aplomb, Charlie experiences a momentary reversion to his inferior social status as he mistakes the chair for a shoeshine stand and, transforming a dental napkin into a polishing rag, starts shining his patient's shoes. When she reminds him of her problem, he dismisses his lapse lightheartedly as an intentional jest. Charlie interprets her slightly nervous giggle as assent to his playful overture and proceeds to sling his leg over her lap and press his usual all-out amorous assault. Employing every trick in the book, he takes her for a spin in the chair and ingeniously uses a pair of dental forceps to extract a kiss by gently grasping her upturned nose to correctly reposition her mouth.

While Chaplin the comedian's dental antics were sufficiently sidesplitting to satisfy the audiences of 1914, whose level of cinematic sophistication was the same as his, Chaplin the director's clumsy editing of this cleverly conceived sequence detracts from the full brilliance of his highly original material. Dividing that one long take of his operating room seduction scene into bits and pieces by repeatedly intercutting it with frenzied shots of the departed dentist, who eventually returns to discover his employee's malfeasance, Chaplin the fledgling filmmaker sacrifices wit for suspense in his only partially successful attempt to master the Griffith-like technique of using parallel editing to keep an audience on tenterhooks until a last-minute comic climax.

Each of the remaining fourteen Keystones that Chaplin wrote and directed after *Laughing Gas* taught him lessons in modern filmmaking technique as it was rapidly evolving during that remarkable turning-point year in the film industry. Tearing a page out of Griffith's book, he even experimented with adapting a poem into a one-reeler — "The Face on the Barroom Floor," by Hugh Antoine d'Arcy. While the clumsily overtitled film of the same name is one of Chaplin's least interesting and inventive Keystones, creating it was an instructive exercise in narrative technique, since the original tale employed psychological flashbacks that required proficiency with time dissolves, irises, and fades — all useful storytelling devices to add to his cinematic bag of tricks.

By the time of his final Keystone, *His Prehistoric Past*, we find Chaplin the storyteller beginning to experiment with greater structural complexity as his narrative depicts the Little Tramp's first dream. Alone on a park bench, the Little Fellow falls asleep and enters a prehistoric kingdom. Hungering for libidinal adventure, he thoroughly enjoys his reverie of deposing the monarch of a polygamous society and stealing his wives until a tough cop bops him over the head with his nightstick and tosses him out of the park.

Later, Chaplin would depict dream scenes and rude awakenings with greater nuance and sophistication in *The Bank* (1915), *Shoulder Arms* (1918), *Sunnyside* (1919), *The Kid* (1921), *The Idle Class* (1921), *The Gold Rush* (1925), *Modern Times* (1936), and *Limelight* (1952). But even as early as November 1914, when he finished his final Keystone, Chaplin felt confident in his ability to write, cast, direct, and edit commercially successful films and adamant in his determination to make movies on a more personally lucrative basis at a less hectic pace — even if it meant leaving Keystone.

He had made thirty-five films (forty-five and a half reels) in ten months of continuous shooting at Sennett's Edendale factory. He now needed a more leisurely production schedule that would allow him time to become more intimately acquainted with his screen character's psychology and to concentrate on improving the quality of each individual picture. He also needed breathing space between films to get off the treadmill, take his bearings, and begin to experience some semblance of a personal life.

As his Keystone contract drew to a close, the bids rolled in. Chaplin began to get feelers, nibbles, straightforward salary offers, and creative business propositions from reputable film executives with plenty of production experience and distribution know-how. Would Charlie be interested in forming a fifty-fifty profit-sharing production company with no salary? asked Marcus Loew. How about a flat rate of twelve cents a foot of film shot with all production costs born by Universal? asked Carl Laemmle. When Keystone management lowballed him with a comparatively modest salary offer, Chaplin told Sennett to tell New York no — "All I need to make a comedy is a park, a policeman, and a pretty girl."[24] The most generous feeler came from Essanay Films in Chicago. Charlie liked Mack and genuinely regretted parting ways, but "business is business," he wrote Syd.[25]

As Sydney Chaplin well knew, there was one concern that beset his kid brother as his incredibly successful first year in films at Keystone drew to a close. The moviegoing public was fickle, and Charlie was keenly aware of the capriciousness of fame and the impermanence of fortune. Sydney and he had seen Charlie Sr.'s swift descent not so many years ago, and Charlie was determined to make hay while the studio lights still shone bright on his Little Tramp:

> At the end of my Sennett contract, I wanted a thousand dollars a week for my services. They thought I was crazy, but I thought, "Well, I have made a name for myself — it's now or never!" So I told them I'd go out and get it.[26]

As Mack pointed out, he did not receive anything remotely near that sum in his own weekly paycheck. But as Charlie reminded Mack, he was not the funniest man in America.

What Happened Next

The Zulus know Chaplin better than Arkansas knows Garbo.

— Will Rogers[1]

WHEN HE SIGNED A ONE-YEAR CONTRACT WITH ESSANAY in 1915, Chaplin was able to cut his production schedule in half and yet raise his weekly compensation eightfold (including the signing bonus). He remained an employee but gained tighter artistic control of his productions. The Essanay comedies had heftier budgets and less-pressured deadlines, which meant he could create more polished skits with production values and narrative complexity much superior to those of the comedies he had been obliged to turn out at breakneck speed at Keystone. Chaplin wasted no time in playfully satirizing his ex-boss's original refusal to take his pleas for artistic freedom seriously, by portraying Sennett as the hard-of-hearing chief executive of Lockstone Studio, complete with a geezer ear trumpet and a bad case of earwax, in *His New Job*, his first Essanay film.

The most invigorating feature of his new contract was the opportunity it afforded him to become more intimately acquainted with his screen character. At Essanay, "Charlie" and his creator became more complex, more mature. They would cavort before the studio lights for twenty years, but to Chaplin (and to posterity) the duality felt lifelong.

> I would have to spend the rest of my life finding out more about the creature. . . . he was fixed, complete the moment I looked in the mirror and saw him for the first time, yet even now I don't know all the things there are to be known about him.[2]

The author-character relationship was self-consciously impersonal, but clandestinely autobiographical. In conversations with friends and family, Chaplin protected his privacy, firmly maintaining his boundaries. He always discussed "Charlie" in the third person and never referred to him as "I" or "me." By inventing a proxy mouthpiece, who allowed him to share artistically disguised and comically revised childhood memories with his audiences, he could open his heart to a public that reciprocated by falling wildly in love with the Little Fellow.

After he left Keystone, Chaplin wove his magic through thirty tramp films including four feature-length masterpieces: *The Kid* (1921), *The Gold Rush* (1925), *City Lights* (1931), and *Modern Times* (1935). Reflecting on that global Chaplin mania, it would seem that posterity's attachment to his tramp remains much more passionate than the public's interest in his films, despite the fact that three of them still appear regularly on the American Film Institute's hundred-greatest-films list. Young people today recognize the image of Charlie Chaplin. But very few of them have actually seen a Chaplin movie or know very much about his career — either at the peak of his international popularity or during his final years.

*　　*　　*

Chaplin's tramp was not the first international pop icon in entertainment history. Those laurels must go to Buffalo Bill, whose instantly recognizable character image was known throughout North America and Western Europe. But the Little Tramp was the first *global* icon in entertainment history and probably the most enduring — with the possible exception of his fellow trickster Mickey Mouse who Disney claimed was inspired by Charlie. In Chaplin's heyday, Will Rogers's remark about his fame extending to African tribesman was no exaggeration. A *New York Times* reporter wrote from Ghana:

"There's a cinema . . . in Accra," said my hosts. "We'll all go down and see what they have tonight. It's the only cinema house on the coast, the only movie within thousands of miles of country."

. . . We were whisked inside . . . the lights flashed on for the intermission. There was a wild burst of shouts and yells and we looked down into a sea of black faces.

Here were Fanti savages from Ashanti land, up-country Kroo boys who work along the docks, . . . Haussas from the north of Nigeria, with red fezzes and huge white turbans, . . . Gamen, natives of Accra, dressed in henna reds and dark blues and brilliant oranges of Manchester print cottons. Some had wrapped them round like a toga; others wore simply a loin cloth . . . naked to the waist, their black bodies shining in the gleam of the electric lamps. . . .

At last the lights went out. No title flashed on the screen, but a funny little man with wide wondering round eyes appeared — a strange wandering walk, a little cane and a derby hat. It was Charlie! My own recognition was no quicker than that of the wildly transported native audience. There was an immediate chorus of shouts, "Charlee! Charlee!" Few of them knew any more English than that, but they did know his funny little hat, his hobbled walk, his amazing shoes.

It was a film from the remote antiquity of filmdom. . . .

Charlie kicked the villain in the usual place, and the villain responded by slamming the door on Charlie's nose. . . .

. . . every time that Charlie kicked the villain and every time that the villain kicked Charlie the audience roared and shouted approval. . . .

There is a traveling moving picture show, equipped with films and projector and an old Ford car, which goes all over the west coast of Africa. It has been in the east, too, and right up in the jungle and the bush among savages who have never seen a white man before. In the larger towns the operator sets up boards across oil cans in a cocoa shed and the pictures are shown on a sheet stretched across one end of the shed. In smaller places the theatre is simply out of doors.

The operator has covered over 30,000 miles. What tales he must be able to tell! How did the natives first receive this white man's juju? Were they frightened? What did the witch doctors think? . . . Some day, when I go back, I am going to get an interview with that man. I want to know, too, what the witch doctors think of Charlie![3]

During his heyday, it has been estimated, as many as 300 million people watched the Little Tramp's movie screen antics.[4] That heyday lasted at least from 1915 through the mid-1930s. In those days, as one of the most famous and universally admired human beings in the world, Chaplin met and mingled with men like Einstein, Churchill, Roosevelt, and Gandhi. In his 1935 essay *Everybody's Language*, Winston Churchill placed Chaplin on an equal artistic footing with Dickens. George Bernard Shaw — a Nobel Prize and Academy Award winner in his own right — declared him the only genius the cinema had produced. And a *New York Herald Tribune* reviewer wrote: "Praising one of Mr. Chaplin's pictures is like saying that Shakespeare was a good writer."[5] Lenin described him as "the only man I ever wanted to meet." Apart from Chaplin's undisputed reputation as the first actor-writer-director genius of cinema, the most important reason for such glowing praise from Lenin and other world leaders was that Charlie (his screen character) was still considered an archetypal symbol of the common man.

A less famous but equally notorious visitor to the Chaplin Studio in 1921 was William Z. Foster — a former IWW "Wobbly" and leader of the 1919 steel strike, who had recently returned from the Red International of Labor Unions conference in Moscow. Clandestinely monitored by one of J. Edgar Hoover's special agents who recorded that innocuous social visit as the very first entry in what eventually became Charlie Chaplin's two-thousand-page FBI file, Foster later ran for the U.S. presidency as the Communist Party's candidate in the elections of 1924, 1928, and 1932.

Chaplin's extraordinary common touch explained his appeal to such a diverse group of political radicals, world leaders, celebrities, and intellectuals, as well as to working-class audiences throughout the Western world. Then there was his remarkable ability to communicate wordlessly with Asian coolies, Hindu natives, African tribesman, Latino peasants, and others for whom language and culture were no barrier. "I am known in parts of the world by people who have never heard of Jesus Christ," Chaplin could (and did) matter-of-factly state without exaggeration.

His intuitive feel for the personal psychology and daily predicaments of the little guy was a direct outgrowth of his years of schooling in the proletarian theatrical traditions of British music hall, coupled with his childhood experiences with poverty and social inequality. Importing the narrative techniques of topical comedy from late-nineteenth-century music hall into early-twentieth-century American filmmaking, Chaplin's silent film masterpieces were eloquent personal musings on contemporary issues of the day, as seen through the eyes of a social underdog.

The Immigrant (1916), for example, affectionately if comically portrayed the trials and tribulations of newcomers, whose official welcome to the promised land consists of being herded like cattle and impersonally labeled with ID tags by Ellis Island clerks under the shadow of the Statue of Liberty. Determined to preserve his dignity through nonconformity but not to risk deportation by openly challenging bureaucratic authority, trickster Charlie slyly back-kicks a shipboard immigration official in his authoritarian behind while ostensibly permitting himself to be tagged and rounded up with the rest of the herd. That two-reeler was Chaplin's take on the immigration experience at a period in American history when fully one-third of all people in the country were either foreign born or had at least one foreign-born parent. For moviegoers around the world, the film was his comic valentine to the American Dream. There was nothing bitter in his social satire: the film ends happily with Charlie marrying a beautiful fellow immigrant whom he has met in steerage during their transatlantic crossing. (Some of the newsreel-like footage from this film is so realistic that it is still used in contemporary documentaries as a visual illustration of what the immigration experience was like.)

Another short film, *Shoulder Arms* (1918), paid a similar affectionate tribute to America's fighting men by simultaneously expressing Chaplin's unblinking view of the gruesome realities of World War I and his profound sympathy for the little-guy doughboys who were still fighting and dying at the time of that film's release. In that antiwar masterpiece, which Jean Cocteau aptly described as moving like a drum roll, Charlie, the klutzy-but-graceful recruit Charlie endures the hardships and perils of trench warfare before bravely volunteering to undertake a dangerous mission behind enemy lines, where he captures the Kaiser, thereby singlehandedly ending the nightmare of war. Or almost ending it. The film concludes with a reality jolt: back in boot camp, Charlie, the romantically naive and patriotic doughboyin-training, rudely awakens on his stateside bunk bed from his heroic dreams of glory, having not yet been shipped overseas to face the horrors that await him. Not only was *Shoulder Arms* the inspiration for Jean Renoir's equally nuanced antiwar classic *Grand Illusion* of 1937, it also was personally requisitioned by General Eisenhower and used as a morale-boosting propaganda film during World War II.

Chaplin's ability to take the temperature of his times and to comment insightfully on the important social issues of the day was sometimes almost accidental. His first feature-length comedy, *The Kid*, was a remarkably intimate film which served to transform personal pain into comic artistic expression. Begun as a direct response to the tragic loss of his own infant, the film follows Chaplin's tramp as he finds, adopts, and lovingly raises a lost child. Production of that masterpiece began only two and a half weeks after his own son died shortly after birth. Serendipitously, the film's themes of emotional loss, displacement, and homelessness resonated with contemporary social concerns. On everyone's mind were the displaced refugee children of World War I. Many people were still grieving for loved ones killed in that war. And among intellectuals, Charlie's cinematic lost child spoke to an equally lost generation looking for self-expression. No moviemaker and no other film — with the exception of Griffith's *Birth of a Nation* — did as much to earn worldwide recognition for the cinema as a legitimate art form. When he went abroad after making *The Kid*, Chaplin was mobbed in both London and Paris, the latter city declaring a public holiday for the premiere.

Modern Times, the last silent film Chaplin made, was the antithesis of *The Kid*: it was an entirely self-conscious meditation on the most pressing social issue of the day, the Great Depression. During the worldwide economic crisis of the 1930s, Chaplin attempted to place the grim problems of society into a comic perspective through the film's running satiric commentary.

Stationing his Little Tramp squarely in the middle of the mess by casting him as a black-sheep factory worker, who was no more a member in good standing of the organized masses than of the ruling classes, Chaplin poked good-natured fun at both sides. Kidding profit-conscious management for its indifference to the welfare of workers, he ribbed strike-happy organized labor for its equally myopic unwillingness to let big business get back on its feet. Steering clear of collective utopian solutions, the film ended with his own signature exit, a stroll down life's highway, Charlie shuffled off into the dawn of a new day arm in arm with an equally scruffy female companion, Paulette Goddard. "Buck up — never say die! We'll get along" are his final, comforting words to her and his Depression-conscious audience.

His next picture, *The Great Dictator* (1940), got Chaplin into political hot water that ultimately forced him out of the United States permanently. While he was on a visit to England in 1952, his reentry permit was revoked as retribution for his alleged Communist sympathies and dubious moral character. It was an ironic twist that Chaplin himself had forecast such a mishap in a famous gag sequence in *Modern Times*.

Wandering in the street, naive Charlie sees a red danger flag fall from a passing truck and picks it up, running and waving the flag in an innocent attempt to catch the driver's eye. He is entirely unaware that he has just been joined from the rear by an angry mob of striking workers. Rallying behind his flag, they chant the Communist "Internationale" until they are dispersed by the cops, who scoop up Charlie the Red and toss him in the clink.

Just four years later, during a remarkably rapid shift of political contexts, Chaplin the filmmaker earned the enmity of isolationist America's political establishment for creating *The Great Dictator*. Abandoning traditional pantomime technique and his classic tramp character in order to play two talking parts — Adolf

Hitler and a little Jewish barber — Chaplin spoke for the first time on film. His closing speech, an artistically flawed but emotionally eloquent plea for concerted international intervention against Hitler's persecution of the Jews, earned Chaplin a subpoena to appear before a hastily formed, isolationist, antiwar Senate subcommittee on war propaganda in September of 1941. The popular, financially successful film — which helped shape American public opinion in favor of the war — also helped earn him, in the files of the FBI, the quaint political epithet "premature antifascist." In the terminology of the day, that was a euphemism for someone with strong left-wing leanings who was not officially a member of the Communist Party.

As Talleyrand remarked, "treason is a matter of dates." Chaplin's passionately anti-Nazi views, about which he was outspoken from the late 1930s to war's end, never changed. But America's relationship to Russia and Germany did. During the years of the Hitler-Stalin Pact, America's official position was isolationist, and Chaplin's speech in *The Great Dictator* was seen as inciting to war. But by the time the United States was involved in World War II, alliances were shifting. Politics during this period made for strange bedfellows. Before the war, the American Communist Party and the right-wing America First Committee were united in their adamant opposition to this country fighting against Germany. It was precisely during this period that Chaplin filmed and released *The Great Dictator*, which openly urged Americans to wage war against the Nazis regardless of whether that war harmed or benefited the Soviet Union. When, a few years later, the Soviet Union and America became allies in a life-and-death struggle against the Axis powers, Chaplin continued voicing his vehement anti-Nazi attitudes. But now he also championed Soviet interests as identical with our own. Throughout 1942 he campaigned vigorously on behalf of Russian War Relief and a Second Front.

Because of Chaplin's worldwide stature as an artist, and the ability of a Chaplin satire to tickle funny bones on such a mass scale, those who disliked and distrusted the Soviet Union viewed him as a formidable adversary. But if his ability to influence were to be effectively neutralized, Chaplin's popular image had to be taken down several notches.

The backlash against Chaplin gathered momentum in late 1942. Westbrook Pegler, a conservative journalist whose syndicated column ran in hundreds of newspapers, kicked off the campaign with two scathing diatribes. Characterizing Chaplin's activities in support of our military alliance with the Soviets as pro-Communist and therefore anti-American, he recommended deportation. And with even more vehemence, Pegler also suggested that the actor's three previous divorces were clear proof of his unpatriotic contempt "for the standard American relationship of marriage, family and home."

The last charge proved to be the one that stuck most easily. When he was younger, Chaplin had a reputation as a libidinous ladies' man, who frequently indulged his weakness for teenage girls. And a juicy sex scandal involving a famous movie star made good reading.

In June of 1943 an unmarried twenty-two-year-old woman with whom Chaplin had been intimate filed a paternity suit, claiming he was the father of her unborn child. Independently administered blood tests would conclusively prove that he was not the child's father. But before those results were made known, Chaplin was well on his way to being publicly branded a "moral leper."

Daily front-page coverage of a sensational trial on lurid charges of white slavery, unflattering photos of him being fingerprinted like a common criminal, and a running series of hostile articles by politically conservative Hollywood columnists, led by Hedda Hopper, contributed to the precipitous decline in Chaplin's public image, as did the behind-the-scenes activities of the FBI. Careful analysis of that agency's security files on Chaplin suggests he was frivolously charged under the antiquated Mann Act in spite of abundant evidence of his innocence — which was eventually proved. It also suggests that the FBI supplied gossip columnists with information from those files and that the bureau even suppressed, and physically hid, indications of judicial impropriety that, if known, would have forced the federal judge hearing the case to disqualify himself on ethical grounds.

Since the widely publicized and unduly protracted series of paternity hearings and trials did not end until a month after Germany's surrender, Chaplin's political influence was effectively curtailed. But he remained fervently committed to an idealistic postwar crusade against all forms of domestic political repression. Like many American liberals in those days, he was quicker to identify and protest the encroachments on civil liberties in the United States than the excesses of Stalinism.

With his image tarnished, the government's political strategy for containing Chaplin became the reverse of what it earlier had been. Keeping Chaplin off the witness stand was now the single most effective way to further damage his reputation and impugn his loyalties. He was, in effect, labeled a Communist in a campaign of rumors and innuendoes. For as the House Un-American Activities Committee and the FBI well knew (and the files of the latter indicate), he never had been a member of the Communist Party. Had he been allowed to testify under oath, he could have set the record straight. HUAC subpoenaed him in 1947, but his hearing was postponed three times, and finally canceled.

Chaplin fought back with the tenacity of a true childhood "invulnerable" — someone who is accustomed to routinely overcoming any and all obstacles, no matter how great.[6] He obliged his attackers by responding to their inflammatory rhetoric with passionate indignation. Goaded into defending himself, he rapidly made himself a convenient symbol of dangerous leftist leanings.

He was determined, no matter the personal cost, not to be

intimidated. That deep and abiding faith in his ability to prevail in the face of adversity had always been his personal credo:

> Even when I was in the orphanage, when I was roaming the streets trying to find enough to eat to keep alive, even then I thought of myself as the greatest actor in the world. I had to feel that exuberance that comes from utter confidence in yourself. Without it you go down to defeat.[7]

That very survival characteristic had endeared his Little Tramp to moviegoers around the world for more than forty years. It was natural that the invulnerable child in Charlie automatically assumed that the same coping strategy would serve him equally well in his struggles with HUAC and the FBI.

"Proceed with the butchery . . . fire ahead at this old gray head" were his opening words to the reporters who gathered at the press conference after the opening of *Monsieur Verdoux* in 1947. Not the least bit interested in discussing his film, they were there to report on his politics. They bombarded him with questions about his patriotism. The Cold War was heating up. His good-natured attempt to deflect their hostility by describing himself as a "peace monger" did not go over.[8]

Afterward, when conservative political pressure groups demonstrated their ability to induce Americans to boycott his film as an act of patriotism, Chaplin began to appreciate the extent to which he had underestimated his opponents.

Limelight, the last film he made before leaving the United States in the fall of 1952, suffered an even more drastic fate. Right-wing lobbyists were able to bring so much political pressure to bear on major exhibitors that bookings were canceled at hundreds of theaters. By the following spring, Chaplin was living in permanent political exile in Switzerland — a decision he announced symbolically by turning in his American reentry permit.

Although he would not set foot in the country again for another twenty years, daily reminders of his absence were present in the subliminal consciousness of millions of Americans during that summer of 1953. Chaplin's theme song from *Limelight*, which he composed, became a hit. The haunting refrain of his sentimental swan song drifted over America's airwaves.

Through an odd twist of fate and a technicality in the rules of the Academy of Motion Picture Arts and Sciences, his theme song would also win Chaplin and his arrangers an Oscar when *Limelight* was rereleased. Back in 1952, to have been considered for an Oscar, the film would have had to play for a minimum of one week in Los Angeles. So successful had the *Limelight* boycott been that year, the film had never lasted that long in one single theater.

Times had changed when Chaplin returned to receive a Special Academy Lifetime Achievement Award in 1972. The former firebrand was in his declining years. And the thirty-seventh president of the United States, Richard Nixon — a former HUAC member and one of the most outspoken anticommunists at the time of Charlie's unceremonious departure — was too busy with his own political problems to comment on Chaplin's return. Within a few months he would be attempting to explain a break-in that had recently taken place at Democratic Party headquarters at the Watergate.

Eighty-two-year-old Chaplin was so choked up that he could barely speak when Jack Lemmon presented him with his honorary Oscar. The physically fragile and emotionally labile actor was genuinely afraid that his former stardom and lifetime professional achievements were fast fading to oblivion. Despite these fears, he received what remains the longest standing ovation in the history of the Motion Picture Academy of Arts and Sciences.

It was a lovefest made all the more poignant by the fact that Chaplin was returning to a Hollywood he had helped shape when it was still a backwater. He was being applauded by an industry he had elevated from its lowly social origins as a cheap novelty amusement that cost only a nickel into the culturally and intellectually prestigious art form known as cinema. Many of the actors in the Dorothy Chandler Pavilion that night considered him the greatest actor in film history. And none of the actors present would dispute the fact that Chaplin pioneered the fundamentals of film acting technique at a time when stage acting techniques were still being crudely imported and adapted wholesale into the new medium. And they were congratulating him, too, for leaving his indelible stamp on twentieth-century culture itself.

Three years later, the former Cockney urchin from the slums of London would be knighted by the Queen of England. Two years after that, he would die peacefully in his sleep at the age of eighty-eight, surrounded by his wife of thirty-four years and seven of their eight children.

Afterword

Falsehoods or
False Memories:
Where's Charlie?

History as such only arouses my skepticism — whereas a poetic interpretation achieves a general effect. ... there are more valid facts and details in works of art than there are in history books.

— Chaplin[1]

ALTHOUGH GERALDINE CHAPLIN IS RIGHT ON THE MONEY when she says I've had her father in analysis for years (twenty to be exact), she has no idea how much time I've also spent cadging second opinions from colleagues in an effort to distinguish fact from fiction in conflicting versions of Charlie's early life story, as told by Chaplin himself on two occasions fifty years apart. In a Chaplin seminar at the Washington Psychoanalytic Institute in 1988, seven doctoral candidates and I spent many long hours poring over those two autobiographies before meeting weekly to discuss our impressions of some glaring disparities in Charlie's accounts of emotionally traumatic events in his early childhood. One of those books, *Charlie Chaplin's Own Story*, was narrated by Charlie in 1915 at the age of twenty-six. The other, *My Autobiography*, was published in 1964 when he was seventy-five.

To seduce those budding analysts to sign up for my course

and take on the talmudic exercise of doing side-by-side comparative text passage readings, I had to sweeten the deal. While we
would systematically examine Charlie's two memoirs, we would
also use some of his greatest movies as texts: *The Kid, The Gold
Rush, City Lights, Modern Times*, and *Limelight*. A fundamental
premise of our seminar (and this biography as well) was that a
filmmaker's life can be used to read his film, and the films can be
used to read his life — *if* he retains such extraordinary control of
his films as Chaplin did. Looking back, I might have advertised
my course in the Institute's academic catalogue as "Hollywood
meets Sigmund Freud." To peddle my proposed curriculum to
the Education Committee faculty as serious psychoanalytic
scholarship rather than frivolous escapist entertainment, I quoted
the father of psychoanalysis himself:

> In the last few days, Chaplin has been in Vienna . . . but it was too
> cold for him here, and he left again quickly. He is undoubtedly a
> great artist; certainly he always portrays one and the same figure;
> only the weakly poor, helpless, clumsy youngster for whom, how-
> ever, things turn out well in the end. Now do you think for this
> role he has to forget about his own ego? On the contrary, he always
> plays only himself as he was in his dismal youth. He cannot get
> away from those impressions and humiliations of that past period
> of his life. He is, so to speak, an exceptionally simple and trans-
> parent case. The idea that the achievements of artists are inti-
> mately bound up with their childhood memories, impressions,
> repressions and disappointments, has already brought in much
> enlightenment and has, for that reason, become very precious
> to us.[2]

To motivate my fellow seminar members to rise to the occasion and grapple conscientiously with that poorly written and
sometimes confusing early memoir, I underscored a heated controversy that still surrounded the book's disputed authorship.
The as-told-to life story (told to journalist Rose Wilder Lane)

was originally authorized by Chaplin for publication in a twenty-nine-part newspaper series that ran in the *San Francisco Bulletin* from July 5 to August 4, 1915. Those articles were reprinted verbatim, but not distributed as planned in book form by Bobbs Merrill in the fall of 1916. At the last minute, sales were blocked by Chaplin's attorney.

When he saw the completed version of his as-told-to memoirs in book form, Chaplin got cold feet. Indignantly disputing its accuracy and authenticity, he behaved as if he had never before seen any one of those original twenty-nine newspaper articles, which contained so many intimate personal details and painful memories of his London childhood only he could have revealed. Four final chapters covering Chaplin's historically unprecedented and meteoric rise to international film stardom between early 1915 and 1916 were tacked on to bring his life story up to date. How, where, and when all of the information in those final four chapters of *Charlie Chaplin's Own Story* was acquired is unclear. Robinson suggests that Lane could have easily culled and embroidered historically accurate information secondhand from published Chaplin interviews by other journalists. But Robinson completely ignores a claim Lane makes that she and Chaplin met in person *in Los Angeles* for a follow-up interview *after he had left northern California*. That claim can be found in a letter from Lane to Chaplin that Robinson reprints in his biography. In it she says, "You were so very courteous in giving me a great deal of time, and all of the information on which to base the story, while I was in Los Angeles, that I have been assuming that your attitude toward me was quite friendly."[3] Ignoring this passage, which directly contradicts his own view of what transpired, Robinson asserts that Lane and Chaplin met once (and suggests that it was probably only once) in northern California between March and April of 1915. He's right that such a meeting did take place. And the outcome of that meeting (or the several northern California meetings, I believe) was the basis for the original twenty-nine-part newspaper series. And the outcome of that subsequent Los Angeles meeting she refers to would seem to be the basis of those final four chapters. Those add-on Hollywood chapters were entirely flattering. They contained no emotionally charged, deeply personal, potentially offensive private information whose accuracy he could dispute.

Having never authorized in writing the republication of the original newspaper series as part of a book, Chaplin was able to obtain a legal injunction to kill the distribution of the thousands of copies that had already been printed. Still, a few copies survived, including a copy in the Library of Congress.

When the book was republished seventy years later, after the copyright expired, the original controversy surrounding its hotly contested authorship resurfaced. Since those memoirs were an as-told-to version of Chaplin's life story, blame for the book's verbally unsophisticated narrative, glaring factual inaccuracies, and obviously distorted memories could easily be ascribed to the twenty-nine-year-old journalist, Rose Wilder Lane. Serving as Charlie's "faithful transcriber" and "editor" — as she referred to herself in the foreword — Lane, whose claim was vigorously contested by Chaplin's lawyer, was characterized in Chaplin's complaint as an unscrupulous journalist who lacked professional standards. Whether she was unprincipled or merely a writer of limited talent becomes the pertinent question.

Apart from that quashed 1916 memoir, Lane later in her career faithfully transcribed and edited — or embroidered and willfully mistranscribed — as-told-to life stories of Henry Ford, Jack London, and Herbert Hoover. Although Hoover disliked the unflattering way his quotes from those original interviews were presented in book form, he never disputed their authenticity. He and Lane eventually became friends, and her papers reside in his presidential library. She also published articles in *Harper's, Ladies' Home Journal, Good Housekeeping,* and the *Saturday Evening Post,* ending her fifty-year career as a war correspondent in South Vietnam for *Woman's Day* at age 78. Her mother, Laura Ingalls Wilder, was the author of the greatly beloved *Little House on the Prairie* books. Rose also helped edit that series, which is considered a classic of American children's literature.

Whether Lane doctored the narrative and fiddled with the dialogue of Chaplin's life story throughout her interviews, as his lawyer charged, or faithfully transcribed all or nearly all of it verbatim from hastily scribbled reporter's notes, as she claimed, is impossible to say. All we know for certain is that she interviewed Chaplin in person.

Taking their lead from Chaplin's repudiation of *Charlie Chaplin's Own Story*, his biographers have generally given this memoir short shrift, ignored its valuable psychological contents, and categorically rejected it as a valid text or legitimate research document. David Robinson is one of Lane's harshest critics (and Chaplin's staunchest defenders). Expressing his exasperation with one particularly egregious passage in the 1916 original, Robinson wrote:

> The book is full of such romantic and misleading nonsense, which has nevertheless continued to supply and confuse gullible Chaplin historians for seven decades.[4]

Robinson ended his discussion of the book by lamenting that "one or two copies had leaked out to be the bane of film historians."[5]

When one of those original copies was reprinted by Indiana University Press, Robinson took up the cudgels on Chaplin's behalf once more. The next year in a 1986 book review in the *Times Literary Supplement* entitled "An Imposture Revived," he again dismissed it as "a flagrant autobiographical fake," adding:

> Is there any value to the text at all? Anyone familiar with Chaplin interviews of the period (he interviewed often and well in his early Hollywood days) will recognize passages which are undoubtedly

authentic and probably recorded from the original interview. . . . some untruths may have come directly from Chaplin. . . . It may be good in parts: but in the end, the areas between what is Chaplin's own story and what is pure fiction are so misty that we would probably do better to discount and discard it all.[6]

As for Harry Geduld, a highly respected Chaplin scholar and emeritus professor of literature at Indiana University, Robinson accused him of being "culpably gullible in the degree of trust he places in the book's authorship." But Geduld was nobody's fool. Aware that he could be made to look ridiculous for publishing such a factually inaccurate book, Geduld clearly stated his reasons for doing so in the introduction to *Charlie Chaplin's Own Story*. He wanted to call future scholarly attention to this previously suppressed autobiography in the hope of getting a second opinion. He wrote:

> Yet for all its naiveties and its pseudo-Dickensian flavor it offers us many unique glimpses into Chaplin's childhood. If, with caution, we choose to regard some of these glimpses as fact, they can be read as a complement to Chaplin's later autobiography. If, on the other hand, we view them as pure fiction, they are no less significant, for, like Chaplin's films we must regard them as the fantasies of a great artist — self-imagings that were more meaningful to their creator than the humdrum reality. As such, *CCOS*, whose import has been lost on virtually every biographer, must await the insights of the psychoanalyst.[7]

Bingo! The game was afoot. We were going to be psychoanalytic sleuths. Professor Geduld had just invited our entire seminar to use its skills as childhood memory experts, and our clinical training as life-story auditors, to add our thoughts and conclusions to this ongoing controversy between two equally qualified Chaplin scholars over the legitimacy of this previously denigrated text.

We started the seminar by discussing the pitfall of oversimplification and arbitrary true-false distinctions that failed to leave room for shades of interpretation. We explored the parallel tacit assumptions and psychological rules of evidence in the way psychoanalysts listen to their patients and read other people's life-story narratives.

We touched on some fundamental issues in psychobiography without, of course, coming up with definitive answers. Truthfulness, accuracy, and witness reliability can be assessed from equally valid but entirely different perspectives in the courtroom, the consulting room, and the biographer's study.

What is a provable fact? What is a psychological truth? How are they different? Are they both legitimate?

What about the question of Chaplin's personal myth that Geduld raised in his introduction? Can a childhood fantasy ever become a historical fact? Can the life that a grown man leads dramatize or actualize self-myths that he invented, or that other family members bestowed on him, as a child? Why do kids invent self-myths? What role do their parents' dreams and life examples play in inspiring them?

What is a lie? Can a lie reveal a truth? What's the difference between free-associating, fibbing, conning, fantasizing, daydreaming, bullshitting, inventing, imagining, exaggerating, embroidering, and outright prevaricating, to name but a few overlapping forms of fact-distorting storytelling and self-reporting.

How are falsehoods, false memories, and screen memories connected? Can a drastic change in childhood memory occur spontaneously at different stages of life? In a previous published monograph on multiple autobiographies written by the same person at different ages, I described how Frederick Douglass's memories of his father shifted dramatically at different stages in his life.[8]

What about Chaplin's father? How could we reconcile Chaplin, at twenty-six, vividly describing his father to Rose Wilder Lane as a drunken brute who cursed and mistreated his mother, with the same Chaplin, fifty years later, recalling with equal certainty, and independently verifiable accuracy, that he had never even seen his parents live together, his parents having permanently separated when he was one.

It was that demonstrably false characterization of Charlie Chaplin Sr. as a mean-spirited brute that originally prompted Chaplin's lawyer and subsequently motivated David Robinson to assert confidently that *Charlie Chaplin's Own Story* was a fake. Both men sincerely believed that Lane's irresponsibly written book was packed with false stories that *she* invented in order to plug holes in a flimsy narrative based on scanty personal information casually supplied by Charlie Chaplin in passing.

The final answer to that particular piece of the psychoanalytic puzzle did not become clear until twenty years after our seminar when I came across a 1915 article written by Sydney Chaplin in a film magazine discussing a man Syd referred to as "my father at the time."[9] That unnamed father, whom Syd described as a music hall star with the signature song "The Miner's Dream of Home," turned out to be a mean-spirited brute by the name of Leo Dryden. He had indeed lived with and drunkenly abused Charlie's mother before stealing their infant son, Charlie's younger half-brother Wheeler, and running off to Canada.

And so Rose Lane's allegedly invented story turned out to be Charlie's false memory: a screen memory combining Leo Dryden and Charlie Chaplin Sr. into one father figure, the description of whom Lane "faithfully" transcribed. Faithfully, that is, apart from the difficulties she and every other interviewer in 1915 experienced in understanding Charlie's nasal twang, Cockney slang, and aitches — an embarrassing speech pattern that the upwardly mobile actor became determined to shed as part of his drive toward self-improvement, coupled with informal elocution coaching from his actress friend Constance Collier, whose later pupils included Katharine Hepburn and Marilyn Monroe.

Describing what Charlie was like around the time of his interview(s) with Rose Wilder Lane, Jeffrey Vance wrote:

> Perhaps the most touching discoveries made were the images documenting Chaplin's early life. Many of these photographs, including shots from his music-hall days and a handful of candid pictures from his early career in films, are inscribed with Chaplin's own writing and remembrances. It is somewhat jarring to see how unsure his writing and spelling were during this period. The inscriptions stand in stark contrast to the urbane and sophisticated personal image that Chaplin perpetuated . . . during his many years of self-education. These photographs, highlighted by his wayward spelling, are a testament to his phenomenal effort and ambition to rise above his impoverished Cockney beginnings.[10]

A typical example of Chaplin's Cockney dialect translation problems was Lane's misspelling Pownall Terrace as "Palermo Terrace."[11]

It would be a gross error to infer strictly on a literary or linguistic basis that Chaplin's primitively expressed, factually inaccurate, and mawkishly told early-life memoir is an invalid research document because it is poorly written. Conversely, it would be wrong to assume that all of the personal information contained in his polished and seamlessly flowing late-life autobiography is also factually accurate because it is persuasively written. By way of example, let us take a look at the profoundly moving opening pages of *My Autobiography*.

Unconsciously condensing two crucial life events that actually occurred two years apart into one memory, Chaplin begins his life story by evocatively limning an incident that was the turning (or termination) point of his childhood. Describing himself as a *twelve-year-old* spending a melancholy Sunday morning wistfully hanging around a theatrical pub where the famous music hall stars of South London congregated, Charlie recalls returning home to the garret at 3 Pownall Terrace where he lived with his mother, only to discover that she was in the process of becoming quietly psychotic. Actually, the psychotic episode he writes about took place when he was fourteen, not twelve. While it is tempting to dismiss his error as one of those randomly generated fact failings of a seventy-five-year-old, certain questions nag the mind of a trained psychoanalytic investigator. Why twelve? Why not ten or thirteen? And why all the nostalgia about spending that sad Sunday morning at a theatrical pub like the one his departed vaudevillian father frequented until his untimely death when Charlie was twelve?

Age twelve! So that's it: Chaplin confounded the date of one personal tragedy — the final loss of his father to alcoholism when he was twelve — with the date of another tragedy, the final loss of his mother to psychosis when he was fourteen. An interesting psychological connection, but so what?

The psychoanalytic wheels begin to spin. Are there any deeper emotional reasons why Chaplin telescoped the two events by fusing his two ages into one? Why not go back and check some dates: when did his father die and when did his mother go mad? Answer: Charlie Chaplin Sr. died on May 9, 1901, and his estranged wife was committed to the asylum on May 9, 1903.

Yet common sense and psychoanalysis would seem to agree that no woman would be driven mad with depressive grief on the anniversary of her ex-husband's death if their emotional attachment had in fact been thoroughly severed thirteen years earlier. And so, what emerges in the narration of Chaplin's boyhood story is evidence of strong residual threads connecting Charlie Chaplin Sr. and Lily Harley, who lived in the same Kennington neighborhoods, no more than a few streets apart from one another, in the 1890s.

Of course their paths crossed. And their relationship was ongoing — not some piece of ancient history that ground to a halt and atrophied in 1890. No wonder their son Charlie romantically idealized their stormy teenage love story as a boy growing up, yearning for a complete family. And it was only fitting that those boyhood idealizations of his parents' adolescent romance would later play such an influential if unconscious role both in the plots of Charlie's films and in his private life inspiring a lifelong romantic nostalgia for pure and innocent adolescent girls.

Returning to that Chaplin seminar and our classroom attempt to resolve the thorny question of whether or not the personal information recorded in Lane's book was narrated sufficiently by Charlie to consider it a legitimate research document — it is important to clarify the issue of who Chaplin was when Lane interviewed him. The internationally renowned and understandably image-conscious celebrity who ordered his high-priced New York attorney to kill *Charlie Chaplin's Own Story* in 1916 was not the same fellow who had spilled the beans a year earlier.

Lane's interview(s) took place early in 1915. Chaplin was well aware that Charlie the screen character was already becoming famous and his films were earning record sums at the box office. But Chaplin had no idea of precisely what his own current level of career success as a professional actor meant, except for the money involved, about which he was streetwise and Cockney-shrewd. When Chaplin hopped a Pullman from L.A. to Chicago that winter to sign a lucrative contract with the Essanay Film Company, nobody recognized him or pestered him for autographs. He traveled incognito and enjoyed an ordinary citizen's sense of personal privacy on that four-day trip to Chicago. He was riding high professionally, but he could come and go as he pleased. Chaplin's traveling companion on that 1915 journey was a cowboy movie star by the name of Broncho Billy Anderson. It was Billy, not Charlie, over whom their fellow passengers fawned. But on Chaplin's next trip East one year later, huge crowds with brass bands greeted him at every stop along the way and the

NYPD actually found it necessary to disembark him from the train at 125th Street in order to avoid the mass mayhem that awaited his arrival at Grand Central Station.

When Charlie had first arrived at that rural studio in northern California where Lane would interview him two months later, his new cameraman, Rollie Totheroh, was astounded by the already wealthy actor's scuffed valise and threadbare belongings. Unaccustomed to fame or luxury, twenty-six-year-old Chaplin lacked pretension. And it was that unsophisticated and poorly educated Cockney actor whose interviews Lane tried to transcribe.

The Chaplin craze was about to start. But at the time Lane and Charlie met, he still thought of himself as "a little nickel comedian,"[12] not the artist in slapshoes he later described. He felt slightly bewildered by the journalistic attention and studio-generated publicity he was beginning to receive.

Chaplin's way of dealing with social insecurity and interview anxiety would always be to do what he knew best — to act. Whenever he felt afraid, he put on a show and charmed his audience by razzle-dazzling them. A much more insightful reporter than Lane, who observed Chaplin thoughtfully while interviewing him several years later, offered this description:

> "I'm an awful chump at being interviewed," he said. "I can talk a bit when it's all informal . . . but when any one starts an interview I lose my head and choke up."
>
> . . . Outside of myself, I have never met any one who has as much fear of meeting people under formal circumstances as Charlie Chaplin. . . .
>
> Then to protect himself he acted. Whenever he gets nervous he acts, and so forgets himself in his outlay of energy.[13]

Extrapolating from this thumbnail description of how Chaplin responded to interviews and interviewers, it is safe to assume that he relaxed himself and tried to win Lane's sympathy by putting on a vivid improv performance of his life story, colorfully dramatizing and spontaneously reenacting scenes from his Dickensian boyhood on the streets of London.

Either by inclination or by intellectual limitation, Rose Lane functioned more like an archivist than a portraitist. She tried to transcribe Chaplin verbatim insofar as she was able to keep up with his rapid-fire delivery and understand his Sam Weller–like Dickensian speech, which he undoubtedly exaggerated from time to time for dramatic effect during the course of his narrative.

And what about the influence of Dickens himself? Apart from his stylistic influence on *Charlie Chaplin's Own Story*, what were his unacknowledged contributions to its story line and plot contents? David Robinson suspects that Lane was the culprit who lifted and transposed whole scenes from *Oliver Twist* and used them as filler to plug holes in her story. Every informed Chaplin scholar concurs that someone cribbed from that novel. It also happened to be Charlie's favorite novel, from youth to old age. In fact, we recall, one of his earliest character monologues was his portrayal as a ten-year-old of Little Nell's grandfather in Dickens's *Old Curiosity Shop*.[14]

Either Chaplin or Lane was technically guilty of "plagiarizing" from Dickens. Given the fact that Chaplin was a consummate sketch artist, and the son of two sketch artists, I believe he was the one who consciously snatched, or unconsciously snitched, those scenes from *Oliver Twist*, commingled them with his own life story, and delivered them in the form of another Bransby Williams–style monologue for his own amusement and Lane's edification.

The question of who seduced whom during those interviews is intriguing. Was Lane gullible? Or did she play along with Charlie and act credulous because he was giving her good copy? Were the interviewer and interviewee on the make? Regardless of whether their encounter was a mutual seduction, it seems obvious that Chaplin was the one who controlled the interview process itself. Throughout his career, from stage to screen, he fought for, gained, and maintained ironfisted control over every aspect of his art. The only thing he couldn't control in this instance was the way Rose Lane wrote her serialized newspaper accounts of their interviews. But he could and did regain control, by killing the book and completely disavowing any responsibility for its authorship.

On the debatable question of *Charlie Chaplin's Own Story*'s authorship, then, take your choice. Neither Robinson's theory nor mine is provable. But what I have tried to suggest here is that *Charlie Chaplin's Own Story* — warts and all — is a legitimate text and a previously overlooked research document that justifies a new Chaplin biography. I hasten to add that this new biography was written, of course, on the shoulders of Robinson's superbly researched work. Without his meticulous, comprehensive scholarship, my own book would not have been possible.

Acknowledgments

I WANT TO THANK Jeffrey Vance, Justin Kaplan, and David Robinson for generously sharing research materials that helped shape the foundations of this book. A special debt needs to be acknowledged to Dr. George Pollock, editor of my Coleridge biography, for encouraging me to begin my psychoanalytic research, and thanks also to the members of my Charlie Chaplin seminar at the Washington Psychoanalytic Institute. Geraldine Chaplin and Pato Castilla have been a wonderful source of support and encouragement. Thanks to Jerry Epstein for spilling the beans on Charlie's mother's tragic story. Kevin Brownlow and Jeffrey Vance were expert readers. Dan Kamin was a helpful fact checker. Frank Scheide gave me two critical Chaplin documents. Kate Guyonvarch at Roy Export was generous in her photo permissions for this book and its Web site. My agent Victoria Skurnick, my editor Dick Seaver, and my copy editor Ann Marlowe all deserve special thanks. And my profound debt to my wife Carole Horn and our daughter Annie Weissman for supporting, encouraging, and critiquing the entire project can never be completely expressed. Lastly, my Granny Ray deserves my loving thanks for babysitting me on Saturday afternoons in the Bronx by shlepping me to Charlie Chaplin films when I was a small boy.

Notes

Chapter One

[1] Denis Gifford, *Chaplin* (Garden City, N.Y.: Doubleday, 1974), 13.
[2] Thomas Burke, *City of Encounters* (Boston: Little, Brown, 1932), 169.
[3] David Robinson, *Chaplin: His Life and Art* (New York: McGraw-Hill, 1985), 194.
[4] Charles Chaplin, *My Autobiography* (New York: Simon and Schuster, 1964), 34.
[5] Robinson, *Chaplin: His Life and Art*, 6.
[6] Chaplin, *My Autobiography*, 34.

Chapter Two

[1] Richard Meryman, "Ageless Master's Anatomy of Comedy," *Life*, March 10, 1967, 91.
[2] Chaplin, *My Autobiography*, 20.
[3] Ibid., 24.
[4] Unpublished letter from Jan Wahl to the author, May 30, 1989.
[5] Stephen M. Weissman, "Charlie Chaplin's Film Heroines," *Film History* 8:4 (1996), reprinted in *The Essential Chaplin*, ed. Richard Schickel (Chicago: Ivan R. Dee, 2006), 65–75.
[6] Claire Bloom, *Limelight and After* (New York: Penguin, 1982), 88.

Chapter Three

[1] Chaplin, *My Autobiography*, 14.
[2] Robinson, *Chaplin: His Life and Art*, 93.
[3] Chaplin, *My Autobiography*, 21.
[4] Konrad Bercovici, "Charlie Chaplin: An Authorized Interview," *Collier's*, August 15, 1925, 6.

[5] Chaplin, *My Autobiography*, 19.
[6] Beverley Nichols, *The Star Spangled Manner* (London: Jonathan Cape, 1928), 265–67.
[7] Robinson, *Chaplin: His Life and Art*, 115.
[8] Chaplin, *My Autobiography*, 18.
[9] Ibid., 289.

Chapter Four

[1] Quoted in Charles Chaplin Jr., *My Father, Charlie Chaplin*, with N. Rau and M. Rau (New York: Random House, 1960), 9.
[2] Harry C. Carr, "Charlie Chaplin's Story: As Narrated by Mr. Chaplin Himself," *Photoplay* 8:2 (1915).
[3] His mother's Nell Gwyn impersonations were so riveting that thirty years later Chaplin commemorated them by leaking a story to the *New York Herald Tribune* (September 27, 1926). The headline read: "Genealogy of Chaplin Traced to Stuart Line: Screen Comedian May Be Descended From Charles II and Nell Gwyn Actress." As for her turns as Josephine de Beauharnais, Charlie laid symbolic claim to French ancestry as well by straight-facedly informing reporters on four separate occasions that he had been born in Fountainbleau. In her sixties, living near her son in California, Hannah Chaplin regularly referred to him as "The King." That is, when she wasn't shocking immigration officials at U.S. Customs by introducing herself as the mother of Jesus Christ.
[4] Harry Crocker, *Charlie Chaplin: Man and Mime* (unpublished manuscript, Margaret Herrick Library, Motion Picture Academy of Arts and Sciences, Los Angeles, n.d.), ch. 1, 18.
[5] *Mundella Report: Report of the Departmental Committee, appointed by the Local Government Board to inquire into the existing systems for the Maintenance and Education of children under the charge of Managers of District Schools and Boards of Guardians in the Metropolis, and to advise as to any changes that may be desirable* (London: Her Majesty's Stationery Office, 1896), 164.
[6] Ibid., appendix 5.
[7] Crocker, *Charlie Chaplin*, ch. 1, 18.

[8] *Mundella Report*, minutes, 23.

[9] John McCabe, *Charlie Chaplin* (London: Robson, 1978), 61.

[10] Chaplin, *My Autobiography*, 31.

[11] Ibid., 31, 32.

[12] Crocker, *Charlie Chaplin*, ch. 1, 17.

[13] Ibid.

[14] Chaplin, *My Autobiography*, 26.

[15] Quoted in "Old London Friends Mourn Mrs. Chaplin," *New York Times*, August 30, 1928.

[16] Lita Grey Chaplin, *My Life With Chaplin*, with Morton Cooper (New York: Bernard Geis Associates, 1966), 140.

Chapter Five

[1] Chaplin, *My Autobiography*, 303.

[2] Admitting physician's note on Hannah Chaplin, September 6, 1898, *Lambeth Hospital Register of Lunatics*, Hl/L/B17/16 (vol. 16: February 1898–October 1898), 364. Courtesy of David Robinson.

[3] Chaplin, *My Autobiography*, 34.

[4] Anticipating his famous *Modern Times* factory scene of 1935, Charlie in 1916 quoted Hannah Chaplin during one of her later psychiatric hospitalizations:

> "Is — it — morning?" mother said painfully. "Three dozen more to sew. He shouldn't keep out the money for spots, there were no spots at all. Twelve make a dozen, and that's a half-crown, and then a dozen more, and then a dozen more, and then a dozen more —" She did not know us at all.

See Harry M. Geduld, ed., *Charlie Chaplin's Own Story* (Bloomington: Indiana University Press, 1985), 49.

[5] Frank Scheide, *The History of Low Comedy and Nineteenth and Early Twentieth Century English Music Hall as Basis for Examining the 1914–1917 Films of Charles Spencer Chaplin* (Ph.D. diss., University of Wisconsin–Madison, 1990), 101.

[6] Chaplin, *My Autobiography*, 24–25.

[7] Anita Leslie, *Clare Sheridan* (Garden City, N.Y.: Doubleday, 1977), 174.

[8] Crocker, *Charlie Chaplin*, ch. 11, 38–39.

[9] *Mundella Report*, 69.

[10] Geduld, *Charlie Chaplin's Own Story*, 157; Chaplin, *My Autobiography*, 57–58.

[11] Chaplin, *My Autobiography*, 289.

[12] Robinson, *Chaplin: His Life and Art*, 19.

[13] Charlie Chaplin Sr.'s unique stage character genre was known as the *lion comique*. Other famous *lions comiques* were Alfred Vance, George Leybourne, Arthur Lloyd, Harry Rickards, G. H. MacDermott, and Harry Anderson. Chaplin's father was neither the first nor the foremost member of this bibulous fraternity of sartorially elegant man-about-town character actors who sang the praises of the good life and the grape both to whet the thirst and to lighten the wallets of their fans and vicarious admirers. But to his credit, Charles Chaplin Sr. had the confidence (or arrogance) to bill himself as *the* Lion Comique, according to his good friend and colleague George Carney. Chaplin memorialized and satirized his father's stage character and *lions comiques* in general by creating the Little Tramp. By donning boots that were far too big for him and doing his signature Rummy Binks walk while impersonating a shabby but elegant would-be man-about-town, Charlie more than filled his father's shoes while remaining a comparative teetotaler.

[14] For many years, "The Miner's Dream of Home" was a standard in British homes, traditionally sung on New Year's Eve along with "Auld Lang Syne."

[15] Chaplin, *My Autobiography*, 35.

[16] Ibid., 35–36.

[17] Ibid., 36.

[18] Ibid., 40.

[19] Charlie Sr. and Louise had a four-year-old son. Charlie recalled no personal interactions with this half brother and was unable to remember his name.

[20] Chaplin, *My Autobiography*, 39–40.

[21] Ibid., 38.

[22] Ibid.

[23] John McCabe, *Charlie Chaplin* (Garden City, N.Y.: Doubleday, 1978), 159.

[24] The park scene was shot before the stock market crash in October 1929. The title card ("Peace and Prosperity") was inserted in December of 1930 and written to underscore the topical relevance of the park scene to the Great Depression that was taking place.

[25] John Bengtson, *Silent Traces: Discovering Early Hollywood Through the Films of Charlie Chaplin* (Santa Monica: Santa Monica Press, 2006), 256.

[26] James Agee, "Comedy's Greatest Era," *Life*, September 5, 1949, 77.

[27] Chaplin, *My Autobiography*, 34.

[28] A more precise word might be "semiautobiographical." For example, Chaplin did not faithfully translate every single detail of his father's alcoholism into his screen character's alcoholism. Charlie Sr. was charming when sober. Chaplin's millionaire is charming when drunk and icy when sober. The word "autobiographical" is not used here in its strictest sense any more than the word "Cockney" is. Technically, a Cockney was someone born within the sound of the Bow Bells of St. Mary Le Bow in Cheapside. Neither Chaplin's nor either of his parents' geographical origins meet that very narrow criterion. But all three of the Chaplins were as much Cockney as *City Lights* is autobiographical. "Cockney" is used here to refer to a London-born-and-bred member of the underclass in the late nineteenth century. This is not to be confused with the twentieth-century bastardized "Estuary English" accent of today, which crosses class lines and affects a working-class "attitude."

[29] Robinson, *Chaplin: His Life and Art*, 393.

[30] The chronological account of *City Lights* presented here is based entirely on Robinson. I was refused access to the Chaplin archive by Chaplin's children and am therefore relying on Robinson's version of the creative chain of events. Robinson was able to reconstruct those events by carefully reviewing the *City Lights* production materials in the Vevey archives with permission from Oona O'Neill Chaplin. After discovering Chaplin's method of jotting down his creative ideas in pencil and then sanitizing any deeply personal memories and feelings they contained for privacy purposes, I approached Kate Guyonvarch, the Chaplin family's current representative, and requested access to the six separate drafts of *My Autobiography* — both handwritten and typed. That request was denied without explanation. I am indebted to my friends Justin Kaplan and Jeffrey Vance for their generous help in

sharing information from the Vevey archives. Unfortunately, neither Justin nor Jeff saw the earlier drafts of *My Autobiography* or Chaplin's handwritten notes.

[31] "Chaplin Interviewed by Richard Meryman, 1966," in *Chaplin: Genius of the Cinema*, by Jeffrey Vance (New York: Harry N. Abrams, 2003), 362.

[32] Crocker, *Charlie Chaplin*, ch. 1, 12.

[33] Chaplin, *My Autobiography*, 37.

Chapter Six

[1] Chaplin, *My Autobiography*, 49.

[2] Jim Tully, "Charlie Chaplin — His Real Life Story," *Pictorial Review*, January 1927.

[3] Chaplin, *My Autobiography*, 40.

[4] Ibid.

[5] Thirteen-year-old Syd Chaplin found a low-paying job as a telegram delivery boy at the Strand Post Office.

[6] Robinson, *Chaplin: His Life and Art*, 71.

[7] Crocker, *Charlie Chaplin*, 13.

[8] Peter Haining, ed., *The Legend of Charlie Chaplin*, (Secaucus, N.J.: Castle Books, 1982), 81.

[9] Chaplin suffered from dyslexia and was unable to read more than one or two words at a time. (Unpublished interview of Chaplin by Meryman, Vevey Archive, courtesy Justin Kaplan).

[10] Peter Honri, *Working the Halls* (Farnborough, Hants.: Saxon House, 1973), 83.

[11] Alistair Cooke, "Fame," in Schickel, *The Essential Chaplin*, 136.

[12] PeoplePlay UK Theatre History Online, "Pantomime Guided Tour: Dan Leno," www.peopleplayuk.org.uk/guided_tours/pantomime_tour/pantomime_stars/leno.php.

[13] Quoted in McCabe, *Charlie Chaplin*, 34.

[14] Glenn Mitchell, *The Chaplin Encyclopedia* (London: B. T. Batsford, 1997), 170.

[15] Chaplin Jr., *My Father, Charlie Chaplin*, (New York: Random House, 1960), 93–94.

[16] Alistair Cooke, "Charles Chaplin: The One and Only," in *Six Men* (New York: Knopf, 1977), 137–38.

[17] Chaplin, *My Autobiography*, 46.

[18] Charles Chaplin, *Footlights* (unpublished) and "The Story of Calvero" (unpublished); Chaplin, *My Autobiography*, 50, 58.

[19] Ibid., 50.

[20] Ibid.

[21] Robinson, *Chaplin: His Life and Art*, 7.

[22] Chaplin, *My Autobiography*, 56, 57; McCabe, *Charlie Chaplin*, 17.

[23] Chaplin, *My Autobiography*, 58.

[24] Raoul Sobel and David Francis, *Chaplin: Genesis of a Clown* (London: Quartet, 1977), 62. N.B.: The fact that Chaplin's claim that his father's funeral was an elegant ceremony contrasted with the provable fact that his father was buried unceremoniously in a pauper's grave has been interpreted by Sobel and Francis as proof positive that Chaplin was a "liar" (on this and many other subjects in *My Autobiography*). Perhaps so. But an alternative explanation is that both statements are true. During my background research into Cockney culture, I encountered descriptions of how the outward display of colorful ceremony and pomp for a funeral was sometimes accompanied by the cost-cutting measure of dumping the corpse in a pauper's grave. Nothing short of exhuming Charlie Chaplin Sr. and discovering whether he was buried in a plain pine box or a polished oak coffin could settle this matter definitively. And unlike Charlie himself, whose coffin actually was exhumed by an inept pair of grave-robbing "resurrection men" (who hoped to extract a hefty corpse ransom from Chaplin's heartbroken widow), it's not likely that any literal-minded, truth-seeking biographers will ever go that far. For further discussion of the clinical distinction between memory falsification and false memories, see the "Afterword" chapter of this book.

[25] Chaplin, *My Autobiography*, 59.

[26] Robinson, *Chaplin: His Life and Art*, 41.

[27] Chaplin, *My Autobiography*, 13.

Chapter Seven

[1] R. J. Minney, *Chaplin: The Immortal Tramp* (London: George Newnes, 1954), 6.

[2] Employing a high-powered telescope from the window of his Hollywood home to achieve the same end, Chaplin would later relive that window-gazing game with his son Charlie Jr. and crack him up with his hilarious long-distance improv takes on neighbors and passersby in Beverly Hills.

[3] Burke, *City of Encounters*, 163-64.

[4] Chaplin, Charlie, *My Trip Abroad* (New York: Harper, 1922), 89.

[5] Unpublished interview, Vevey Archive, courtesy Justin Kaplan.

[6] McCabe, *Charlie Chaplin*, 91.

[7] Meryman, "Ageless Master's Anatomy of Comedy," 83.

[8] Crocker, *Charlie Chaplin*, ch. 1, 30–31.

[9] Chaplin, *My Autobiography*, 62, 64.

[10] Ibid., 60.

[11] Ibid., 61.

[12] Ibid., 61.

[13] Ibid., 60.

Chapter Eight

[1] Geduld, *Charlie Chaplin's Own Story*, 81.

[2] Ibid., 154.

[3] Chaplin, *My Autobiography*, 12.

[4] Ibid., 70.

[5] Tabes dorsalis is a sensory-motor disturbance of gait coordination that could easily be mistaken for alcohol-induced clumsiness in any patient who also happened to be disoriented and incoherent for another independent reason (such as severe malnutrition). Tabes dorsalis is caused by degeneration of the posterior columns of the spinal cord and commonly occurs in advanced cases of untreated neurosyphilis.

[6] Geduld, *Charlie Chaplin's Own Story*, 47.

[7] Ibid., 48.

[8] Robinson, *Chaplin: His Life and Art*, 22.

[9] Chaplin, *My Autobiography*, 78

[10] Ibid.

[11] Ibid.

[12] Gifford, *Chaplin*, 19.

[13] Geduld, *Charlie Chaplin's Own Story*, xviii.

[14] Chaplin, *My Autobiography*, 85.

[15] Ibid., 86.

[16] Ibid.

[17] Ibid.

[18] Ibid.

[19] Ibid., 87.

[20] Dana Burnet, "Garbo and Chaplin Talked to Me," *Photoplay*, June 1936.

Chapter Nine

[1] Geduld, *Charlie Chaplin's Own Story*, 103–4.

[2] Ibid., xxi.

[3] *The Green Room Book; or, Who's Who on the Stage* (London: T. S. Clark, 1906), 68.

[4] Chaplin, *My Autobiography*, 88.

[5] Geduld, *Charlie Chaplin's Own Story*, 82.

[6] Chaplin, *My Autobiography*, 92.

[7] The term "fresh part" is used advisedly. Chaplin recalled being out of work for the next three months. Independent evidence (advertisements and notices in the *Era*) reveals that he again toured as Billy in *Sherlock Holmes*. Either way, he found his next *fresh* part, playing slapstick in *Repairs*, three months after this encounter with Madge Kendal. While the anecdote is clearly an embellishment, I include his version of this incident from *My Autobiography* because it is too difficult to entirely resist the obvious pleasure he took in fabricating a good story.

[8] Geduld, *Charlie Chaplin's Own Story*, 98.

[9] Ibid., 86.

[10] Chaplin, *My Autobiography*, 93, 94.

[11] John M. Garrett, *Sixty Years of British Music Hall* (London: Chappell, 1976), song 32.

[12] Geduld, *Charlie Chaplin's Own Story*, 51.

[13] Chaplin, *My Autobiography*, 97.

[14] Honri, *Working the Halls*, 139.

[15] Geduld, *Charlie Chaplin's Own Story*, 98.

Chapter Ten

[1] Gifford, *Chaplin*, 21.

[2] Robert Lewis Taylor, *W. C. Fields: His Follies and Fortunes* (Garden City, N.Y.: Doubleday, 1949), 2.

[3] Chaplin, *My Autobiography*, 45.

[4] Geduld, *Charlie Chaplin's Own Story*, 98–99. Charlie must have gotten a huge kick out of inventing this cock-and-bull story of his *Casey's Circus* audition for Rose Wilder Lane, a young reporter for the *San Francisco Bulletin*. It first appeared in the *Bulletin* on July 24, 1915.

[5] Will Murray, "How I Discovered Chaplin," *Glasgow Weekly Record*, September 10, 1921, quoted in Robinson, *Chaplin: His Life and Art*, 66.

[6] Murray, "How I Discovered Chaplin," quoted in Robinson, *Chaplin: His Life and Art*, 67–68.

[7] Agee, "Comedy's Greatest Era," 74.

[8] Sandy Powell, *Can You Hear Me, Mother?: Sandy Powell's Lifetime of Music Hall*, with Harry Stanley (London: Jupiter, 1975), 15.

[9] Geduld, *Charlie Chaplin's Own Story*, 101.

[10] Robinson, *Chaplin: His Life and Art*, 67.

[11] Geduld, *Charlie Chaplin's Own Story*, 101.

[12] Ibid., 102.

[13] Gifford, *Chaplin*, 21.

[14] Honri, *Working the Halls*, 6.

[15] For an excellent discussion of this topic, see George Wead, *Buster Keaton and the Dynamics of Visual Wit* (New York: Arno, 1976), 134, 321.

[16] Geduld, *Charlie Chaplin's Own Story*, 103.

[17] Chaplin, *My Autobiography*, 94.

[18] Burke, *City of Encounters*, 137.

Chapter Eleven

[1] Fred Karno, "The Birth of a Star," in *The Legend of Charlie Chaplin*, by Peter Haining (Secaucus, N.J.: Castle, 1982), 25–26.

[2] Chaplin, *My Autobiography*, 115.

[3] This seven-month period of irregular employment (July 1907 through February 1908) probably was that dissipated period of "whores, sluts and an occasional drinking bout" that Chaplin misremembered or purposely embellished in *My Autobiography* in his colorful description of the immediate aftermath of his prideful confrontation with Madge Kendal.

[4] Chaplin, *My Autobiography*, 96.

[5] Ibid., 97.

[6] Robinson, *Chaplin: His Life and Art*, 68.

[7] Chaplin, *My Autobiography*, 97.

[8] Gerald Mast, *The Comic Mind*, 2nd ed. (Chicago: University of Chicago Press, 1979), x. See also Richard Schickel, *D. W. Griffith: An American Life* (New York: Simon and Schuster, 1984), 185.

[9] David Robinson, *Chaplin, the Mirror of Opinion* (Bloomington: Indiana University Press, 1983), 119.

[10] *Hilarity, Jail Birds, Early Birds, His Majesty's Guests, The Football Match, The Casuals, Moses and Sons, Mumming Birds, The Thirsty First, The Smoking Concert, The Diving Birds, New Woman's Club, Thumbs Down, Cinderella, Saturday to Monday, Dandy Thieves*. And more would follow.

[11] Chaplin, quoted in McCabe, *Charlie Chaplin*, 28–29.

[12] In *My Autobiography*, 100, Chaplin describes the role of the crooked gambler in *The Football Match* as the "trial engagement" that won him his first Karno contract. He did, however, first play a bit part in *London Suburbia*, a sketch Syd was starring in at the time. Evidently Chaplin considered that brief walk-on appearance as the music hall equivalent of a Hollywood screen test rather than an acting credit.

[13] Chaplin, quoted in McCabe, *Charlie Chaplin*, 28.

[14] Powell, *Can You Hear Me, Mother?* 13–15.

[15] Chaplin, *My Autobiography*, 101.

[16] Ibid.

[17] Ibid.

[18] Ibid., 102.

[19] Ibid.

[20] Chaplin, *My Autobiography*, 103.

[21] Ibid., 95.

[22] Ibid., 104.

[23] Ibid., 105–7.

[24] Ibid., 102–3.

[25] Ibid., 115.

[26] Ibid.

[27] Powell, *Can You Hear Me, Mother?* 108.

[28] Chaplin, *My Autobiography*, 97.

[29] Minney, *Chaplin*, 18.

[30] Quoted in Robinson, *Chaplin: His Life and Art*, 33.

[31] Lillian Ross, "A Reporter at Large: Moments From Chaplin," *New Yorker*, May 22, 1978, 102.

[32] Grace Simpson, interview with Groucho Marx, *Motion Picture*, May 1936, excerpted in Haining, *Legend*, 147–50.

[33] Robert Payne, *The Great God Pan: A Biography of the Tramp Played by Charles Chaplin* (New York: Hermitage House, 1952), 144.

[34] Mack Sennett, *King of Comedy*, with Cameron Shipp (Garden City, N.Y.: Doubleday, 1954), 97.

Chapter Twelve

[1] Quoted in McCabe, *Charlie Chaplin*, 38–39.

[2] Chaplin, *My Autobiography*, 118.

[3] McCabe, *Charlie Chaplin*, 27.

[4] Ibid., 28–29.

[5] Joyce Milton, *Tramp: The Life of Charlie Chaplin* (New York: Harper-Collins, 1996), 46.

[6] Robinson, *Chaplin: His Life and Art*, 87–88.

[7] Richard Findlater, *Joe Grimaldi: His Life and Theatre*, 2nd ed. (Cambridge: Cambridge University Press, 1979), 59.

[8] McCabe, *Charlie Chaplin*, 28.

[9] Benny Green, ed., *The Last Empires: A Music Hall Companion* (London: Pavilion, Michael Joseph, 1986), 137, 142.

[10] Buster Keaton, "My Friend Charlie Chaplin," reprinted in Haining, *Legend*, 187–89.

[11] Dan Kamin, *Charlie Chaplin's One-Man Show* (Metuchen, N.J.: Scarecrow Press, 1984), xiii.

[12] Chaplin, *My Autobiography*, 119, 120.

[13] McCabe, *Charlie Chaplin*, 41.

[14] Chaplin, *My Autobiography*, 134.

[15] Ralph Waldo Emerson, "Self-Reliance," in *Essays and English Traits*, vol. 5 of Harvard Classics (New York: P. F. Collier & Son, 1909), 79–80.

[16] Karno, "Birth of a Star," 25–26.

[17] Chaplin, *My Autobiography*, 128.

[18] Ibid.

[19] Ibid., 132.

[20] Ibid., 120.

[21] Ibid., 134.

[22] Haining, *Legend*, 15.

Chapter Thirteen

[1] Which explains why, more than half a century later, IBM would pay twenty-five million dollars in fees to the Chaplin estate for the commercial use of his effigy in their worldwide sales campaign for user-friendly personal computers aimed at the so-called common man that the Charlie Chaplin character's iconic image still epitomizes to this day, even for people who have never even seen a Chaplin film in its entirety.

[2] Robinson, *Chaplin: His Life and Art*, 383.

[3] Geduld, *Charlie Chaplin's Own Story*, 138.

[4] Burke, *City of Encounters*, 149–50.

[5] Chaplin, *My Trip Abroad*, 11.

[6] Chaplin, *My Autobiography*, 141.

[7] Ibid., 139.

[8] Sennett, *King of Comedy*, 148.

[9] Gary Carey, *Doug & Mary: A Biography of Douglas Fairbanks & Mary Pickford* (New York: Dutton, 1977), 18.

[10] Chaplin, *My Autobiography*, 138.
[11] Geduld, *Charlie Chaplin's Own Story*, 117.
[12] Ibid., 118.
[13] Sennett, *King of Comedy*, 50.
[14] Schickel, *D. W. Griffith*, 116.
[15] Sennett, *King of Comedy*, 51, 54, 55.
[16] Ibid., 51.
[17] Schickel, *D. W. Griffith*, 352.
[18] David Bordwell, Janet Staiger, and Kristin Thompson, *The Classical Hollywood Cinema: Film Style & Mode of Production to 1960* (New York: Columbia University Press, 1985), 121.
[19] Schickel, *D. W. Griffith*, 23.
[20] Ibid., 24.
[21] Ibid., 31.
[22] Edward Wagenknecht, *The Movies in the Age of Innocence* (Norman: University of Oaklahoma Press, 1962), 101.
[23] Schickel, *D. W. Griffith*, 270.

Chapter Fourteen

[1] Sennett, *King of Comedy*, 156.
[2] Ibid., 148.
[3] Ibid., 152.
[4] Meryman, "Ageless Master's Anatomy of Comedy," 90.
[5] Chaplin, *My Autobiography*, 140.
[6] Sennett, *King of Comedy*, 153.
[7] Chaplin, *My Autobiography*, 141.
[8] Ibid., 120–21.
[9] Ibid., 123.
[10] Sennett, *King of Comedy*, 99.
[11] Walter Kerr, *The Silent Clowns* (New York: Knopf, 1975), 64.
[12] David A. Yallop, *The Day the Laughter Stopped: The True Story of Fatty Arbuckle* (New York: St. Martin's Press, 1976), 38.
[13] Sennett, *King of Comedy*, 94.
[14] Chaplin, *My Autobiography*, 142.

[15] Sennett, *King of Comedy*, 152.

[16] Ibid., 153.

[17] Geduld, *Charlie Chaplin's Own Story*, 124.

[18] Chaplin, *My Autobiography*, 143.

[19] Ibid., 144.

[20] Ibid.

[21] Betty Harper Fussell, *Mabel* (New York: Ticknor and Fields, 1982), 71.

[22] Sennett, *King of Comedy*, 154.

[23] Ibid., 157.

[24] Ibid., 157–58.

[25] Chaplin, *My Autobiography*, 144.

[26] Kerr, *The Silent Clowns*, 22.

[27] "Chaplin Interviewed by Richard Meryman, 1966," in Vance, *Chaplin*, 360.

[28] Chaplin, *My Autobiography*, 146.

[29] Ibid., 146–47.

[30] Meryman, "Ageless Master's Anatomy of Comedy," 90.

[31] Ibid., 84.

[32] Frederick Martin, "An Evening with Charlie Chaplin." A photocopy of this article was kindly provided by Frank Scheide. The periodical and publication date are unidentified, but the author is described as the advertising manager for Great Britain of Paramount-Artcraft. He was an old friend of Charlie Chaplin Sr. who visited with Chaplin while on a business trip in Los Angeles. They talked about old times, and apparently Charlie let his hair down.

Chapter Fifteen

[1] Quoted in Gilbert Seldes, "I Am Here To-day," in Schickel, *The Essential Chaplin*, 104.

[2] Meryman, "Ageless Master's Anatomy of Comedy," 90.

[3] Harry C. Carr, "Mack Sennett — Laugh Tester," *Photoplay*, May 1915, 71.

[4] Chaplin, *My Autobiography*, 149.

[5] Ibid., 148.

[6] Sennett, *King of Comedy*, 181.

[7] Chaplin, *My Autobiography*, 149.

[8] Ibid.

[9] Ibid., 151.

[10] Ibid., 150.

[11] Sennett, *King of Comedy*, 163.

[12] Gerald D. McDonald, Michael Conway, and Mark Ricci, *The Films of Charlie Chaplin* (New York: Bonanza, 1965), 28, 32, 42.

[13] In *Sherlock Jr.* the same characters go back and forth between the movie-within-the-movie story and the "real life" screen story as doubles of themselves.

[14] McDonald, *The Films of Charlie Chaplin*, 13.

[15] Sennett, *King of Comedy*, 180.

[16] Crocker, *Charlie Chaplin*, ch. 6, 14.

[17] Chaplin, *My Autobiography*, 152–53.

[18] Sennett, *King of Comedy*, 152.

[19] Carr, "Charlie Chaplin's Story."

[20] Chaplin's $200/week Keystone salary was equivalent to more than $4,000/week in 2008 (using the Consumer Price Index). As to the earning power of his films: the CPI translation of the $160,000 rental earnings *Dough and Dynamite* generated in 1914 would have exceeded $3.4 million in 2008 (according to measuringworth.com). Chaplin made thirty-five Keystones. Although it had not yet dawned on Charlie at the time of that showdown with Mack, he was big business.

[21] Theodore Dreiser, "The Best Motion Picture Interview Ever Written," *Photoplay*, August 1928.

[22] Sennett, *King of Comedy*, 187.

[23] Kalton Lahue and Terry Brewer, *Kops and Kustard: The Legend of Keystone Films* (Norman, Okla.: University of Oklahoma Press, 1968), 67.

[24] Chaplin, *My Autobiography*, 159.

[25] Robinson, *Chaplin: His Life and Art*, 132.

[26] Crocker, *Charlie Chaplin*, ch. 6, 18.

Chapter Sixteen

[1] Alistair Cook, *Fun & Games with Alistair Cooke* (New York: Arcade, 1996), 220.

[2] Edward Wagenknecht, *Stars of the Silents* (Metuchen, N.J.: Scarecrow Press, 1987), 92.

[3] Erick Berry, "Charlie Captures Africa's Gold Coast," *New York Times*, July 5, 1925.

[4] Wagenknecht, *Stars of the Silents*, 92.

[5] Haining, *Legend*, 132.

[6] Lives like Chaplin's are now being systematically studied by social scientists. They are finding that children subjected to homelessness and other forms of emotional stress and abuse don't all turn out the same way. While the vast majority become severely impaired or socially disadvantaged adults, a small handful, like Charlie Chaplin or the equally world-famous Oprah Winfrey, surprisingly turn into smart, resourceful, streetwise superkids; the psychological shorthand term to describe them is "invulnerables." These resilient children go on to lead high-achieving and remarkable lives as valued members of society. Chaplin was such a person, and his famous film character and alter ego "Charlie" was as well.

[7] Chaplin Jr., *My Father, Charlie Chaplin*, 9.

[8] Robinson, *Chaplin: His Life and Art*, 538.

Afterword

[1] Chaplin, *My Autobiography*, 323.

[2] Sigmund Freud to Yvette Guilbert, quoted in Crocker, *Charlie Chaplin*, ch. 14, 2–3.

[3] Robinson, *Chaplin: His Life and Art*, 183.

[4] Ibid., 182.

[5] Ibid., 185.

[6] David Robinson, "An Imposture Revived," review of *Charlie Chaplin's Own Story*, ed. Geduld, *Times Literary Supplement*, June 27, 1986, 716.

[7] Geduld, *Charlie Chaplin's Own Story*, ix.

[8] Stephen M. Weissman, "Frederick Douglass, Portrait of a Black Militant — A Study in the Family Romance," *Psychoanalytic Study of the Child* 30 (1975): 725-51.

[9] Syd Chaplin, "A Few Reminiscences," *Bioscope*, March 11, 1915, 957.

[10] Vance, *Chaplin*, 17.

[11] Geduld, *Charlie Chaplin's Own Story*, 26.

[12] Carr, "Charlie Chaplin's Story."

[13] Walter Vogdes, "Charlie Chaplin: Rather a Quiet Little Guy Who Takes His Pantomimic Art Seriously," *New York Tribune*, December 30, 1917, quoted in *Charlie Chaplin: Interviews*, ed. Kevin J. Hayes (Jackson: University Press of Mississippi, 2005), 28–29.

[14] One year after those interviews with Rose Wilder Lane, in the early winter of 1916, Chaplin played the role of the Artful Dodger in a one-night benefit performance of a stage version of *Oliver Twist* at the Mason Opera House for the Los Angeles News Boy Fund. Constance Collier played Bill Sykes's Nancy and Sir Herbert Beerbohm Tree played Fagin.

Index